Digital Signage

About the Series

NAB EXECUTIVE TECHNOLOGY BRIEFINGS SERIES

A series developed jointly between Focal Press and National Association of Broadcasters

The NAB Executive Technology Briefing Series consist of titles addressing current and future industry technologies, authored by experienced and well-known professionals, often industry consultants, for managers and investors in the industry. Readers should have an introductory to an intermediate level of knowledge of the technology. The primary goals of each title in the series are as follows:

- Provide the reader with a working knowledge of the topic. Each title clearly explains the technology discussed, the end-result providing the reader with a general technical understanding to adequately converse with industry engineers and other technology professionals.

- Discusses the impact (past, present and future) that the technology had/has/will have on the industry. This includes-but not limited to: financial implications, human resource implications, how the technology will change the industry, competitive considerations, advertising/marketing considerations, legal/legislative ramifications.

- Identify investment opportunities in the industry. Each title outlines not only areas of opportunity but also the risks that may be involved.

NAB Disclaimer
The opinions, findings, and conclusions expressed in this publication are those of the author(s) alone, and not necessarily those of the National Association of Broadcasters.

NAB EXECUTIVE TECHNOLOGY BRIEFINGS

Digital Signage: Software, Networks, Advertising, and Displays

A Primer for Understanding the Business

Jimmy Schaeffler

AMSTERDAM • BOSTON • HEIDELBERG • LONDON
NEW YORK • OXFORD • PARIS • SAN DIEGO
SAN FRANCISCO • SYDNEY • TOKYO
Focal Press is an imprint of Elsevier

Acquisitions Editor: Angelina Ward
Assistant Editor: Katy Spencer
Marketing Manager: Amanda Guest
Developmental Editor: Beth Millett
Publishing Services Manager: George Morrison
Project Manager: Paul Gottehrer
Design Direction: Joanne Blank
Cover Design: Maria Mann
Cover Images: ©Getty Images

Focal Press is an imprint of Elsevier
30 Corporate Drive, Suite 400, Burlington, MA 01803, USA
Linacre House, Jordan Hill, Oxford OX2 8DP, UK

Library of Congress Cataloging-in-Publication Data
Application submitted

British Library Cataloguing-in-Publication Data
A catalogue record for this book is available from the British Library.

ISBN: 978-0-240-81041-6

For information on all Focal Press publications
visit our website at www.books.elsevier.com

08   09   10   11   5   4   3   2   1

Printed in the United States of America

Working together to grow
libraries in developing countries

www.elsevier.com | www.bookaid.org | www.sabre.org

ELSEVIER   BOOK AID International   Sabre Foundation

This book is dedicated to my family. I especially highlight my friend, my wife, of nearly three decades, Diane, who has constantly spotlighted my talents, and consistently helped me to address my flaws. Thank you all, and for your help in "getting it done." I sincerely hope you will share my excitement for all that digital signage will become.

Contents

Acknowledgments

Three people are key to the production of this book. The first two are the two people who worked with me to complete this book, and to complete it on time. They are Robb Hawkins and Chris Dempsey. Both, quite simply, worked extremely hard to help complete this project. I commend them both. Similarly, I owe much to Jeff Bixler of HughesNet, who became my early mentor and without whom this book's quality would likely never have published.

In addition, I am indebted to all those who provided case studies, which because of their efforts have become very important individual lessons within each chapter of this book.

And finally, I commend a handful of people who, from the outset, showed great patience and gave generously of their time as we researched and analyzed the book's early parts. This list includes Lyle Bunn, Laura Davis-Taylor, Bill Gerba, Fabian Keller, Lars-Ingemar Lundstrom, Xavier Orriols, Graeme Spicer, Lionel Tepper, and Adrian Weidmann.

Thank you all once more.

About the Author

Jimmy Schaeffler is the chairman and CSO of The Carmel Group, (see website www.carmelgroup.com) a telecommunications, computer, and media industries consultant, conference organizer, and publisher. Since 1995, The Carmel Group has provided these services to a broad range of clientele in the private, public, government, and non-profit sectors.

While being widely sought for his expertise on satellite TV, cable, wireless, and telephony, Schaeffler has already earned a position as a leading authority on such new, advanced cable, telco, DBS, broadband, and broadcast services such as video-on-demand, digital video recorders, Video on Demand (VOD), high-definition TV, satellite radio, and digital signage, to name just a few.

Today, scores of the world's largest telecommunications, computer, and media companies seek Schaeffler's insights for studies and conferences, etc., and his views are reported regularly in such publications as *The Wall Street Journal*, *Investor's Business Daily*, *Business Week*, and *Time* magazine and Schaeffler is the author of numerous telecom books, and has been a frequent participant in industry conferences and activities, around the world, going back to the mid-1990s. A "google" of his name delivers literally thousands of entries.

Schaeffler holds a bachelor's degree, with honors, from the University of California, Berkeley, and a Doctor of Jurisprudence degree from the University of Pacific, McGeorge School of Law in Sacramento, CA, where he served as a staff member on the law school's *Pacific Law Journal*. He is licensed to practice in CA, MN, CO, Washington, DC, and before the U.S. Supreme Court.

Executive Summary

Digital signage is emerging at a rapid rate.

It is doing so because of a combination of drivers. These include large or small, flat-panel, high-resolution monitors; receiving signals either from an in-house server or PC, or one located on the other side of the world; sent via the Internet and via wired, wireless, or satellite-delivered files; which files are video, audio, still, or animated; and several of which can be shown concurrently on different "regions" of the same monitor; and all of which can be made especially *relevant* and *targeted* to specific audiences; often down to the individual recipient. In North America alone, millions of digital signage screens are just a few years away from deployment.

Digital signage is happening because it is bringing success to more groups of businesspeople globally. This is especially the case with the group of executives related to the advertising worlds of today and tomorrow. Indeed, for this group of executives, the fact that the book focuses heavily on the importance of on-screen content should be particularly revealing. This executive cadre will also find the specific focus on digital signage business models to be of great interest.

In addition, and most importantly, digital signage, as this book clearly states, has answers for those in the advertising community who seek viable responses to communities and audiences lost because of DVRs, MP3 players, satellite radio, and other ad-avoidance software and hardware. Yet, as a measure of its true effectiveness, digital signage will work in many communities beyond the standard, commercial environment: indeed, health, education, production, and government are but a few of the genres where digital signage is being used and tinkered with.

Moreover, while this book takes a lot of time and effort to explain the basic "where," "what," "when," and "why" of digital signage—especially aimed at those new to the digital signage business—it also looks to the impact of digital signage products and services in the trend-setting global arena.

In short, digital signage is emerging at a rapid rate, because, in general thus far, it works. Yet, as the book stresses, the future of the digital signage industry (and the future receptivity of all of its audiences) lies best in the able hands of those that do their homework, do it carefully, and do it right. This book is written with the express vision of making that happen.

Introduction

Pure and simple, digital signage is an *answer*.

The more I researched the basics supporting its hardware, software, operations, business models, and its future, the more its solutions became clear.

It is an answer because, as a technology, it presents new opportunities and alternatives for those like advertising agencies, innumerable global advertisers and retailers, as well as their vendors, each of which is faced with huge challenges to remain *relevant* in the minds (and in the eyes) of the consumer audiences it must address daily, in order to move its business forward.

When all is said and done, the best description of digital signage comes down to the three-sentence summary provided in Chapter 3: "What's driving the adoption and growth of the digital signage phenomena? Put another way, why would someone use, or want to use this remarkable new application? The short answer is to *convey a message*, presumably one that is important both to the displayer and to the audience."

In sum, having completed the research and analysis of this project, this book was written almost entirely for the purpose of helping new (and old) digital signage players find those *answers* and convey those messages, especially as they relate to their own businesses.

About This Book

Nearly 20 case studies support the work in the 11 chapters in this book. These case studies are intended to present additional answers, especially for digital signage neophytes who need as many answers as possible, and ideally, with those answers coming from real-life experiences. These case studies are thus specially recommended to help put the chapter lessons into context. One example is the Mayo Clinic experience in Chapter 1, focused on the not-for-profit medical, educational world. Another example, on the complete opposite side of the business world, is the Clear Channel Outdoor for-profit, commercial case study that helps conclude the book in Chapter 11. Both are also great examples of where first-rate businesses are taking the best digital signage. In addition, because of the effectiveness of photographs, charts, and diagrams, several chapters offer more than a dozen figures aimed at helping to best and most simply tell the story of digital signage. Overall, the book offers scores of photographs showing examples of digital signage deployments around the world.

Chapter 1 offers an introductory view of digital signage for the average business person (who has minimal or no real understanding of what digital signage is made of). It presents the topic in the form of answers to questions about how big it may get, what are its major components, what are its purposes, what are the trends behind it, who are its stakeholders, and what are its costs? In addition to the Mayo Clinic case study, case studies exploring the advertising sides of National Malls and AccuWeather are presented.

Chapter 2 presents a detailed look at digital signage's basic history, forms, technology, software, hardware, installation, maintenance, key players, and trends, as well as its challenges and opportunities. A case study reviewing the experience of California-based emebaVet, and its veterinarian TV network of digital signs, sheds light on successful digital signage deployed in a small, individualized, medical facility environment.

Chapter 3 looks at the drivers behind the new medium called digital signage. Ten unique factors are expected to have a special impact on the growth and development of the digital signage, both in North America and abroad. A case study of a digital signage deployment by Logical Solutions into dozens of Carmike Cinemas across the United States is offered, as well. Chapter 3 also offers another helpful grouping of charts and photos to help readers understand the digital signage story.

Chapter 4 looks at ideas for when and where to use digital signage. It's case study is that of The Salon Channel Network, supported by digital signage operator, Airplay America. The focus of the chapter is on the use, display, control, and reliability of digital signage networks.

Chapter 5 examines the all-important content that is the center of the compass that guides digital signage. The chapter looks at proponents of, strategies for, and types of, digital signage content. This chapter, too, is replete with photos that enhance the educational process. The case study features digital signage pioneer, Scala, and its numerous client deployments through the years. Sub-topics include understanding the customer, placement, types, dwell time, audio, and future content.

Chapter 6 delves into the organizations that are already into, or those that will want to be into, digital signage deployments. Case studies examine Orkin pest control, the Children's Hospital of the University of Pittsburgh, and retail giant JC Penney. Quite a lot of focus in this chapter is given to advertising agencies and their clients, including a special focus on retailers.

Chapter 7 tells business people how to choose the type of digital signage they wish to utilize. Top-level choices include turn-key and piecemeal, with a particular focus on reliability as a not-to-be-forgotten choice element. Another first-rate case study from the digital signage deployments on hundreds of gas station pumps in North America is the lesson model here.

Chapter 8 is another particularly important chapter, because it is written for business people who are looking to understand the core business models behind digital signage. Case studies examining digital signage deployments in a bank, a mall/supermarket, and an airport are presented.

Chapter 9 dissects international digital signage, with an emphasis on the key areas of Europe and Asia. Many instances and examples of digital signage are presented, noting that in many ways—because of the absence of typical government and related restrictions—overseas deployments of digital signage are quite likely to be more innovative and more inventive than those in North America. Baby-TV, as well as lessons learned from deployments in Woolworths, Spar, and The Mall retail centers are the case study and related lessons in this chapter.

Chapter 10 is a specific look at where and how to start the implementation of a digital signage network, no matter what the size of the organization or the network is. Another bank operation, this one in the southeastern United States, is the case study supporting this chapter. This chapter is critical for those looking to decide and then actually deciding to implement a new digital signage operation.

Chapter 11 concludes the book with a look at the future of digital signage. This chapter attempts to predict areas of development and the implementations thereof. The Clear Channel Outdoor case study takes the reader from an academic to a reality view of this side of the digital signage world.

Of note also are an excellent glossary of terms related to digital signage, as well as a quite helpful map, and first-rate directory list.

Ultimately, a lot of people and businesses will figure out digital signage, make a lot of money, and satisfy and positively engage a lot of people along the way. A lot of good business will come from a shift to digital signage.

It is the author's sincere intent that many of them will at one point look back on the process of getting there and determine that this book helped.

Jimmy Schaeffler
Carmel-by-the-Sea, California, USA

1   The Big Picture: An Overview of Digital Signage

Digital signage has evolved into a highly efficient, appealing means of providing multimedia content for business owners, brand marketers, and advertising agencies, who realize its benefits of informing, promoting, and entertaining specifically targeted consumers. The days of providing static content are behind us.

—Tom Perchinsky, CEO, Adek Corporation

Labor- and material-intensive, static, traditional advertising signage, such as posters and billboards, is being replaced by flat monitor screens and quite-active digital content, often in a network, controlled from nearby or afar, often via the Internet, from any imaginable global location. Non-commercial digital displays offer huge upside potential, as well. Projections of revenue growth in the digital signage industry hit $2.6 billion (yes, billion!) by year-end 2010.[1]

What Is Digital Signage?

For most people, the first key message to understand about digital signage is, just what is it? Indeed, as a technology and as a communications medium, it is so relatively new, undeveloped, and untested, that most both inside and outside the industry of digital signage cannot adequately describe its features and capabilities.

A most simplistic definition of digital signage is that of a "remotely managed digital display, typically tied in with sales, marketing, and advertising."

---

1. The Carmel Group, 2007, www.carmelgroup.com.

As is often the case when new technologies develop and are defined, the industries behind the term "digital signage" chose and accepted its name somewhat hastily and conveniently, rather than with the goal of properly capturing the full essence and scope of what this new medium and technology involve. Indeed, it is important to realize that "digital signage" includes monitors that will do much more than deliver mere content representing signage (or commercial) messages. One example includes digital displays used in travel centers to relay travel information.

Nonetheless, the moniker "digital signage" has morphed through the years to become the recognized standard term used to describe the core software and hardware that comprise this dynamic industry sector. Meanwhile, other terms used to describe "digital signage" (or its equivalent) within the industry include, alphabetically, those such as "Advertising Networks," "Captive Audience Networks (CANs),""Captive Audience TV," "Digital Advertising," "Digital Display," "Digital Media Advertising," "Digital Media Networks," "Digital Messaging," "Digital Point-of-Purchase (POP)," "Digital Signage Broadcasting," "Digital Signage Networks," "Digital Signs," "Dynamic Communications Network," "Dynamic Digital Signage," "Dynamic Display Engagement Media," "Dynamic Out-of-Home," "Dynamic Signage," "Electronic Signage," "In-Store TV," "In-Store TV Networks," "Kiosk System," "Narrowcasting Networks," "Out-of-Home Advertising," "Out-of-Home Media Networks," "Out-of-Home (OOH) Video," "Place-Based Media," "Retail Digital Media," "Retail Media," "Retail Media Networks," and "Screen Media."

That said, the better definition and the one used frequently throughout this work is simply that of "digital signage" (although this book is about more than just commercially based digital signage). This book is really about all of the global digital display media, of which the digital (commercial) signage is a large part, but certainly not all. Indeed, the title of this book, *Digital Signage—Software, Networks, Advertising, and Displays: A Primer for Understanding the Business*, was chosen, in part, to accommodate this concern. To sum up, for the purposes of this book, "digital signage" will refer to both commercial implementations of the technology, as well as all other uses.

Wikipedia defines digital signage as "… a form of OOH advertising in which content and messages displayed on an electronic screen, or digital sign, can be changed without modification to the physical sign, typically with the goal of delivering targeted messages to specific locations at specific times."

FIGURE 1.1 *Digital Signage Can Set the Mood and Provide Information to Its Viewers, Such as in The Lobby of the Cancer Center at the Mayo Clinic (Copyright 2007. Property of the Mayo Clinic. All rights reserved.)*

Yet, as is often the case with Wikipedia entries, the entry falls short of a thorough and accurate academic description of its meaning. For example, the proper definition of digital signage will likely also include in-home applications. Chapter 11 discusses those types of future applications. In addition, the content displayed by digital signage will not be confined to mere advertising messages; instead, non-commercial digital displays, today (and in the future) include (and will include) educational and environment-setting or mood-enhancing messages, to name but a few. A perfect example of a non-commercial digital display is depicted in Figure 1.1. It shows a digital signage display created by the Mayo Clinic, in Rochester, MN, used almost entirely for the purposes of information and mood setting.

Mayo Clinic

Rochester, MN-based Mayo Clinic's system is one of the best known digital signage deployments by a not-for-profit organization. It has been directed for the past half-dozen years by Warren Harmon, whose title is Section Head, Media Production, for Mayo Clinic. The system is planned for and directed to Mayo Clinic's patients and staff. Institutionally, the facility has 30 screens spread throughout 50 Mayo Clinic buildings on the Rochester campus. Plus, there are six "customized projects," each with one to six screens, which occur where a particular unit of the hospital, or administrative supporting department, requests to purchase and operate its own system within the larger system.

When initiated, Mayo Clinic's biggest motivator was the desire to achieve a consistency and timeliness of multiple messages for the staff and patient audiences. Because the staff is so large, so diverse, and so spread out across the Mayo campus, delivering messages in the traditional, static sign way was inefficient and wasteful. Posters were unsafe for patients, hard to manage and coordinate, creating undue clutter and inconsistency of the Mayo Clinic brand, and unduly expensive in light of the value delivered. "Posters on easels just didn't work, people were ignoring the paper. You can meet demands with digital signage, that you can't with paper signage," notes Harmon.

Harmon begins each digital signage implementation in the Mayo Clinic with a formal needs assessment, and on occasion, a pilot test in areas with diverse messaging and audiences. Decisions such as the type of screen for the specific locale are determined, for example, and whether a landscape (horizontal) or portrait (vertical) is the best presentation format. Systemwide choices of either liquid crystal displays (LCD) or plasma are provided, which Harmon has identified as the best for all of the screens that make up the Mayo Clinic digital signage system. Organic light emitting diodes (LEDs) are being considered for the future, due to their ability to display remarkable pictures and to fit into the different Mayo Clinic environments. Content delivered includes photos, text, graphics, charts, and pictures (but no audio). Screen locations include elevator bays, hallways, bus stops, and almost everywhere indoors (especially cafeterias and conference rooms).

A specific example of the appropriateness of digital signage in the Mayo Clinic environment is its use to convey emergency messages, both on a local and national basis. Every monitor tells the audience how to respond in case of emergencies. Harmon offers that, "The digital signage system is designed to manage all components of an emergency situation." Scala and Alpha Video's CastNet system are the software management brains behind the Mayo Clinic digital signage program. And although targeted messaging is used only "occasionally," more is planned for the future. System management is done remotely via the Internet.

Intending to maintain a high level of control and message, Mayo Clinic decided early on to abstain from third-party advertising. Mayo Clinic's main goals are (1) to communicate with patients and employees, (2) to enhance and influence their experience, as well as (3) to convey important and timely messages.

Financially, Mayo Clinic's digital signage program began a handful of years ago with a budget of $200,000, which built a core system of 30 monitors fed by one server via coaxial cable. As digital signage grows at Mayo Clinic in several clinical and administrative areas, average annual costs come to somewhere in the range of $150,000–$200,000. Because the digital signage system was not built with the goal of a financial profit, but rather for its efficiency and the well-being of its audiences, no clear return on investment (ROI) benchmark was created to prepare for its implementation.

Installation of the Mayo Clinic digital signage system is at times challenging for Harmon and his colleagues. One of the reasons is that installing a monitor into a wall is often the best solution, but that means additional expenses, as well. Other questions involve safety, as well as determinations on how to distribute the signal from the servers to the monitors (e.g., via Ethernet, cable, or coax). Standardization of items, such as which monitors and where they should be placed, created additional challenges, including factors such as a logical deployment and replacement plan.

On the maintenance and service side, Harmon has learned from years of experience that requiring a multi-year service and maintenance agreement is something over which he will not compromise. These minimum 3-year agreements include coordination of training for the new deployment, as well as frequent periodic software updating sessions and on-site service. Message and content creation is put into the hands of the Mayo Clinic's individual department "customers." All content is submitted on scheduled intervals for the specific signage application. Content creation sessions are designed to be browser based and user generated, creating enhanced efficiency and user friendliness for Mayo Clinic staff members.

It is extremely unlikely the Mayo Clinic will drop its digital signage system, but an over-proliferation of screens on the campus, where audiences would not easily distinguish messaging, or if the content were to become irrelevant to audiences over time, might result in removal of the system (or parts thereof). Harmon noted that there is always room to improve the design of the system and how the content furthers the consistency of the Mayo brand (because the Mayo Clinic is such a dynamic, fluid, and ever-changing environment).

Concludes Harmon, "Digital signage is only one of Mayo Clinic's media channels, and is part of our overall corporate communications strategy. Growth potential for digital signage as a strategy in a corporate environment is huge, especially as it relates to overall employee communication and satisfaction."

One of the better known and better versed champions of the recent digital signage movement, Lyle Bunn describes digital signage (which is probably better suited for the readers of this book who wish to acquire an accurate understanding of what digital signage means and what it represents) as "a network of digital, electronic displays that are centrally managed and individually addressable for display of text, animated or video messages for advertising, information, entertainment, and merchandising to targeted audiences."

Digital signage, as described in this book, shall also include utilizations and content or devices such as flight and train information/screens, corporate communications (e.g., in conference rooms, lobbies, and training facilities), command and control center displays tied to security applications, removable media such as DVDs that are delivered by foot (often termed "sneaker-net" delivery), and specialty channels for specialty audiences, such as those in waiting rooms.

An example of a "typical commercial digital sign"—which, because the majority of digital signs are commercial, also happens to be an example of a "typical digital sign"—is shown in Figure 1.2.

It's Not TV

Also helpful is an understanding of what digital signage is not. Digital signage is not like standard over-the-air broadcast television. Instead, modern-day digital signage typically depends on more than one audio, video, or data file that gets delivered concurrently to a single screen for concurrent display. Yet, free over-the-air broadcast signals can and do typically become one of many parts of a digital display, whether for digital signage or other purposes. Thus, a typical

FIGURE 1.2 *A Typical Commercial Digital Sign at Nike Town in San Francisco (Copyright 2008. Property of Jimmy Schaeffler. All rights reserved.)*

digital display may involve multiple sets of images that are displayed on the same screen at the same time, and broadcast or multichannel TV content may be part of that.

Indeed, digital signage images emanate from numerous sources at the same time, such as a broadcast, cable, or satellite signal, and mix together on the same screen, at the same time, together with photo images, or data, animation, or other video images via signals sent from a computer or server, close by or far away. One of the wonders of digital signage is the pure and unbridled flexibility of the content that can be delivered to the medium. Where TV involves real-time content, the digital signage display features content that can be live (or "real-time"), as well as other content that is not live and is stored somewhere in a form of memory.[2]

Further, although broadcast-oriented TV content is usually created at and delivered from one or more TV stations, the content delivered to digital signs comes concurrently from many different files, and sometimes, many different places. Inasmuch as the audience for TV shows typically finds itself sitting, the same audience for digital signage content tends to be more active and mobile.

And finally, TV involves but one protocol, form, and stream to carry both analog and digital TV, whereas digital signage offers users a great variety of protocol, forms, and displays. Digital signage offers this flexibility and variety primarily via its foundation as a medium built around an Internet Protocol TV (IPTV) format.[3]

Note also that other forms of signage, such as well-lit displays on trucks and at stationary locales that offer transparent scrolling paper or cloth panels, are not examples of digital signage. Scrolling signage like this also tends to be more static and less adaptive to the elements that make digital signage so attractive to today's advertisers, vendors, and audiences: that is, instantly changeable content; in the form of a concurrent display on a single screen of slides, video, animation, audio, and/or scrolling digital data (for example); offered on a single screen or on many screens

---

2. Note that in a manner that is purposefully consistent with the sister NAB-Focal Press publication, Lars-Ingemar Lundstrom's *Digital Signage Broadcasting: Broadcasting, Content Management, and Distribution Techniques*, this book also utilizes the terms "real-time," "non-real-time," and "near-real-time," to refer to the different forms of content delivered to a digital display, and their relation to "live" versus "non-live" coverage of places, people, and events.

3. See, Lundstrom, Lars-Ingemar, *Digital Signage Broadcasting: Broadcasting, Content Management, and Distribution Techniques*, published by NAB-Focal Press, for a specific and detailed introduction to each of the technical sides of digital signage.

concurrently; presented on bright and ever-cheaper flat-panel displays; controlled from close by or incredibly afar; via the Internet and IPTV (for example).[4]

The Scope of Digital Signage

Some, if not many, of the cognoscenti who recognize and study its future, predict that digital signage will burgeon to the point where it reaches to every imaginable civilized locale. This will include structures and displays inside and out, both commercial and non-commercial, as well as in homes everywhere. In addition, at no point in the future can they foresee some form of digital signage not being a significant part of our future lives. Rather, the question becomes merely the forms it will take, and the quantity of applications, as well as—and perhaps most importantly—the controls human populations will place on this new industry.

Various business measurements are typically deployed to indicate the predicted future of a new medium. These usually involve things such as units deployed, subscribers, annual revenues, and costs per thousands of consumers reached (CPMs).

The underlying foundation of the digital signage industry is the global advertising industry, which is big and getting bigger. According to the advertising research and intelligence firm TNS Media Intelligence, U.S. ad spending in 2005 delivered an estimated $144 billion. On a global scale, according to the global accounting firm PricewaterhouseCoopers, global advertising spending reached $385 billion in 2005. By 2010, PricewaterhouseCoopers projects that global ad spending will reach half a trillion dollars.

According to Neilsen Monitor-Plus, the total dollar volume of the U.S. outdoor advertising industry in 2006 measured $5+ billion. From another source, Infotrends, the specific 2006 measure of digital signage spending was an estimated $1+ billion. Figure 1.3 shows digital signage (part of outdoor signage) at 3% among the plethora of different advertising types and locales.

The point is that digital signage remains relatively dwarfed compared to spending on cable and network TV, for instance, yet that former figure is ripe for change, as most reading this book will agree.

---

4. Not to belabor the obvious, but it is important to note that digital signage is also not the Internet. For example, whereas almost all Internet use by the public is done in what is a fairly intimate and typically private, person-to-monitor space, digital signage is almost always used out in the open by all of the audience that makes up the passing public at the time.

In Figure 1.4, the advertising spending picture is presented yet again through another set of research eyes, this one by Veronis Suhler Stevenson, TNS Media Intelligence Report, Universal McCann, the Outdoor Advertising Association of America, and IAB/PWC. This chart shows the overall estimates of U.S. advertising

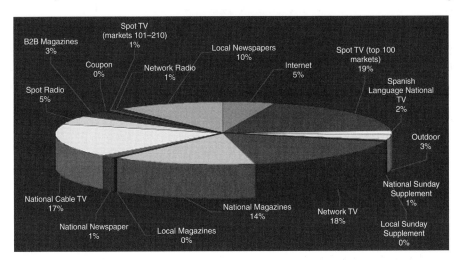

FIGURE 1.3 *2006 Advertising Dollars Indicates Only 3% Spent on All Outdoor Signage, of Which Digital Signage Is an Even Smaller—Yet Quickly Growing— Percentage (Infotrends)*

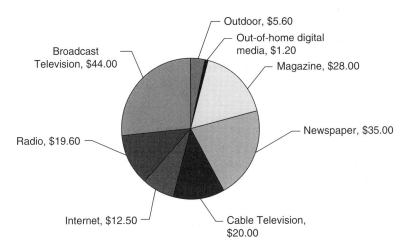

FIGURE 1.4 *2006 U.S. Advertising Spending by Media Type, with a Total of $165 Billion (Veronis Suhler Stevenson, TNS Media Intelligence Report, Universal McCann, the Outdoor Advertising Association of America, and IAB/PWC)*

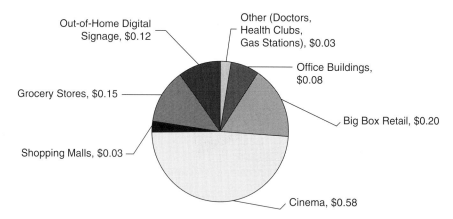

FIGURE 1.5 *2006 U.S. Advertising Spending on Out-of-Home Digital Media, with a Total of $1.2 Billion (Veronis Suhler Stevenson, TNS Media Intelligence Report, Universal McCann, the Outdoor Advertising Association of America, and IAB/PWC)*

market size, as well as the breakouts by percentage among the different ad types. Digital signage makes up a relatively small percentage and sum of the OOH digital media market, at $1.2 billion for 2006 (see Figure 1.5), however, that sum in future years is realistically expected to rise exponentially.

New York City-based Arbitron notes a study that found: (1) shoppers are very receptive to retail video via digital signage; (2) as such, retail video tends to stem the tide of commercial avoidance; and (3) retail video reaches consumers at a critical point when they are ready to purchase a product or service. Figure 1.6 further elaborates these phenomena.

While there are many variations in the estimates presented by the various research organizations presented here and elsewhere in this book, the point here is simple: The lucrative and powerful advertising industry recognizes, and thus will drive, the future of digital signage in the U.S. and globally, probably because digital signage works and it will undoubtedly work better in the future. Figure 1.5 helps make this point.

Part of the reason the advertising industry is willing to consider the potential of new media such as digital signage has to do, ironically, with the development of other new media, such as DVRs, MP3s, VOD, and the Internet. For example, a recent study by The Conference Board and YNS indicates that nearly 16% of American households that use the Internet watch television broadcasts online and

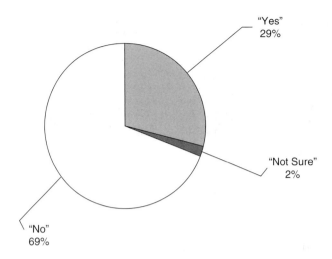

FIGURE 1.6 *Digital Signage Increases the Likelihood of Unplanned Purchases, in the Retail Environment—One in Three People Made an Unplanned Purchase After Seeing an Item Featured in a Store's Video Programming (Arbitron)*

that year over year the rate has doubled. The research firms said personal convenience and avoiding commercials were the top two reasons why consumers are flocking to the Internet for video.

Looking solely at the consumer electronics (CE) hardware behind the digital signage movement, the Arlington, VA-based Consumer Electronic Manufacturers' Association of America (CEMA), using data from a study conducted by Isuppli/Stanford Resources, projected that the overall worldwide retail signage market was $501 million in 2003, with a growth projection including a 29% CAGR, growing to $2.35 billion in 2009. 2003 display revenues were comprised of plasma at $310 million with LED video at $156, rear projection at $19, and LCD at $16 million. By 2009, plasma displays are expected to generate $1.14 billion in revenues, followed closely by LCDs at $996 million. In the same year, LED and rear-projection displays are expected to achieve $220 million and $30 million sales, respectively. Figures 1.7 and 1.8 depict an important cross section of this digital signage CE growth.

As further referenced in Chapter 3, some analysts are suggesting that the overall U.S. digital signage industry will produce revenues nearing $2.5 billion by year-end 2010. Pointing toward numbers like these, of the 450,000 billboards around the country, about 500 are digital, and all have been erected within the past 2 years or so. Hundreds more are planned to go up in 2008, according to the

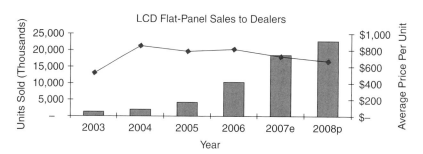

FIGURE 1.7 *The Actual and Expected Growth of Flat-Panel Plasma Screens for 2003–2008 (Consumer Electronic Manufacturers' Association. Used with permission.)*

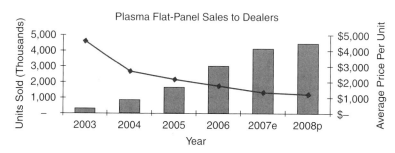

FIGURE 1.8 *The Growth of Actual and Estimated Sales to Electronics Dealers of the Other Major Digital Signage Screen Format (i.e., LCD, for 2003–2008) (Consumer Electronic Manufacturers' Association. Used with permission.)*

Outdoor Advertising Association of America, the outdoor advertising industry's Washington, DC, lobby group.

On another level of measurement, examples of digital signage networks include estimates of Wal-Mart's 75,000 displays, McDonald's 43,000 displays, and CompUSA's 8,240 screens in 103 stores, with as many as 80 screens per store in some locations.

Core Opportunities and Challenges

As detailed in Chapter 3, there are a great number of opportunities and a handful of critical challenges ahead for the digital signage industry.

Key among the challenges are education, unrealistic expectations, costs, finding appropriate business models, and the relative newness of the digital signage medium.

Key among the opportunities are some of the same things that we label above as "challenges." Thus, there is true opportunity in educating business and consumers about, finding ways to lower the costs of, finding appropriate business models for, and exploiting the newness and uncharted territories that make up today's (and tomorrow's) digital signage world.

Digital Signage Today

Digital signage can be found in the following key locales, especially ones where there is a so-called "captive" (or waiting) audience:

- Malls
  - Kiosks
  - Information displays
- At retail
  - Supermarkets, department and drug stores
  - Gas stations, convenience stores
- Streets, freeways (i.e., billboards)
- Trade shows
- Cinemas, theaters
- Hotel and motel lobbies
- Vehicles
  - Busses, taxis, and airplanes
- Travel centers
  - Customer terminals
  - Airports, subways, and train stations
  - Elevators (and waiting areas in front of elevators)
- Stadiums and arenas
- Public buildings and places

- Hospitals
- DMVs
- Public authorities
- Municipal crossroads
- Houses of worship
- Amusement parks
- Gambling and gaming centers
- Restaurants
- Banks
- Health facilities
    - Salons, health spas
    - Doctors', veterinarians', and dentists' offices
- Factories and manufacturing
- Any place selling digital screens should be using digital signage (and use inventory on the floor in the form of digital signage).

Future locales for digital signage are also worth noting in this section because, as noted in Chapter 11, many are being experimented with today, and some beta tests are ongoing to bring them into more and more places. These include:

- in car navigation systems (huge need tied-in appropriately with use by the consumer);
- in clocks at the airport (few have it; every gate needs one; they should be ad-sponsored, including a discreet, relevant, and changeable advertisement);
- just imagine it (but do deploy it correctly, so that the audience enjoys, is and helped by, and appreciates the message).

Purposes of Digital Signage

Digital signage can today be used to deliver content that falls primarily into four distinct (but often overlapping) forms: commercial, informational, experiential, and behavioral.

Commercial

There is little doubt that commercial versions of digital signage are the most important part of the phenomenon. This is, in large measure, because this is the side of the industry where the money resides. Furthermore, commercial utilizations of digital signage are an answer to the rather chaotic environment advertisers and their patrons find themselves in as they enter a new century. The reasons for this chaos are tied to consumers' abilities (and desire) to turn off or ignore ads, together with the lack of relevant or meaningful advertising content to address their consumption needs.

Several key forms of digital signage will lead the pack of future commercial uses. First will be the traditional form of product or service sales. Second will be the implementation of brand and image introduction and enhancement. Another will be tied in with behavioral digital signage, where, as noted in greater detail later, potential customers will be encouraged to go into a retail outlet or stay longer and spend more money.

Informational

From Paris, France, to Shanghai, China, travel center usage of digital signage and displays has proliferated in recent years. As airports upgrade to place themselves more in the forefront of modern-day travel, installation of large and vivid digital displays is becoming quite commonplace. To date, most of these displays are limited to mere flight information and data, however, future displays recommend the possibility to tie in directly with commercial, behavioral, and experiential usages as well.

Another example is the wait-queue for international travelers entering a new country and preparing for an interview with a local customs agent. This is a unique chance to inform the visitor, in his or her language, of the why, who, and how of immigration, thus easing the visitor's or new resident's anxiety and helping him or her to better assist and communicate with the customs representative. In short, the proper implementation of digital display in this environment helps each party to do the job better.

Another ideal example is a waiting room of a medical facility, where patients are introduced to various medical products and services via digital displays. Chapters 2 and 9 offer case studies where these digital signage systems in medical facility waiting rooms are operating successfully.

Experiential

Picture a medical clinic or doctor's office where patients are waiting to be examined. Nerves and anxiety are high, and time passes slowly. Typically, much of the worry is driven by an acute lack of information about what malady afflicts, and how it can be treated.

In this scenario, new digital signage services such as Baby-TV and emebaVet, have been introduced. Another example, as indicated in Figure 1.9, is the Mayo Clinic digital display system, which actively deploys digital signage for use by its doctors, nurses, and related staff members, as well as its thousands of annual patients. In each of these instances, there is a sincere effort being made by the business owner, content provider, and operator to put the patient and his or her loved ones at ease, to inform them about their condition, and/or to help them pass the otherwise difficult time waiting for service.

Another example would be digital signage placed in hospitality centers, such as hotels, spas, and restaurants. Like hospitals and veterinarians' offices, digital signage content affects perceived waiting time. As importantly, content messages provide anything from recipes and descriptions of meals served to public service announcements; to information on health center treatments, products, and other services; to information about various visitors' attractions from the hotel concierge. Indeed, as is true of so many present-day applications of digital display,

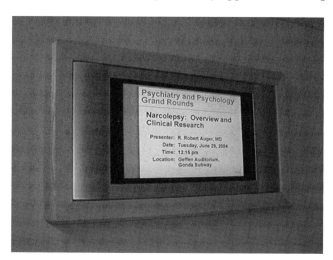

FIGURE 1.9 *An Example of a Typical Mayo Clinic Digital Poster in Rochester, MN, That Informs Employees and Patients (Copyright 2007. Property of Mayo Clinic. All rights reserved. Used with permission.)*

these examples scratch the surface of what can and will be displayed in the future. Chapter 11 will more completely address these possibilities.

Behavioral

At a convenience store, a bank, or a post office facility, for example, customers either wait in line or wait for the completion of their service. In these types of situations, consumers are, in essence, part of a "captive audience." Indeed, absent something such as a form of digital signage, they either do nothing, get aggravated waiting, or wile away the time daydreaming, or checking a personal digital assistant or cell phone.

A well-positioned and well-presented digital sign, with first rate content that is relevant and stimulating, can serve not only to pass the time, but as importantly, to also engage other products or services in, nearby, or at another similar facility. Thus, a bank patron might be encouraged to activate an automatic payroll check deposit service, rather than wait in line every other week. Or a post office patron might be encouraged to use a lobby machine to weigh his or her package himself and then use a credit card to pay for the postage, place the postage himself on his parcel, and place the parcel in the pick-up bin. And a gas station-convenience store customer can be conveniently addressed while pumping his or her gas, given important information about weather, stock markets, and other relevant content, and motivated to go inside to buy certain convenience store products because of certain offers or sales.

Screens or Displays

Understanding the "big picture" of digital signage also requires a basic understanding of the basic types of screens (or display devices), where the content is shown, and how the consumer receives and reacts to the on-screen message. These devices are another part of the package that is driving this industry's new-found success. One thing they all have in common is a compact form, usually meaning the screen or display is much, much thinner than old-style cathode-ray TV sets, and thus able to be cost-effectively, conveniently, and attractively displayed in a huge range of locales. Digital signage is also working because of its ability to be displayed in a large range of screen sizes, from huge arena screens to the smallest of 1.5 inch by 1.75 inch personal digital assistants. Also importantly, digital signage is working because the screens provide such high-definition quality resolution. The author advises spending the time to investigate and understand and/or hiring someone who does, to get a proper handle on the proper implementation of quality and acceptable performing digital signage hardware.

> For a more complete review of the technical specifics of these types of screens, readers are recommended to see chapter two of Lars-Ingemar Lundstrom's NAB/Focal Press book, *Digital Signage Broadcasting: Broadcasting, Content Management, and Distribution Techniques.*

Scrolling Message Boards

Scrolling message boards, also known as Betabrite screens (see Figure 1.10), are the type seen in modern movie theaters, where the data delivered on-screen is usually displayed in a moving fashion right to left or vice versa, or up and down, in a single color (typically red on a black background), in anything from a near-static positioning to a constant movement.

Plasma Displays

As is true for television screens, in digital signage, for screens larger than 42 inches (107 cm) in width, plasma flat-screen monitors are the acceptable norm. Because of their contrast capabilities, plasma screens are ideal for retail environments.

FIGURE 1.10 *A Scrolling Message Board Advertising Off-Track Betting at the Monterey, CA, Fairgrounds (Copyright 2008. Property of Jimmy Schaeffler. All rights reserved.)*

LCDs

For screens smaller than 40 inches (102 cm), LCDs are flat-screen monitors that have contrast ratios that are not quite as good as those of plasma screens, which should be a consideration when making screen choices. Conversely, obtaining high-level resolution is an easier chore using a LCD than it is using a plasma screen. In addition, LCDs may also include a class of screens called thin film transistor (TFT) LCDs, often used with computers, and can offer "touch screen"-type interactivity, which most other types of screens cannot.

LED Displays

LEDs are based on the principle that light is emitted in certain organic compounds when electrons and electron holes (the lack of electrons) are joined. Today, LEDs are used primarily in very small displays like mobile phones, MP3 players, and digital cameras. There are, however, prototypes for up to 40-inch TV displays. LCDs and plasmas will likely face tough competition from LEDs in the next few years.

Electronic Billboards

The only large screens that can truly handle harsh outdoor temperatures outside are LEDs, however, they are big consumers of electricity. LED techniques are also used for smaller digital signs, such as for text messages on busses, at railway stations, and in airports. Figure 1.11 shows an electronic billboard in use in California.

Projection Screens

Two main types of projector screens, LCD and digital light processing (DLP), highlight the technology behind these kinds of digital displays. Typically, projection systems are most suited for cinema- or theater-like environments. Nonetheless, newer technology is permitting the application of projection screens in retail and public environments. Projection screens are also a relatively cheap way to conduct a digital signage project, although they do require a place to house the projector and a wall on which the image can be projected.

Round Screens and Images on Windows

A few other types of digital signage screens are in development or already entering the market. For example, companies like German-based Litefest are rolling out round screen, kiosk-like, 2- or 3-foot diameter free-standing round screens, such as the one shown in Figure 1.12. These are being deployed in places like malls and airports, especially where high visibility is important and floor space is at a premium. Moreover, some today are discussing the concept of digital signage in the

FIGURE 1.11 *A Large Electronic Billboard on a California Freeway (Copyright 2007. Property of Clear Channel Outdoor. All rights reserved. Used with permission.)*

FIGURE 1.12 *A New, Narrow, Round, and Tall Kiosk-Like Digital Signage Application (Copyright 2008. Property of Jimmy Schaeffler. All rights reserved.)*

form of an entire side of a large, high-rise building, every window of which would make up part of the total screen. Cities like New York, Chicago, and Tokyo are expected to be ideal candidates for major unveilings of these types of mass-image digital signage.

Electronic Paper

Electronic paper (also known as e-paper) is another form of digital signage technology, one that tries to duplicate the look of regular ink on paper, yet reflects light-like ordinary paper and is capable of holding text and images indefinitely without drawing electricity. It will also allow the image to be changed later. Unlike traditional digital displays, e-paper can be bent or crumpled like regular paper, making it ideal for certain applications. It is lightweight, durable, and very flexible, compared with other display technologies.

Self-Illuminating Digital Paper

E-paper should not be confused with digital paper. Digital paper is also called interactive paper, in large measure because it can be used together with a digital pen, allowing the user to create handwritten digital documents. The digital pen acts to store the handwriting or other creations and then upload them to a computer.

Hardware Infrastructure

Beyond the displays, probably the next most important piece of practical hardware supporting a digital signage and display system is the server. Many simpler systems use basic personal computers or laptop computers as servers. They collect, store, arrange, and display the multilayered content and present it for delivery to the screen. Yet, recognizing a PC's or laptop's processing and storage limitations, many more sophisticated digital signage networks are deploying larger and more capable dedicated servers. These are complex computers that have the size, storage, and capability to do many things on a single screen at one time—or to do the same thing or something different on many screens at the same time, often in dozens, scores, hundreds, thousands, or tens of thousands of screens scattered around the world.

Additional hardware pieces typically include those on the receiver side, and those of the transmit side. On the receiver side, a single digital signage display is comprised of the display device itself, the server/player, and any applicable wiring (unless wireless antennas are deployed, which isn't always the case given the questions about the quality delivery of video via wireless), and either a digital sub-scriber line (DSL) router or satellite antenna. Some businesses, such as theaters, also deploy additional servers, often called "side" or "edge" servers, which are often used to store advertisement files.

On the transmit side, a network operations center (NOC) and a content man-agement server (for software control and monitoring) are typically involved. Some of the more advanced satellite delivery systems use multicasting, which would include a multicasting server and IP encapsulator. On the "extremely low-tech" side of digital signage, a DVD player might also be termed a form of digital signage hardware, even if it includes the even lower-tech form of DVD distribution and delivery, that is, "sneaker-net" (or foot) delivery of the DVDs to the digital signage locale.

Content

Some would rather call the "software" side of digital signage the "creative" side. This is because the content or software is where the greatest range of long-term creativity arises. Indeed, the importance of this side of the business cannot be underestimated. On the software side of digital displays, specific details include on-screen content, planning and scheduling, content security, proof of playback, dynamic screen zones, and network control, as well as applications software.

The on-screen content on digital signage devices is typically quite varied, which is another reason the medium is flourishing. In addition to audio and video signals from over-the-air broadcast television, cable, Direct Broadcast Satellite (DBS), and telephone company video (telco), Internet streaming and IPTV are the basis for the content that populates today's digital signage and display devices. These signals will typically fill up just one section of a device (or screen), which is usually called a region, a zone, or a ticker. Other content shown concurrently on other zones, regions, or the like include still pictures, PowerPoint slides, anima-tion, and other forms of full-motion video.

In short, the sky becomes the limit when it comes to the creative uses of dif-ferent types of moving and moveable content being shown at the same time on different parts of the screens and displays that make up the digital signage world. Indeed, some new advertising and retail commercial entities are moving to cre-ate content presentations that are more like their own in-house or in-store custom networks. A typical list or "log" of content will include multiple images shown concurrently, involving still photos, animation, live video (both real-time and non-real-time), and varied audio feeds, all aiming to educate, entertain, inform, modify behavior, and send an appropriate advertising message to a unique, identifiable, and typically mobile audience.

Worth also including in a listing of basic software is the proprietary middleware that operates programs and makes the content work on screen, and the content files that end up being actually displayed on the digital display (or screen). Select server and media player software is also a very important part of this middleware. More and more people in the digital signage world are calling middleware the "software control system," to better describe its functioning.

Interestingly, the recent introduction of digital signage software that is provided free of charge to the end user might well increase the number of potential digital sign users. Free software makes much more attractive the economics of digital signage. This is especially the case with small businesses and non-commercial digital sign users, such as educational institutions, hospitals, and churches.

Distribution

Three key methods of distribution are behind the content delivered to today's digital signage networks and devices.

First is the traditional wireline form of distribution. This form includes wires from cable, telco, and Internet service providers (ISPs), whose wires and signals are delivered to a server and then relayed further by wires to a user. It also includes specially installed wiring, for example, that done for an in-office computer system, such as a local area network (LAN).

Second is the terrestrial wireless distribution form. This is the form used by cell phones.

Third is the delivery of content via satellites. Companies such as HughesNet and Convergent (today owned by Technicolor, a subsidiary of French-owned Thomson) offer systems and services that employ the use of satellites positioned anywhere from hundreds to tens of thousands of miles above the earth. These satellites serve as relay stations for data starting at one point in a region on earth and coming back down into another point in the same (or another) region or "footprint."

Whatever the distribution form, one strength that digital signage holds from a vendor point of view is the ability of certain retail or other outlets to send content simultaneously to one or to literally tens of thousands of locations. Figure 1.13 provides a Nielsen example of 11 of the U.S.'s largest retailers and where their

FIGURE 1.13 *Retail Networks Offer Massive Coverage of the Entire U.S. (Nielsen. Used with permission.)*

stores are located. Such retailers are ideal for the implementation of large-scale digital signage network operations.

Nonetheless, as noted previously, some digital signage distribution is still stuck in the low-tech days of old distribution of media, such as hand delivery of (or sneaker-netting) DVDs to the digital signage displays within some networks.

Trends Propelling Digital Signage

Wisdom and telecom industry experience suggest it is a matter of when the digital signage revolution truly takes off, rather than if. The future appears that obvious.

Five specific trends point to the rapid development of the global digital signage industry:

(1) The personalization of messages to individual consumers.

(2) The transfer of content from device to device and person to person.

(3) The global deployment of High Definition Television (HDTV) and IPTV.

(4) The enhancement of storage and digital technologies across continents, media, and devices.

(5) The need for enhanced advertising opportunities offered to the world's producers of products and services.

Yet, the changes ahead for broadcasters, multichannel operators, telcos, advertisers, and their allies are hard to estimate when it comes to the combination of technology, software, and hardware that makes up digital signage.

Digital Signage Stakeholders

Absolutely necessary to a clear understanding of the dynamics behind digital signage is the comprehension of the different constituents and, especially, where a newcomer might fit in. Although not entirely inclusive, the list below categorizes the different roles occupied by many of the industry's key stakeholders.

Advertisers

As noted frequently throughout this book, the real driving force behind the development and deployment of global digital signage will be advertisers, many of whom will be driven to deploy digital signage by their advertising clients. Nonetheless, it is critical for today's advertisers to realize how different digital signage is today from traditional advertising, be it the difference between static signage and digital content on digital screens, on one hand, or the difference between a traditional broadcast TV ad and a digital signage ad, on the other.

Network Operators

Network operators are usually businesses that work with location owners and end users to create and manage the core system that delivers the content to the digital signage screens. The network operator is usually capable of supplying everything on the creative (i.e., content) and the technical (i.e., hardware) sides of the digital signage business, although it can also deliver a mere part of the infrastructure and allow the location owner or similarly situated vendor to contract with other vendors for specialized parts or services. A good example of a network operator in this mold is Germantown, MD-based HughesNet, which offers turn-key systems (including content delivery), as well as separate, individual digital signage components.

Plus, the actual operational details, day-to-day and month-to-month, are typically the responsibility of the network operator.

Mobile, Interactive, Touch Screen, and RFID Technology Providers

Mobile, interactive, touch screen, and RFID technology providers might be looked at as the "cutting edge" and sometimes "future" providers of the digital signage world. That is because these are the key areas where digital signage is moving beyond the traditional views of content and hardware delivery. These providers are constantly thinking up new ways to enhance the receptivity and enjoyment of consumers as it relates to the new medium of digital signage. Indeed, as it relates to future trends and converging technologies, these mobile, interactive, touch screen, and RFID technology providers are most likely to pave the way to new digital signage activities and growth.

ISP, Satellite, Cable, Telco, and Wireless Providers

One way or another, each of the ISP, cable, telco, wireless, and satellite (or Very Small Aperture Terminal (VSAT)) providers is a media transport solution. These operators have the backbone infrastructure that allows them to send the signal from point to point and, eventually, to the digital signage or display screen. ISP providers include AOL, Earthlink, and NetZero; cable providers include companies such as Comcast and Time Warner; telco providers are those such as AT&T and Verizon; wireless providers are exemplified by Verizon and Cingular; and satellite providers again include VSAT operators, such as HughesNet and ViaSat.

Ultimately, it becomes their job to transport and distribute the content from place to place. Some in the industry refer to these initial distributors of content as "back end" providers, meaning they are often much further away from the point-of-presence/point-of-purchase near the end user or audience (as it relates to the delivery of the digital signage on-screen content).

Traditional Billboard Companies

These are the companies that should be quite concerned about digital signage, because, already, companies are beginning to replace static, vinyl billboards with large electronic billboards, especially in larger cities like Los Angeles and Las Vegas. In fact, for these companies, the transition suggests a remarkable example of businesses possibly being left behind and left irrelevant if they do not keep up with emerging trends. In many recent cases, the traditional billboard companies are looking toward digital signage alternatives because of enhanced economic and regulatory hurdles. Chapter 11 features a case study discussing the experiences of an industry-leading outdoor digital signage operator.

Kiosk Providers

Mall walkways for the public are the locations where round, narrow, and tall kiosks are typically found. These are stands incorporating video and audio to inform, entertain, and encourage people to buy products or services or to visit certain mall areas. Increasingly, these kiosks are not only delivering sophisticated digital content, but are also locales where the best in new, two-way interactive customer-to-vendor/advertiser interaction is taking place. Types of interactive screens include touch screens, and screens that interact with credit and smart card operations. Consumers tend to find these types of interactive digital signs more and more helpful and acceptable, especially when the creators do their jobs well. ATMs are yet another example of digital signs that serve people particularly well.

Flat-Panel Display Providers

Once the standard TV screen moved from the days of huge and heavy cathode-ray tube screens to so-called flat-screen displays, the digital signage industry had yet another of its key developmental elements in place. Today, the thin screens are also being termed "flat-panel displays." The technology that goes into these devices is becoming more and more sophisticated and is offering better quality and even slimmer designs. More than any other digital signage hardware item, flat-panel displays are the core hardware item supporting the medium and its recent growth. This is in part because they are the final display device for presentation of the actual content to the viewing audience, and thus have perhaps the greatest effect on the reliability and the quality of the content displayed.

System Contractors

A "system contractor" is typically a company that undertakes a contract to build a digital signage system. These contractors are to be differentiated from network operators, the latter of whom actually handle the day-to-day operations behind the particular functioning digital signage system.

Software Suppliers

There are two types of software suppliers. This book refers to those that create and provide the on-screen video, slides, pictures, animation, and data as the content providers. The other suppliers are those that provide the software control systems, also known to some as middleware providers. These companies that provide the software control systems are referred to by many in the digital signage industry as the "glue that holds the network together."

Store Fixture Providers

These are the companies—typically local and small- to mid-sized companies—whose on-site personnel install and maintain the in-store networks and display devices. Store fixture providers are often hired by system contractors to complete the in-store installation of digital signage deployments.

Digital Printers

Digital printers are those that send digital pictures and billboards via the Internet, offering on-site digital printing services to retailers and the like. Essentially, this service allows shops to print out their own posters or billboards. And like traditional billboard providers, digital printer operations have much to learn from close tracking of the blossoming digital signage industry.

Audio/Visual Professionals

For traditional audio–video rental, service, and installation vendors, digital signage offers an additional new opportunity to broaden their portfolios of services, adding installation and maintenance of digital signage to their list of products and services.

Buyers and Location Owners

Those who pay for and therefore decide to actually implement a new digital signage deployment are typically in this category of buyers and location owners. Nonetheless, as seen clearly in Chapters 6 and 8, these stakeholders also typically do not actually implement all or any of the system themselves, but rather bring in digital signage experts to set it up and do it correctly the first time.

Restaurateurs, Hospitality, and Entertainment

Each of these categories of commercial providers is in a position to dramatically enhance their customers' experience, and generate revenue from partners who want to advertise on their networks. It is important for these vendors to appreciate just how important these two objectives, enhancing customers' experiences and creating revenues, can be toward the achievement of their ultimate business goals. Any location, from a diner, to a small motel, to an amusement park, would be one where its constituents would get a lot out of relevant and helpful digital signage content.

Retailers

Among all the actual and would-be stakeholders, the group of retailers is perhaps the most important single group when it comes to the long-term future and success of the digital signage industry. This is in some measure because, as the old bank robber adage goes, "That's where the money is." Focus for this audience will be on getting proper digital signage deployments to help retailers make money, by cost effectively selling advertising time on their networks, pushing sales, and imprinting their corporate brands in consumers' psyches. Yet this audience must always be cautioned: do it with relevance and sensitivity, and do it right!

Integrators

Different from the ISP, satellite, cable, telco, and wireless providers, the companies that label themselves integrators are tasked with bringing together all of the hardware and software elements and constructing a digital signage network or smaller system. Like the system contractors, these are often local entrepreneurs, although they can also be headquartered far away from various digital signage locales, instead traveling temporarily from site to site for installation.

Banks and Financial Institutions

One of the better known waiting places for modern-day adults is the bank teller line in the local bank. It creates the perfect convergence of an audience that is idle (and perhaps not happy about the wait and thus prime for a mood change) and the opportunity to inform and educate that audience about the bank's or institution's goods and services. Chapters 8 and 10 contain case studies examining this financial environment.

Transportation Hubs

Business people and their families are frequent travelers. As such, few have visited modern airports, bus stations, and train stations—and gas station and convenience stores—without seeing and using a digital sign. These digital signs are used to convey commercial messages and digital displays of visitor entertainment and information. A huge part of the transportation industry's future will be tied to digital signage, and vice versa. Chapter 8 contains a case study reviewing a typical digital signage environment (i.e., an airport).

Costs

As further noted in Chapter 3, "typical" digital signage costs can range widely, dependent on the individual choices made throughout the process on the hardware, software, and even the installation sides of the implementation. Nonetheless, a set of figures from a respected, yet anonymous, vendor shows in Table 1.1 what a conservative outlay of funds might involve in 2008. These expenses are represented relative to one another in the chart in Figure 1.14.

On the content, installation, and maintenance sides of a cost presentation, as noted in more detail in Chapter 3, up-front and longer-term costs vary widely, dependent upon a huge variety of criteria. These criteria include the number of outlets, screens per outlet, sophistication of the files making up the content, the number of files, plus whether a PC or a larger server is utilized, just to name a few.

Single monitor	$1,500/site
Single media server	$1,500/site
Remote installation	$1,500/site
Network terminal	$2,000/site
Network services	$40/site/month
Digital signage services	$50/site/month
Remote maintenance	$45/site/month
Content creation fees	$20,000/month

TABLE 1.1 *Typical Digital Signage Costs*

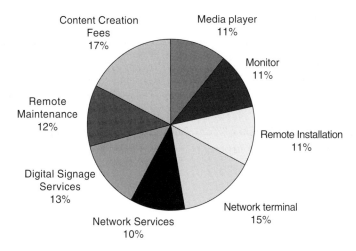

FIGURE 1.14 *A Percentage Breakdown of Total Costs for a "Typical" Digital Signage Deployment*

Consumer Receptivity

Regardless of which research and measurement company conducts the data gathering, Arbitron or Nielsen, both indicate that consumer receptivity to quality digital signage is surprisingly high. As Figure 1.15 shows, theater viewers prefer digital signage in the form of cinema ads to the mere re-airing of TV ads in the same theaters. Moreover, almost two-thirds of moviegoers in the Arbitron study recited solid recall of digital signage ads presented before a movie. One in five of all moviegoers state they are more interested in a product or service after they see it featured on a movie screen. More than half of consumers believe it is acceptable to show ads before a movie, a number that is even higher than the 46% who feel it is acceptable to show ads on television; 36% surveyed felt it was acceptable to show ads before movies presented at home on DVD, 18% on the Internet, and 18% by way of embedded ads in video games.

From a slightly different vantage point, the New York City-based Nielsen organization summarized 30 studies observing the digital signage receptivity of large audiences. Nielsen found that these audiences presented two key attributes as they relate to digital signage in general, nationwide. First, respondents stated that digital signage enhanced their visit and made it more enjoyable. Second, they opined that digital signage was a good thing for the site to offer. Put another way, four out of five surveyed reacted positively and less than one out of ten were notably negative.

Nonetheless, key players in the future growth of digital signage will be required to be diligent and careful so as to not upset or alienate one particularly

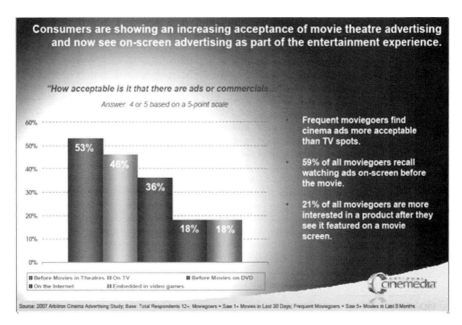

FIGURE 1.15 *An Arbitron Measurement Shows That a Theater Audience's Receptivity to Digital Signage Is High*

important audience: the consumer. If future digital signage applications turn out to be cluttered, intrusive, and insensitive to various audiences' needs, large numbers and percentages of people will be turned off by the new medium. At that point, one of any medium's best sales tools—word of mouth—will instead become its worst enemy. When significant numbers of people begin talking badly about a new product, service, or application, this often dispels its most rapid demise.

Two more studies, both at retail, one by a respected measurement and testing service, Arbitron, and another by a European-based advertising placement company, JC Decaux, pin-point additional causes for consumer receptivity; in short, digital signage is effective. The data from the 2005 Arbitron study and from the 2006 JC Decaux survey is summarized as follows.

2005 Arbitron Retail Study

Over 1,400 U.S. shoppers who viewed digital signage at U.S. malls on the east and west coasts indicated in response to the digital signage experience:

- 40% of them were more likely to make a purchase in stores using digital signage.

- They were 1.56 more times likely to recall a retailer's advertising spot and then make a purchase.

- They added up to seven times the sales lift overall for retailers who used digital signage to boost new-item introductions.

- 81% of the shoppers recalled content that focused on merchandise available in the store.

- 47% of them recalled learning about specials or sales.

- 72% of them in the 18–34-year-old demographic noted they were interested in the digital signage element of music videos playing while they shopped.

2006 JC Decaux/TescoTV Study

The United Kingdom's TescoTV supplier, JC Decaux, conducted research in Tesco supermarket stores, which was made available in March 2006. The study used special camera equipment to track the eye and head movements of 75 shoppers over a 3-week period. The TescoTV Network consists of 100 stores, with 50 screens in each:

- 85% of shoppers looked at a digital screen while shopping at Tesco.

- The average customer passed by 20 screens per visit, actually looking at eight of them.

- Each screen had a 40% chance of being seen, which is equal to the exposure of an outdoor, six-poster advertisement as measured by the U.K. company, Postar.

The Future of Digital Signage

Just looking at the current list of "future digital signage devices" does a lot to excite the imaginations of many observers. That's because things like RFID can be wedded to digital signage in a way that enables digital displays to instantly recognize the identity of a person approaching a digital sign. Then the sign "reacts" to the person by displaying content that is unique and relevant to that individual or the group he or she is in. Moreover, newly developed scanning devices can read a bar code or other message on a name badge or PDA and react by sending that same content to the individual's PDA for storage and later use.

For example, a digital sign might display a message in or near New York City's Times Square, advertising a product such as a premium tied to a certain brand (e.g., M&M candies). The audience member can then walk to the screen somewhere on the street; wave his/her PDA across the message transfer or communication point; have the information/content transferred to the PDA; and later download information on how to easily buy that premium online, often with the push of just a few buttons or a few clicks of a mouse. Or some kind of coupon for future submission might be offered. That is an idea of where digital signage is headed in the future. Figure 1.16 shows a huge 30-foot by 50-foot digital sign in New York City (seen through a second-story restaurant window).

Chapter 11 gives a more complete and detailed listing and description of future digital signage opportunities and applications. The two case studies in this chapter, the first one in a not-for-profit environment, the second, below, in a commercial context (and focused on the actual delivery of the all-important content to the digital signage screen), give the reader an excellent view to actual digital signage implementations, their challenges, realities, and additional views to the future.

FIGURE 1.16 *A Huge Digital Sign in Front of the M&M Mars Candy Store at the Corner of Broadway and 46th in New York City (Copyright 2008. Property of Jimmy Schaeffler. All rights reserved.)*

AccuWeather

AccuWeather, the State College, PA-headquartered entity that describes itself as the "world's leading commercial weather" information company and that also describes itself as a "content provider for digital signage," also focuses on providing value-added services for its digital signage clients, primarily in the areas of merchandising and advertising. There is a high demand for weather information, and that demand was the major motivator behind AccuWeather's launch into its digital signage business. Mike Welsh, the company's Director of Digital Signage Sales, notes "Weather information ranks as the top reason viewers choose a local TV newscast. It is also one of the most-read sections of a newspaper, one of the top three reasons listeners choose a radio station, and one of the most accessed forms of content on the Internet and mobile (wireless) web. What is more, the intense audience interest in weather enhances the value of advertising avails adjacent to it. Weather will play the same role in the next new medium—digital signage." Figure 1.17 shows the AccuWeather content on a typical digital signage display, this one located at an airport in Syracuse, New York.

FIGURE 1.17 *An AccuWeather Digital Sign, Focused on Local Weather, in the Lobby Area of an Airport in the Upstate New York Area (Copyright 2007. Property to AccuWeather. All rights reserved. Used with permission.)*

Welsh notes the significant growth the company is experiencing in its partner and customer base, as the digital signage market takes off. AccuWeather began its foray into digital signage following an in-depth analysis of the state of the industry, growth projections, potential market, competition, sales potential, and what it felt was the required investment to optimize its content and delivery service in the realm of digital signage.

Today, AccuWeather judges the effectiveness of its deployed digital signage content by how engaging it is for that audience. In short, the message from AccuWeather is that effective content needs to be visually appealing to audiences, as well as relevant—the audience's content has to be local, up to date, and reliable.

AccuWeather employs a business model that leaves the advertising potential to its customers (i.e., the ones that actually host the digital signs). AccuWeather itself does not sell advertising in the content it delivers. Instead, AccuWeather empowers its client users to attract the audiences—to their screens and to their advertising—via AccuWeather's content, which AccuWeather commits to make accurate, detailed, local, and always visually appealing. In the end, this model works in a fashion similar to network television: TV viewers tune in to the evening news, for example, and are teased through commercials with the promise of more weather details. Similarly, AccuWeather's digital signage partners use weather to hold viewers' attention to their advertising or the messaging that they provide.

The content AccuWeather currently offers is focused on its most popular weather content pieces. These include genres entitled "Current Conditions," "Today/Tonight/Tomorrow," "5-Day Forecast," "Hour-by-Hour Forecast," "National and Regional High-Resolution Doppler Radar" (with 15 minute updates), and "Presenter Lead Video Forecasts" (i.e., the top 115 DMAs in North America, 2×/day). Additionally, AccuWeather brings weather-related health indices to the industry, such as arthritis, asthma, migraine, pollen, air quality, UV index, and cold and flu. The network also provides news from The Associated Press, including sports, business, entertainment, U.S., the world, health, and science/technology.

Because the AccuWeather service involves content only, the company does not provide any software-based scheduling mechanisms for day parting. Instead, this capability is provided by its partners. AccuWeather has supported weather-targeted advertising on other media for many years, and many of its digital signage customers are currently using sky conditions, temperature thresholds, or health indices as a trigger for particular ads or messages. Examples of weather-triggered advertising in which AccuWeather has participated include links between the weather and products, such as clothing, beverages, and food, as well as more subtle examples, including advertisements for vacation locations shown during inclement weather.

Looking specifically at the weather content, AccuWeather's proprietary "Forecast Engine" produces weather data for 2.7 million points globally. Examples of the range of forecasts provided include the 24/7 comprehensive forecasts produced for all 43,000 U.S. zip codes, all 750,000 Canadian postal codes, and a collection of 40,000 non-U.S. cities. Delivery of AccuWeather content comes via HTTP Web service or File Transfer Protocol (FTP). In most cases, the AccuWeather content is delivered or served to a central server at the reseller's location. The players controlling the individual signs in the field are directed to ping the reseller central server, which forward the AccuWeather data to the player.

AccuWeather supports all major digital signage platforms, including a very wide range of content management software and hardware players. Its content is offered in a number of file types (e.g., XML, PNG, and SWF), which provides optimal solutions for each platform. AccuWeather's business model involves it receiving "cash for [its] content," and AccuWeather leaves the advertising discussion to its customers and their customers.

Some applications, such as hotel lobby digital signage, may incorporate AccuWeather's "Today/Tonight/Tomorrow" forecast as an amenity to guests, to help them better prepare for their business/pleasure in a city away from home. However, AccuWeather's content is most commonly used to attract attention to accompanying advertising content. Finally, although brand awareness is welcomed, most of AccuWeather's customers prefer to incorporate the AccuWeather.com brand as a source of authority, accuracy, and reliability in weather forecasting. The value in the exposure of the AccuWeather brand is an ancillary and welcome bonus.

AccuWeather states that it believes the digital business is poised for significant growth, as additional users of signage come to appreciate the value of weather content in attracting audiences. Early on, when considering moving into the digital signage content realm, AccuWeather created a targeted ROI plan before its initial deployment. The biggest obstacle to further digital signage content deployment is largely a function of the roll-out schedules of the company's customers. "This market is happening, and we're prepared for the demand," claims Welsh. The only question is how soon things will really take off.

Surprisingly, AccuWeather notes little negative reaction to AccuWeather's digital signage content deployment in public/outdoor locations. In all cases of feedback, its partners receive unsolicited praise for bringing to a captive, and sometimes bored, audience content that they want to see and can benefit from. AccuWeather's partner, Transit TV, has conducted impact studies of deployed, outdoor digital signage. The research provides statistics about people who depend on service for their news and weather, as well as information about the retention of commercials that air after the AccuWeather weather segment (see http://www.transitv.com/research.html, for specific details of this research).

2 What Is Digital Signage?

Digital signage provides dynamic real-time, near-real-time, or non-real-time infor-mation that may be individually adapted to the location, time, situation, and who is actually watching the screen. Using simultaneous screen elements such as regions, layers and tickers (or "crawlers"), several messages, originating from different sources (and places), may be combined on one single screen. Though providing information in a fully automated way, the medium also allows for inter-action with the viewer, using touch screens or other means of user control.

—Lars-Ingemar Lundstrom, author, *Digital Signage Broadcasting: Broadcasting, Content Management, and Distribution Techniques*, by NAB-Focal Press

The description of modern digital signage contains a handful of key ingredients. Most who follow the industry agree these generally include at least:

Digital hardware displaying **digital software** (in the form of both on-screen content and software control systems), featured on **screens that are thin and come in many sizes**, **offering constantly changing and refreshed content**, often shown on **many regions of a single screen**, capable of **delivery instantaneously** via satel-lite and the Internet, from a server or personal computer (PC), close by or on the other side of the globe, intended to be particularly **relevant and helpful** to con-sumers aimed largely at **out-of-home audiences** who are frequently **moving from place to place**, yet are often **held "captive"** by a particular situation, event, or environment.

The optimum introduction to the topic, "What Is Digital Signage" includes each of the key elements below: history, forms, technology, software, hardware, installation, maintenance, key players, trends, challenges, and opportunities. Together, these elements make up a mosaic of a remarkable new communications device—indeed, some have called digital signage a "killer application." The pic-ture that represents this new business is a vibrant one, and huge sums of resources, as well as significant consumer perceptions, will shift because of it.

Its history is founded in creative new approaches to the age-old practice of selling things, which also defines its future (as noted specifically in Chapter 11). The forms it takes today range from small, half-foot by 1-foot-sized screens, to very, very large 50-foot by 140-foot stadium screens; to quarter-mile long, 3-foot high "wrap around" arena digital displays; and to kiosk-like round displays of 3 ft in diameter and 6 or 7 ft in height, wherein the content is displayed on a round digital screen, instead of on the normal flat digital screen.

As is true with just about any consumer electronics (CE)-based product and service, a basic understanding of the technology behind digital signage helps not only from an operational point of view, but also from the standpoint of seeing where the hardware and software can go together in the future. In major parts, the software behind the digital signage industry today is comprised of the on-screen content, on the one hand, and of the software control systems on the other. The hardware is typically made up of the screens, servers, media players, PCs, mounting equipment and wiring, as well as the other wires, antennas, routers, and transponders that are part of the distribution and transport infrastructure. Installation is important from a function, safety, and effectiveness point of view. Once the system is operational, professional maintenance reinforces some of the same objectives of quality installation, that is, functioning, safety, and effectiveness, as well as system performance measurement. It also means a system that lasts longer and goes down less often.

A basic understanding of digital signage turns finally on a conceptualization of its key players and the trends that are affecting it, as well as its challenges and opportunities as a burgeoning global telecommunications industry subsector.

History

The genesis of digital signage is actually very primitive: to recognize threats and opportunities in life, human beings instinctively react to sounds and motion. Drawing from this dynamic are the earliest notions of people trying to gather the attention of others to market a product or service. On a 20th-century telecom level, early radio and certainly television—almost all of which was free-to-air advertising-supported—went a long way toward creating the early foundations of digital signage and display. Recognizable voices and faces on screens, especially ones that move, are attractive to audiences just about everywhere. Outdoor billboards are another part of the early bases of digital signage, as are the Internet, and certainly the development of digital devices, content, and standards.

Early Usages

One of the first examples of an application that could logically fall under the rubric of "digital signage" occurred in the late 1970s and 1980s, when fashion houses in places such as New York City would videotape their runway shows, record the content on a VCR, and hand deliver it to show on a bulky TV set in their retail outlets. In Canada, in 1984, the Loblaws grocery chain was among the first to place Sony analog TV sets in front of employees (used primarily to instruct and enhance compliance with rules and directives) and in front of shoppers (used to further sales and enhance merchandising environments). TVs in bars and restaurants followed soon after. At the Canadian specialty retail chain—Athletes World—a cooperative-funded content package that brought consumers a mix of retail messages, key vendor ads, and music—called World TV—was introduced in the early 1990s to mixed success, due to key shortcomings in the areas of technology and compliance.[1]

Fast forward to the late 1990s and the development and implementation of digital media, coupled with the CE industry's efforts to create smaller, lighter, and thinner display screens (or monitors). With the CE industry's development and implementation of the highest-quality images in the form of High Definition TV (HDTV), another foundation is laid. The Japanese-inspired development of digital devices thus set the stage for digital signage. Indeed, Fujitsu's alliance with U.S. PixelWorks in 1997 to offer U.S. buyers the first plasma display device—a $13,100, 42-inch screen of mediocre quality yet revolutionary new size dimensions—was a critical early catalyst. Very few who understood the concept of signage used to sell things (or motivate people to action) could miss the potential new applications that arose for screens this thin and light.

Flat-panels began replacing posters and signs, led by such industry pioneers as Planar's Brad Gleeson, Scala's Jeff Porter, and 3M's Ian Forbes and John Kirkpatrick (the latter of whom many believe was the first to coin the term "digital signage" for the new industry). Others who were early to test and implement the digital signage industry included Bunn Company's DW+ Partners' Graeme Spicer, Marketforward's Manny Almagro, Dawson & Company's Carre Dawson, Broadsign's Dave Haynes, Impart's Thomas Muniz, Adspace founder, Lou Giacalone, and PRN's Sean Moran. One key effort involved using the flat screens to replace the "boxy rear-projection screens," as Gleeson terms them. Companies such as Pioneer, Panasonic, and Philips became early investors in digital signage CE, as well.

---

1. "Compliance," in this sense, refers to employees at screen locations actually operating the digital signage system properly, for example, by making sure that proper tapes get inserted into the digital video recorders (DVRs) and shown on the screen in a timely and scheduled manner.

Nonetheless, finding the right distributors and right business models remained a challenge. In fact, a great deal of assets and revenues were squandered early on, as new developments were perfected. A Women's Shopping Network, assisted by on-air talent Joan Lunden, was an example of early stumbling, tied to improper funding and improper focus on hardware and network concerns, rather than on the all-important content.

Successful Installations

When the focus of digital signage truly turned to trade shows and unique gaming locales, the digital signage industry began to blossom. Looking at individual examples, one of the first true large-scale implementations of digital signage came, not surprisingly, from the minds of several casino entrepreneurs in Las Vegas, NV, who placed more than 100 plasma screens inside the casino at Mandalay Bay, late in 1999.

Moreover, because trade shows were another early hot bed of digital signage development, industry veterans tell humorous stories of their members, mostly from among the hardware and software companies dabbling in digital signage, getting together infrequently at these trade shows, and informally nicknaming their meetings and group as "Digital Signage Super Friends." On the serious side, these meetings were also the genesis for new trade show and publications plans (e.g., new affiliations with the pre-existing POPAI trade organization, as well as shows such as the Digital Retailing Exposition, and publications such as the *Digital Signage Quarterly* and *Digital Signage Resource Directory*).

Industry trade group for retail sales

POPAI stands for the Point-Of-Purchase Advertising Institute. As stated on its website, www.popai.com, POPAI is an international trade marketing association for the marketing at-retail industry. Founded in 1936, POPAI celebrated its 70th anniversary with more than 1,700 member companies representing *Fortune* 500 brand manufacturers and retailers, as well as marketing at-retail producer companies and advertising agencies from over 45 countries around the world.

Trade shows were good places for digital signage because flat screens worked well in cramped quarters, and video and audio did a good job of displaying a booth's products and services. Digital plasma screens were also relatively easy to ship and store [at least compared to their predecessors, 100-lb analog cathode-ray tube (CRT) TVs]. Worth noting is that in this pre-retail, early trade show digital signage environment, the winning message was quite similar to that of today: discover how to educate, influence, entertain, and/or inform an audience.

Looking deeper at the early gaming environment, an example of digital signage and its ability to evoke consumer action was the placement of flat screens in certain areas of casinos, offering content that told of huge jackpots at certain slot machines, often tied to greater pay-off percentages coming from collections of slots in other casinos around the world, labeled "progressive jackpots." "Vegas and the gambling industry understood the potential of digital signage very early," notes Spicer. As such, Las Vegas became the center of such digital signage firsts at retail, in restaurants, and in convenience stores.

Current Opportunities

Today, according to a number of estimates, the total number of digital signage screens in North America is more than half a million. That number is expected to double in the next 2–3 years. A large percentage of this growth is naturally tied to the retail development of digital signage, which is expected to be quite large. Indeed, there are lots of opportunities to use digital signage at retail, many by some who have never tried it before, and many more that have never been tried before by anyone. That said, making digital signage work at retail remains a challenge. As noted further in this book, hundreds of critical questions arise. Can an acceptable return on investment (ROI) be achieved? If not or if it cannot be measured, are there other reasons to justify having a digital signage system? To avoid the harsh light of for-profit measures and concerns, sometimes stores consider their digital signage systems as part of their inventory of store fixtures, which can skirt the black or white issues of payback and margins.

Add to that the ability to create content that is then sent to the display device via the Internet from anyplace in the world where the Internet connects, and the elements for a successful new business are in place. As for today, we've moved past the Wild West of digital signage and display. The formation of rules and guidelines is in its early stages, and lots of new ideas are being tested and perfected. For broadcasters, multichannel operators, and related industry vendors, digital signage offers an attractive prospect, because it offers an answer and an alternative to the business they are losing to the depletion of traditional advertising assets.

Forms

Numerous forms of digital signage exist today, and many more are expected in the future, as the medium develops.

The classic forms of what is truly digital signage involve scrolling message boards, in places such as stadiums, banks, and retail stores; liquid crystal displays (LCD) and plasma displays, ranging anywhere from 3 inch to 80 inch; CRT monitors; electronic billboards in arenas, ball parks, and along freeways; rear- and front-projection screens; and organic light emitting diode (LED) screens. A company in Germany, LiteFast, even offers a digital sign in the form of a 6-foot high, 3-foot diameter round kiosk-like display, which brightly shines the moving digital content on a curved glass surface (see Figure 2.1).

FIGURE 2.1 *A Round Digital Sign Exhibited by the Company LiteFast (Copyright 2008. Property of Jimmy Schaeffler. All rights reserved.)*

Another way to look at the forms of digital signage is to look at the locale in which they are placed. For simplicity, these can be broken down into commercial and non-commercial groupings. Commercial locales are those that are truly signs and thus offered to sell products and services in commercial environments. Non-commercial displays are not as frequently considered "signs" or "signage" in the normal sense of the word, and are seen in places not normally associated with commercial sales.

Non-Commercial

A flat-screen panel placed in the lobby of a college, advising and educating prospective students and parents of the institution's assets, would be better termed a digital display than a digital sign. In some measure because of their slow growth thus far, the entire area of non-commercial digital displays is expected to grow even quicker than that for the commercial side. In this vein, use of digital displays by faith-based institutions has just begun what is expected to be a huge growth pattern.

Other locales for non-commercial deployment of digital signage screens include factories, government and travel centers, as well as churches, temples, mosques, and synagogues. Worship signage might include large screens to project the image of the celebrant to those in the back of the hall. Educational institutions, such as a high school or college, could use digital signage to notify faculty, staff, and students about events, requirements, achievements, etc. These non-commercial digital displays are more fully described in Chapters 1 and 3.

Figure 2.2 shows two screens in the baggage area inside the immigration and naturalization center at San Francisco International Airport. These signs, one a flat screen and the other an old-style CRT, direct incoming residents and visitors through customs. Figure 2.3 shows a French government traffic sign with road and travel information, placed above the freeway entering Paris.

Commercial

Not surprisingly, because rather deep pockets and substantial financial and commercial assets are behind it, as between commercial and non-commercial, the commercial side of digital signage is and will, for some time, remain a much greater part of the digital signage pie.

Locales for the deployment of commercial digital signage are many and quite varied. Nonetheless, four major groupings make up a fairly complete listing of digital signage locales:

- *Retail*: Malls, supermarkets, grocery, drug, clothing, and sporting goods stores, as well as convenience stores, gas pumps, and auto repair centers (Figure 2.4).

FIGURE 2.2 *A Pair of Non-Commercial Government-Operated Digital Signs at San Francisco International Airport (Copyright 2008. Property of Jimmy Schaeffler. All rights reserved.)*

FIGURE 2.3 *A Highway Digital Road Sign in Paris, France (Copyright 2008. Property of Jimmy Schaeffler. All rights reserved.)*

FIGURE 2.4 *A Digital Sign in a Clothing Store (Copyright 2008. Property of Lyle Bunn. All rights reserved.)*

As but one example of its remarkable potential, digital signage inside shopping carts presents great promise.

- *Travel*: Airports, train stations, public transit systems, busses, taxis, walkways, on busy streets in urban locales, in elevators, on billboards beside roads and freeways, and in company lobbies (Figures 2.5 and 2.6).

- *Customer service*: Health facilities (such as spas and health clubs), doctors' waiting rooms, hotels and motels, and cinemas or theaters (Figure 2.7). This

FIGURE 2.5 *A Commercial Digital Sign on a Parisian Roadway (Copyright 2008. Property of Jimmy Schaeffler. All rights reserved.)*

FIGURE 2.6 *An Early Application of Digital Signage in Airports Is Still in Use Today (Copyright 2008. Property of Jimmy Schaeffler. All rights reserved.)*

FIGURE 2.7 *A Digital Sign in the Lobby of a San Francisco Business (Copyright 2008. Property of Jimmy Schaeffler. All rights reserved.)*

FIGURE 2.8 *A Digital Sign above a Loading Dock (Copyright 2008. Property of Jimmy Schaeffler. All rights reserved.)*

chapter's case study, featuring the veterinarian TV service, emebaVet, and the Chapter 9 case study about the U.K.'s Baby-TV, are good examples of this burgeoning digital signage "customer service" subsector.

- *Miscellaneous*: This category is ever growing, and sometimes overlapping the first three, including in factories, in employee break rooms, at trade shows, and in stadiums or arenas (Figures 2.8 and 2.9).

FIGURE 2.9 *Digital Signs Being Used at a Trade Show (Copyright 2008. Property of Jimmy Schaeffler. All rights reserved.)*

A more detailed listing and description of various locales that have thus been the base for digital signage experiments and implementations is in Chapter 1.

---

emebaVet

emeba, a Modesto, CA-based company, offers mid- to large-sized veterinary clinics across the U.S. a waiting room TV experience appropriately called emebaVet. The term "emeba" is essentially an acronym for the phrase "electronic multimedia education and business application." Vets were the first vertical market that happened to take hold for the company, so it ran the emeba name together with Vet. The service today features an "advertiser-supported client education system," according to company VP of technology, Dan Hong. From a company presentation, emebaVet states, "Digital Advertising is the new medium. It can target a captive audience geographically, demographically, and psychographically, in addition to educating the internal customer."

Currently, emebaVet is emeba's core service. Yet other offerings are planned, including those with digital signage applications in the human medical and charter airplane sectors. More than 100 digital signage screens have been deployed by emebaVet. Their goal is to get to 3,000 mid-to-upper-tier locations, where emeba estimates 80% of the vet industry revenues reside.

The service is aimed at delivering animal health-related information to the owners of pets in veterinarian offices nationwide. emebaVet has found that waiting rooms, exam rooms, and staff areas are ideal placement spots for the emebaVet digital screens (Figure 2.10). Categories of content covered include wellness, illness, lameness, nutrition, behavior products, and ancillary hospital services. Data access includes diagnostic and lab results that can be viewed. Web access includes in-room access to credit services, pet insurance, and other information. Specific content offered to waiting room visitors includes:

- Latest products and new services

- Grooming and diet tips

FIGURE 2.10 *An emebaVet Screen Deployed in a Veterinarian's Office (Copyright 2007. Property of emebaVet. All rights reserved. Used with permission.)*

- Preventative care

- Latest technology (DR, scanning)

- Advanced treatments

- Content about the veterinarians, hospital, and staff

- Human interest stories and patients pictures

- Important, national, animal-related news

The biggest motivator for emeba to first deploy emebaVet was the company's identification of a mix of industry demand: (1) by the clients, and (2) by a large, well-defined "captive audience" (in the sense that these clients are tied to the vet's waiting room until they and their pet are seen by the vet staff). The decision to deploy the emebaVet digital signage system was made following "lots of research." The founders, including Hong, visited existing deployments, went to trade shows, attended demonstrations, and did anything they could do to learn about the industry.

Early on, the greatest challenge for emebaVet was the substantial task of educating both the clients and the advertisers to the service. To better accomplish that, Hong wishes his company had, in the early years, spent more time in front of clients and advertisers, such as during group functions and trade shows.

Looking ahead, Hong sees the biggest challenge when it comes to continuing the emeba digital signage system as being that of "balancing and managing rapid growth." On a related note, the sole event that would cause emeba to discontinue its use of digital signage would be emeba moving into another industry of focus.

These days, emeba looks to satisfaction surveys and sales volume reports to assess the effectiveness of its emebaVet digital signage deployment (Figure 2.11). When asked about the primary benefit to emebaVet of using digital signage in advertising, Hong noted site-specific, measurable ROI.

Screens deployed are of either the LCD or plasma variety, while emebaVet's content is described by Hong as, "dynamic, live, information, displayed in high definition." emebaVet's digital signage network is being used for national, regional, and local targeting of vet-related audiences, including targeting down to a single location or single group of digital signs within a single location. emebaVet uses a dedicated platform solution to enable its regional or worldwide content distribution and playback. emebaVet also utilizes Scala and a handful of custom applications to manage its system.

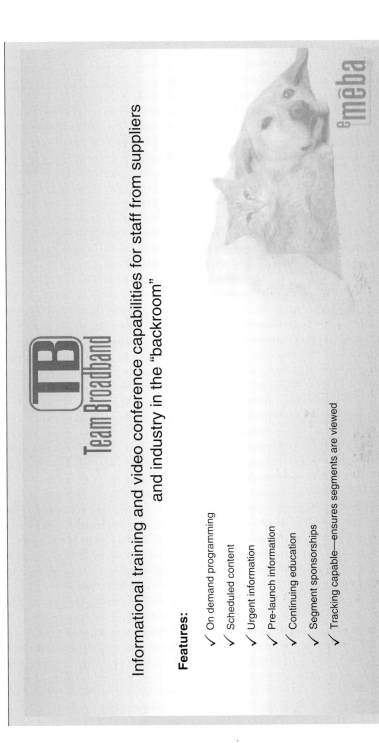

FIGURE 2.11 *An emebaVet Presentation, Showing Specific Staff Benefits That Can Be Achieved from a Digital Signage TV Network-Type of Deployment (Copyright 2007. Property of emebaVet. All rights reserved. Used with permission.)*

Organizational management of the content is controlled for each location by emebaVet. Key locales for deployments of the emebaVet service include veterinary medical facilities, universities, and industry-related sites. emebaVet also deploys advanced scheduling mechanisms for "day parting," "week parting," and its time-based targeting of advertising messages. And the displayed content is also targeted to specific locations at specific times.

Control of the system is handled remotely via the Internet. The system also includes the use of digital signage by third parties for advertising purposes.

A list of the reasons answering the question of "Why emebaVet?" includes the following advantages for would-be veterinarian clients: (1) detailed air-time reports, (2) dynamic programming with no loop play (every hour contains new and unique information and randomization of advertisements, so as to remain fresh), (3) updated programming on the fly (which means no more waiting until next month or for the next issue of a publication), and (4) emergency notifications.

Financially, at the outset in 2003, emeba invested approximately $550,000 into its emebaVet digital signage deployment. Early ROI from the first emebaVet deployed digital sign project was 200%, all of which emebaVet reinvested. This was during the early start-up phase, beginning with a mere 3–4 screens, when emeba landed its first $1 million client, according to Hong. More recently, the current expected ROI from most other deployed digital signage projects comes in at 65%, on average.

emebaVet practiced wisely and prudently at the outset, establishing a targeted ROI plan before deployment. This plan was based on the principals' knowledge of ad spending in the industry. They got to know the ad rates and the size of the network. To measure its ROI, emebaVet uses a calculation involving what Hong calls "the cost per advertiser/per location/product and service sales reports/transactions per location reports."

Moving forward, the biggest inhibitor to further digital signage deployment for emebaVet is the availability of capital needed to grow. The self-financing of the early emebaVet years only goes so far. emebaVet uses period-on-period sales reports to assess the effectiveness of its deployments.

Like several others queried for this book's case studies, Hong was less than eager to focus on a trade organization or a standards-setting body to set technical standards, for advocacy and promotion, research, education, and networking. This is tied, in part at least, to the fact that emebaVet's digital signage (or planned deployments of digital signage) has not yet been affected by regulatory/legal rules and/or statutes.

Technology

As noted in the Focal Press sister publication, *Digital Signage, Broadcasting: Broadcasting, Content Management, and Distribution Techniques*, the core technology behind most digital signage systems can be relatively arcane and complex.

In briefer form, this technology is made up of an understanding of why digital signage works, and how it works based around the idea of content being delivered instantly; in numerous files (i.e., video, animation, data, photo, audio and/or PowerPoint); shown concurrently on multiple zones, or regions, on any given screen. It is not unlike what a viewer sees when he or she observes the Internet. The only thing that is truly different is that with digital signage, usually the audience is not required to interact with the content (although more modern deployments do permit consumer interaction with the on-screen content).

Another important technological matter is the arrival of digital signage inside the household, a trend that some experts believe is just around the corner. Companies such as Kodak have developed home-based systems in the form of digital picture frames, as depicted in Figure 2.12.

FIGURE 2.12 *Digital Signage Is Even in Use in the Home; in This Case It Is a Frame Intended for Changing Display of Photos (Copyright 2007. Property of Kodak. All rights reserved. Used with permission.)*

Yet another important technological aspect of digital signage is its differentiation between traditional television and the Internet. Indicative of its digital variety and flexibility, digital signage can offer real-time, near-real-time, or non-real-time files, concurrently, as well as files from many different sources, as detailed above. In addition, the way the technology is usually deployed, most digital signage today is aimed at audiences that are on-the-move, whereas traditional TV audiences are usually sitting still in their homes. Finally, while most TV content is created at and/or originates from a nearby TV station studio, digital signage content comes from many files assembled in and delivered from a media player, PC, or server located nearby or far away. Important to note, in a similar vein, is that most of these features described above clearly differentiate digital signage from the Internet as well, the latter being an almost purely (almost hyper) interactive medium.

> The content on a digital signage screen can be one of three types, or a combination of any of them. This keeps content appropriate for the digital signage application—for example, a giant display at a sporting event needs real-time content, while a video demonstrating a blender's features at a department store would be non-real-time.
>
> - *Real-time*: Live broadcasts that are immediately distributed and displayed, such as sporting events and breaking news.
>
> - *Near-real-time*: Data that is stored briefly in the process of transferring it from the origination point to the various local installations, such as stock tickers or gambling odds. This kind of data has to be current within a few minutes.
>
> - *Non-real-time*: Content that is stored and available for use long after it has been created, such as product demonstrations or directional signage.

The basic digital signage process involves content, typically, at retail, in the form of prices and promotions (and their descriptions), being created in a computer using a software management package. The content is then stored on a computer and/or on a website, made accessible to store employees through a log-in and password, and via high-speed connections—including Integrated Services Digital Networks (ISDN), Digital Subscriber Lines (DSL), wireless, or satellite—the content files are then transported to computer menu boards (which help those employees select the file they want, at the specific time, for the specific audience).

Technical knowledge of digital signage is furthered by the understanding that often the best content displayed comes from numerous different files being displayed concurrently on the same screen. Thus, content developers can divide a screen into layers, zones, or regions, and populate each one by itself and, simultaneously, in conjunction with the other content elements showing as video, photos, logos, animation, and data. PCs or media players typically utilize various programs to assist the displays. Computer-operated and fully functional automatic playlists make sure that the zone-by-zone display is flawless and snap-second accurate. The potential for on-screen content creativity is obvious, and thus no less huge.

This same content is being delivered via several different sources. The days of manual "sneaker-net" foot-delivery of VHS cassettes, CDs, and DVDs are being replaced by delivery forms that require less and less human effort. These can include content coming from several separate distribution sources [e.g., Internet, PC- and flash-based memory files, live-streaming Internet Protocol Television (IPTV), satellite, broadcast, cable, telco, peer-to-peer networks, unicasting, wireless local area networks (LANs), and so on]. Additional technical flexibility is available to allow content flexibility, based on the audience or the locale. And technical tools exist to ensure that video and audio regions of the inside of a store do not overlap, and do not disturb one another, so as to confuse or annoy the audience.

Indeed, an industry adage has it that anywhere there is a paper sign, there can be a digital sign, and there are lots of ways to make content interesting, for example, to have lots going on at the same time on a given screen; or to show one video or photo pushing aside the other on-screen; or to have a virtual TV channel (such as the U.K.'s Baby-TV). In fact, the beauty of much digital signage is that it goes beyond paper signage, because one digital sign can take the place of dozens or hundreds or even thousands of paper signs trying to display the same content. Further, as it relates to the consumer, allowing him or her to gain information on services and goods can often be more effective as a sales tool than a traditional print advertisement. Following this trend, kiosks and customer terminals today will morph more and more into media players that will offer motion detector-activated or radio-frequency identification (RFID)-activated interactivity (or permit downloads of information to cell phones), for example.

As for the technology inside the screens themselves, the development of the flat panels, with their thin size and good resolution, has indeed made digital signage possible. These types of panels include LCDs, plasma, projection, LEDs (plus outdoor display systems and interactive touch screens), as well as self-illuminating digital paper (electronic paper), most for indoor use, but a handful for outdoor display, as well. A fuller listing and description of these types of screens are included in Chapter 1.

On the back-end of the digital signage technical world, customer billing and on-screen display measurements are critical to the proper operation of most commercial deployments.

As noted earlier in the chapter, *Digital Signage Broadcasting: Broadcasting, Content Management, and Distribution Techniques*, by Lars-Ingemar Lundstrom, is focused on the technological aspects of digital signage and is highly recommended for anyone seeking detailed and specific discussions of the topics discussed generally in this book. Moreover, the book by Laura Davis-Taylor and Adrian Weidmann, *Lighting Up the Aisle: Principals and Practices for In-Store Digital Media*, offers a 15-page technology section. The key takeaways from the latter volume, published in mid-2007, include:

- Content is almost always the ultimate end, whereas technology should be looked upon as the secondary, and yet necessary, means to that end.

- Up-front goal setting and due diligence answers to the "what" and the "why" questions (focused on the audience, the message, and the theme, and how the content achieves that), naturally leads good digital signers to the "how" of technology. *Strategy should be staked before spending.*

- Design the content and technology, indeed, the entire system, for the benefit of your customers, employees, and stakeholders (and in that order).

- Demand media playback and performance measurements of actual on-screen airings or displays.

- Make sure that each part of the hardware (e.g., screen, server, media player, PC, and so on) has been planned for optimum long-term use and build-out of the system.[2]

Software

Two key types of software make up the content side of digital signage and displays. One is the on-screen or on-air content that is displayed on the screen. The other is the software program that actually permits the placement of the on-screen content.

Content On-Screen

Content delivered by digital signage has expanded and proliferated as a result of the Digital Age. This content can now be displayed in multiple parts of the same

---

2. See, Davis-Taylor and Weidmann, *Lighting Up the Aisles: Principals and Practices for In-Store Digital Media*, copyright 2007, Relevant Press, who note, "Make sure that you understand and are comfortable with the manufacturer's business stability, warranty and replacement policies, turnaround times, overall Service Level Agreements (SLA), distribution locations, product stability, and backward compatibility. Also pay close attention to continuity (watch out for this one as we got burnt on this issue twice!), and end-of-life (EOL) policies." Used with permission of the authors.

FIGURE 2.13 *An Example of "Zoned" Digital Signage (Copyright 2008. Property of Jimmy Schaeffler. All rights reserved.)*

screen. This content can include a running data stream at the bottom of the screen, a signal logo displayed in a lower corner, an animation clip displayed in the other lower corner, a photo on the right upper corner, and a live or near-live video displayed in most of the remaining center of the screen—and all at the same time. In addition, with the use of the proper program installed on the proper media player, server, or PC, each item can be changed to another, from close by or far away, instantly, by the second, hour, or day or longer time frame (Figure 2.13).

Software Control System

The other software in a digital signage system is the software control system, which some call the "middleware." This software forms the structure upon which the viewed content rides. The software control system programs are important because without them it is impossible to display on-screen content.

One of the key decisions to make in this realm is what operating system to use (e.g., Linux, Microsoft, or Apple). Each has its own advantages and disadvantages. What to use depends very much on the applications and features that are important to the user. In rough terms, Windows is popular because it supports multiple file formats. Linux has the advantage of being available to use for free. Apple systems are known for their abilities to handle graphics.

Hardware

Pieces of hardware that make up a digital signage or digital display infrastructure are typically anywhere from five or six to a dozen in number. Not surprisingly, the most noticeable hardware is the monitor or flat-screen panel that presents the message to the audience. Wires typically connect this to an electrical supply, as well as to a set-top box or modem, the latter of which often will connect to an outside source, such as a computer, server, and/or the Internet.

On the origination side of the infrastructure, a laptop or a PC is a place where the content is either created, or stored, and transmitted (or all three). Video, audio, PowerPoint slides, data, animation, and graphic files are then either stored and played from the PC to the screen, or, in more sophisticated systems, a media player or server device serves that dedicated function.

Installation

The installation of digital displays involves matching the hardware components to the chosen spot in the digital signage locale where the screens will be mounted. Thus, installers must be equipped with the tools and the knowledge to be able to take screens and mount them safely and attractively to (or inside of) walls and ceilings, or even to simply mount them to a stand on the floor in a store, mall, or other location. Checking to see if an installer is certified and bonded, and whether they have the overall skill required for the project, is also important.

Once the screen is properly mounted, wiring must be properly run through the location, connecting back to the server and other parts of the hardware that run the content through the system and onto the digital screen. Coaxial cable and Ethernet wiring are a couple of commonly used solutions for inside digital signage wiring. Or, if the system is run wirelessly, sometimes a separate antenna must be placed in, on, or near the screen device to receive the content signal. Further, an appropriate spot must be found, typically at the locale or in the specific store, for placement of the server, media player, and/or PC that will manage the content.

Installers of digital signage need to consider the relative costs of installing in different ways, and matters such as safety and security. To optimize the system's capability, monitors should usually be purchased and installed in a standardized fashion. Logical hardware deployment and replacement plans are both examples of a professional installer operating to maximize its effectiveness and value to the property owner, controlling company, and/or network operator.

In addition, when hiring an installer and/or company to maintain a digital signage deployment, one can hire a "turn-key, do it all" vendor (discussed in Chapter 7), such as Hughes Network Systems, or an installation/maintenance-only company, such as Qualxserv, Rhombus Group, or Rollouts.

Maintenance

Once the digital signage hardware has been properly installed by a skilled installer, it must be properly maintained by the same or a similar professional to maximize the functioning of the asset. In any budget for the deployment of digital signage, this is an important item that should not be omitted.

Maintenance of larger systems, in fact, is not only important, but also a requirement.

Many of the larger networks and system operators are requiring that clients commit to a warranty up front, as part of the early planning and implementation. Up-front service agreements are also becoming more and more the norm. Indeed, many larger systems have full- or part-time dedicated maintenance personnel, whose job is to constantly and regularly troubleshoot and maintain digital signage systems.

These dedicated personnel can also be integral to the training of other personnel when it comes to upgrades and new guidelines and directions. A perfect example would be new emergency- and/or security-related content that is developed and needs to be installed and implemented into a new system. Protecting against piracy or signal compromise would be an important part of this process. Maintenance personnel might be integral to seeing that this is done effectively and efficiently.

Key Players

Groupings of key players supporting the digital signage and display world today are comprised of three groups. The first group is the audience, followed by what we call in this book the "stakeholders." Stakeholders are those with a vested interest in the planning, implementation, and ongoing use of digital signage, such as owners, installers, and content distributors. And third, are the investors.

Audience

Whatever one does as a stakeholder in the world of digital signage, a guiding light should remain the question, "What does what I do mean to the audience?" In essence, the audience is the engine that drives the vehicle, wherever it goes. To remember this is to avoid one of the most common mistakes of those deploying digital signage.

Audience group size, age, gender, ethnic background, interests, income level, and abilities (both physical and cognitive) are just a handful of the different criteria a sophisticated student of audiences might study. In fact, the range of demographic data that can be gathered these days—the *what* and the *who* of an audience—is remarkable.

When a given person or group comes to the place in front of a digital sign can also be a critical determinant to the success of the content that is placed on that screen. For example, in a mall environment, content delivered to a morning group of single sales shoppers would probably not be the best content to show to an evening group of families.

Where an audience is, further defines the content. Thus, the content shown to a summertime audience in a New Orleans, LA-based JC Penney would be markedly different from that shown to a wintertime audience in an Anchorage-based JC Penney's. One might be into Hawaiian print shorts and shirts, whereas the other would be focused on snow-blowers.

Why an audience member is in a specific location is another important measurement, the understanding of which can also make a content work or not work. Realizing with specificity the intent and interests and goals of an audience, and what can be done to adapt to or alter those motivations, is another ticket on the road to digital signage success. Closely related to this measure is the understanding of *what they are doing while there*. Thus, the content delivered to an audience of health club members running on treadmills will probably best differ from that of shoppers in a grocery store.

In short, getting audiences to react in the desired way to a given piece of digital content often turns on giving them a value or a benefit, which inevitably turns on knowing that audience. It's that simple (although that doesn't mean it's easy to do).

Stakeholders

Chapter 1 discussed each of the individual stakeholders in more depth. The major grouping of stakeholders listed here reduces itself to just a handful: location owners, network owners/operators, hardware providers, software providers, installation and maintenance providers, distributors, and investors. Note that many of these roles are overlapping and, as business people, this may often place stakeholders in awkward and conflicting positions.

Location Owners

The location owner is the one who owns the mall or the store or other locale where the screens and/or network is operated. The location owner often does have a hand in the digital signage system; however, very often the owner simply sits back and lets the network operators and/or leaseholders run the system. As compensation for providing the place and the audience that is drawn there, location owners usually collect a fee. Barter, perhaps in the form of an ad-for-an-ad, is another form of viable compensation when location owners are dealing with others in their digital signage environment.

Location owners include billboard companies, kiosk vendors, retailers, malls, stadiums, arenas, restaurateurs, factories, hospitality centers, houses of worship, and transportation centers, to name the majority. Among transportation centers or sites are train and bus stations, airports, on busses and inside taxis, at gas stations, and in convenience stores.

Network Operators

Network operators are really in a category all their own. They are what they say they are: they operate the network. Their variety is great, dependent upon things such as the size of the location owner, size of the location(s), amount of investment in the digital signage system, how many functions the network operator fulfills, and so on.

Hardware and Software Providers

Hardware and software providers include many stakeholders, as well. CE flat-panel screen providers are a big player among stakeholders, many annually bringing in hundreds of millions of dollars in screen sales. PC, server, and media player CE makers are another subset of hardware providers. On the software side, companies providing software management programs and systems combine with creators of content, such as video programmers, graphic and other artists, as well as actors, producers, and other on- and off-air talent.

Distributors

Distributors of the content include very basic hand-delivery systems, but as these antiquated distribution systems become fewer, content instead almost inevitably gets carried by Internet service providers (ISPs), as well as cable, telco, electrical, satellite, and wireless operators, for example.

Installation and Maintenance

System contractors, fixture providers, audio/video professionals, system integrators, and those that install and maintain digital signage are among the stakeholders labeled "installers and maintainers."

Investors

Investors typically come in two basic flavors: those that are part of, or involved in, the digital signage system, and those that are not. Typically, the majority of investment comes from those who are wholly ingrained in the day-to-day operations. Nonetheless, of late, more and more banks and venture capital investors, seeking pure investment opportunities, are seeing digital signage systems as attractive choices. Indeed, the future of digital signage will have a great deal to do with how these two classes of investors—the inside and outside investors—work together to make digital signage systems and operations relevant and successful to global audiences.

Trends

Trends are an important and exciting part of digital signage because they speak to the future and how that future might develop. Perhaps the all-important and foremost trend of digital signage today is simply its overall rapid development as a technology application. Indeed, a legitimate argument can be made for the idea that, in a life stage context, digital signage has rapidly moved out of infancy and is now well into its healthy adolescent stage. Yet, that said, the real value focusing on trends is to give readers a feel for a collection of specific trends that are actually making that macro trend occur.

Twenty key trends make up a list of those that are driving today's development of digital signage. These are listed and identified as follows:

- Well-functioning digital signage systems are achieving the goal of enhanced consumer relations and communications (such as between retailers and their customers), as well as enhanced corporate relations and communications (such as between management and employees).

- Digital signage is beginning to exhibit advantages over traditional signage, such as in lower costs, especially in the areas of creating, storing, managing, communicating and presenting media, and information. Digital signage can also do more in one location than paper signs, which increases their value and reduces the waste of paper signage.

- The technology of wireless communications is rapidly affecting the digital signage industry, which offers digital signage vendors the choice of using wired or wireless communications models (or both).

- More advertisers, retailers, and others are making a place for digital signage among their static, TV, and other traditional advertising plans, because the well of traditional advertising is beginning to run drier.

- Among ad agencies and their clients, as well as among many other parts of the commercial enterprise, resources are beginning to shift from traditional advertising and marketing to new alternatives, such as digital signage.

- Retailers and location providers are moving toward ownership of their own digital signage networks.

- Branding by retailers will gain remarkable new momentum, especially as those retailers seek to differentiate their products and services.

- Both store employees and store consumers are getting more savvy. Stores and store employees will enhance their effectiveness at selling and branding by embracing new technologies, thus driving greater space and employee productivity. Indeed, it is foreseeable that some of these sophisticated new retail technologies will eventually replace human resources.

- Similarly, consumers will embrace new technologies that will give them more control over the shopping process, key among which will be technologies that give them more information.

- Consumers will more and more dominate the dynamics between the retailer and the consuming audience dynamics.

- Digital signage is exhibiting a superior ability to accelerate business cycles and the speed of business processes.

- Controlling owners, network operators, and creative services personnel are making better utilization of their existing, in-house content assets (thus saving money and time).

- Screens and display devices are becoming flatter, lighter, larger (if necessary), and of higher picture display quality. Larger-sized LED screens are more frequently an option to more and more new digital signage newcomers.

- Screens are becoming less expensive.

- Media management software is becoming integrated into the actual hardware.

- Small displays (e.g., 7-inch- by 11-inch-sized screens) are appearing on retail shelves.

- Multiple choices among vendors, types of technology, hardware, software, operators, sizes, and types of deployment offerings (from piecemeal to turn-key) are becoming commonplace. Uniform professionalism is also becoming an expected commodity within the digital signage industry.

- Standards and best practices are coming to the digital signage industry (e.g., training standards for installation and management).

- The delivery of instant content to audiences is being triggered by touch screens.

- The delivery of content is being triggered by RFID devices or even by "smart devices" that judge crowd sizes and other crowd or individual dynamics.

As a result of all of these converging trends, digital signage is seen as a true bright spot for those wishing to communicate messages—especially commercial and advertising messages—to audiences of consumers and other end users.

Challenges

In an effort to avoid a tendency to appear overly optimistic or sanguine about the future of digital signage and display, as noted in several other chapters, one inevitably encounters concerns, risks, and cautions about its future. Key among these are those noted in greater detail in Chapter 3, and include the classifications of (1) implementation, (2) profitability (and other measures of success), (3) operations, (4) industry adoption, and (5) audience receptivity.

Implementation

Starting at all and *starting right* are probably the two most important steps toward understanding and adapting the proper implementation of a digital signage project.

Chapters 4, 6, 7, and 10 provide an in-depth understanding of the homework that must be done and the questions that must be asked (and, ideally, answered, at least in part), prior to investing any significant sums in digital signage. These include a plethora of foci on things such as the basics of this chapter (and the basics of a digital signage description), that is, forms, technology, software, hardware, installation, maintenance, some key trends to watch, and important challenges and opportunities. Combined with a dissection of one's and one's company's goals, clear strategies can be set.

Profitability (and Other Measures of Success)

Once the due diligence has been completed, and the team assembled, a quality budget is necessary to complete the earliest steps toward implementation. Tied in with this is a clear view to business models, return on objectives (ROO), and return on investment (ROI). Chapter 8 covers this in more detail. Worth repeating is the idea that measures of success other than economically measured profits and losses—for example, ambience, audience well-being, and brand building—are quite often a part of the digital signage experience. They are also quite often reasonable enough by themselves to justify implementing and keeping a digital signage system.

Operations

Once operational, a digital signage system takes considerable attention to maintain momentum. Not only must the technology and hardware be maintained and even occasionally upgraded or replaced, but more importantly, audiences must be studied to maintain the connection with and relevance of the content that addresses them. Studies of audience movement, numbers, and responses are good ways to maintain and build momentum in the digital signage world. Additionally, the entire system must be kept secure from compromise by competitors and other outside sources. In addition, at this stage, the attention of dedicated company and third-party personnel is an additional "must have" if the project is to succeed longer term. And ultimately, great communications "company-to-employee" and "company-and/or-employee-to-customer" are clearly the most effective operational criteria.

Industry Adoption

Ten years from the publication date of this book, buys-ins, and *real* buy-ins, by certain industry sectors, will mean the digital signage industry has truly succeeded. These successful commitments include those by advertisers and their retail clients, and certainly those by the CE and related hardware industries. Helpful, too, will be strong participation by and creative production by both the creative content and technical sides of the business. Indeed, given that there are an awful lot of plusses in the business for every digital signage stakeholder, each should be a willing player.

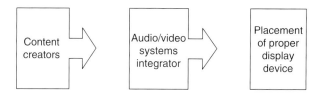

FIGURE 2.14 *The Creative Implementation Process (Copyright 2008. Property of Jimmy Schaeffler. All rights reserved.)*

Figure 2.14 shows a very basic representation of the creative implementation process. The key point here is that the content creators and the hardware/technology implementers need to work closely together to achieve optimum success in just about every digital signage implementation.

Financial investors, such as venture capitalists, should also be watching the digital signage sector for future growth.

That said, doing it right will mean the difference between digital signage stakeholders achieving "good" versus "better" results, and the difference between "solid profits (or ROI)," and "remarkable profits (or ROO)." For example, the CE industry and the multichannel operators have thus far done nothing more than a "fair" job of educating and advising consumers about the value of and technology behind HDTV. This has, in turn, hurt their bottom lines. Similar concerns address the topic of the transition from analog to digital technology that will directly affect broadcasters and multichannel operators beginning February 2009.

An example of steps the digital signage industry can take in this regard include the maintenance of a strong industry trade group and support organization, as well as the lobbying for and implementing of important policy and technological objectives. In this regard, few items will be more important than the setting of key standards within the digital signage industry. In addition, building a rapport with governments and local populations will be critical to the industry's future status.

Audience Receptivity

The end measure of success for individual applications of digital signage, as well as for the industry as a whole (short-, medium-, and long-term), will be audience receptivity and adaption. If the audience likes the content and the display that make up each version of the digital signage experience that they encounter, then it probably succeeds and the overall industry does, as well.

Relevance is a great concern in this arena. Some digital signage installations have failed because the content delivered is not interesting or relevant to the audience at hand. Thus, for example, if a blatantly commercial message is presented to an audience that is decidedly not receptive, not only will the content be turned off, but the audience may end up angered by the intrusion and apparent presumptiveness.

Conversely, the right message, at the right time, to the right audience, can and should motivate the audience to do things that they otherwise would never have done. Indeed, recent studies have shown that while consumers are not receptive to shotgun-type, broad message to broad audience ads, the same consumers are quite receptive to ads that are personalized and relevant to them and their needs. For an audience of potential luxury car buyers, a well-produced ad answering all their key questions can go a long, long way toward getting that audience to be more interested in buying that vendor's automobile. In short, good digital signage means not only getting to the audience, but putting the time and effort into getting to them in an effective manner.

Proper productions of technology, for example, a screen that is the proper size, placed properly, with the proper audio volume and display brightness, and properly displayed relevant content, add greatly to audience receptivity.

Opportunities

It is hard to deny that the future looks bright for those involved in the digital signage industry. Chapters 1 and 3 highlight the development, through the years, of various opportunities that now face the digital signage industry. Summarized, they indicate that digital signage as a future global telecom phenomenon is near-to-inevitable. The only real question is how well that development will be orchestrated by the participants. That will dictate the ultimate success of digital signage, which, again, will ultimately be determined by audience receptivity.

Many of the opportunities discussed in this book are also reflected in the "Trends" section of this chapter. The six key groupings of opportunities are as follows:

- Digital signage vendors stand to make money on what digital signage deployments actually deliver (e.g., in terms of revenues coming from advertising and sales up-lift). In addition, these vendors can save money by, for example, redirecting the spending once dedicated exclusively to traditional print, billboard, and broadcast advertising and media.

- Beyond money and margins, innumerable strategic and marketing objectives are obtainable exclusively via the deployment of digital signage opportunities.

- Vendors are in a position to gain remarkable control and flexibility over the content delivered to targeted consumers, which drives the digital signage message.

- Vendors can use digital signage's remarkable technology to design and implement unique and effective content and messages.

- Digital signage vendors are in a position to educate others in the industry to the benefits of digital signage.

- If they can be properly introduced to and educated about the benefits of digital signage, audiences will ultimately drive the future of the digital signage industry.

3 What's Driving Digital Signage?

It's hard to imagine where [digital signage] can't go.

—Jeff Bixler, Assistant Vice President, Business Development,
Hughes Network Systems

The adoption and growth of digital signage is occurring rapidly because the new medium delivers a customized and changeable message, in a unique way, in places people congregate; it also permits great flexibility, while becoming steadily more valuable, accretive, and cost-effective. Nonetheless, proper growth requires careful attention to guidelines aimed at doing it right the first time. Table 3.1 summarizes the opportunities and challenges facing digital signage. This chapter will review each in depth.

OPPORTUNITIES	CHALLENGES
ROI growth	ROI skepticism
Advertising solutions	Installation costs
Connectivity	Content development
Flexibility	Confusion re: system capabilities
Quality	Scalability
Affordability	Coordinating collaboration between different groups
Manageability	Concerns re: privacy and intrusion
Accessibility	Concerns re: clutter
Adaptability	Industry standards
Longevity	Consumer acceptance

TABLE 3.1 *Digital Signage: Opportunities and Challenges*

Ten Key Reasons Drive the Success of Digital Signage

What's driving the adoption and growth of the digital signage phenomena? Put another way, why would someone use, or want to use, this remarkable new application? The short answer is *to convey a message*, presumably one that is important both to the displayer and to the audience.

The longer (and more complete) answer represents a plethora of reasons, generally in no particular order and depending upon the desires of the participants. Nonetheless, the combination of the 10 reasons here does a solid job of presenting the case for digital signage. For balance, a later section highlights some of the items that tend to slow the growth of the industry.

Return on Investment

Taking most, if not all, of these elements together, they create the opportunity to find additional value in digital signage, especially in the form of return on investment (ROI). When a business can spend several thousand dollars up front on the initial hardware, content and implementation, plus maintenance fees of a few hundred dollars or less monthly, yet at year-end reap increased sales and/or margins in the double- or triple-digit category, the ultimate value of digital signage becomes quite evident.

Ad Solutions

"If you want to sell apples, advertise them where people are buying them." This saying is noted memorably at the conclusion of an animated short film for the trade group Digital Signage Forum.[1] The forum proclaims the ability of digital signage to address the disarray that many believe represents Madison Avenue today.

Because the environment for retail advertising has become so fragmented— due to less reading of newspapers; sparser viewing of traditional media such as over-the-air broadcast TV; and new devices and services such as spam blockers, DVRs, VOD, MP3 players, satellite radio, and remote control devices—*a digital sign display fulfills important advertising needs* for those selling today's (and

---

1. See, Digital Signage Retail Tutorial, http://www.digitalsignageforum.com/digital-signage-retail-tutorial.html.

tomorrow's) products and services. Further, because today's consumers have more opportunities to turn off the advertising messages they dislike, digital display that makes them *want to watch and become involved*—perhaps even via some form of interactivity—resonates not only among consumers, but among those wishing to connect with them.

Digital signage enables vendors to change out the messages more quickly and to target specific viewers much more effectively than traditional forms of advertising. It also allows advertisers to avoid the clutter and waste of traditional paper signs. In these days of "green solutions," that theme can go a long way.

Connectivity

A digital display of any kind builds a *connection* between the person or organization displaying the message and the recipients of that message. Importantly, in almost every instance, compared to static or traditional advertising signage, digital signage does a superior job of attracting and maintaining the attention of the vast majorities of global audiences. Most consider digital signage to be a far superior form of targeted advertising and display, thus further increasing its desirability and audience effectiveness. Branding is but one of the many areas of advertising that industry professionals believe will flourish in a Digital Signage Era. In the end, *digital signage is mostly about enhancing the experience of the viewing audience*, with the results being quite sought after, such as happier customers, greater brand awareness, more ad sales, and sales uplift.

Flexibility

Because of the newly developed *flexibility* of the hardware and software that makes up digital displays, and of the delivery and distribution opportunities, the number of acceptable sites for digital display is increasing incrementally. Indeed, it is probably harder today to think of places where digital displays would *not* work than it is to think of those places where it does, or will, work.

Quality

Also related to the software is the burgeoning *quality and appropriateness of the content* being created for digital signage displays. In addition to photo images, data and high-quality video can be added to or mixed in with other media on a single screen or multiple screens grouped together. The messages and images can be switched by the second, minute, hour, week, or longer. Closely related technology improvements have also been significant and have driven the effectiveness of digital signage deployments (Figure 3.1).

Affordability

Digital display hardware is becoming more and more *affordable*. Indeed, with the global proliferation of low-cost plasma and liquid crystal display (LCD) monitors, the hardware behind some lower-end digital display systems costs hundreds of dollars today (versus thousands of dollars a few years ago). And as flat-screen display monitors replace bulky cathode-ray tube TV monitors globally, the digital display hardware becomes much more efficient and practical for everyday use.

Manageability

Digital signage and related displays can be *installed* and *managed* rather simply. Similar to hardware costs, installation and maintenance costs have declined markedly as digital signage proliferates and competition ensues. On a related note, digital

FIGURE 3.1 *A Glendale, AZ, Outdoor Mall with a Variety of Outdoor Screens, Some of Which Are Traditional Vinyl and Some of Which Are Digital (Copyright 2008. Property of Sean Badding, The Carmel Group. All rights reserved.)*

signage has become particularly efficient in its recent development, such as the ability to change the content on most screens instantly from wherever one can find a computer and a connection to the Internet. New compression formats that can compress large amounts of content into small file sizes have also been a relatively important driver of digital signage growth.

Accessibility

With the advent of the Internet and the ability to connect a personal computer (PC) anywhere to a display screen located almost anywhere, the content displayed on a remote monitor can be managed in real time, 24/7/365. Indeed, changes on the screen can be made almost within the second, one after another. To emphasize the point, with the advent of high-quality video transmission *wireless* Internet services, a wired Internet connection will one day no longer be necessary for those wishing to manage their digital display content from afar. Moreover, Internet Protocol TV (IPTV) is an additional impetus aiding the accessibility of digital signage, and the burgeoning satellite broadband distribution sector is yet another driver. Use of IPTV technology, specifically, together with technical upgrades that have come, or are coming, via digital video compression improvements (e.g., going from MPEG-2 to MPEG-4 formats), will help make the use of more bandwidth for digital signage more efficient and less costly in the future.

Yet another form of "accessibility" includes access to audiences, which digital signage does well. One important form of access to audiences is the positive effect that well-conceived content has on *audience receptivity toward and retention of messages* (after the fact). Studies have shown that this kind of quality digital signage content can be vastly superior to traditional, static signage (such as vinyl billboards) when it comes to effectively delivering the message.

Acceptability

Digital signage's *acceptance* by the top-level advertising and retail management executives is a critical component toward the continued development of the digital signage juggernaut. No longer is digital signage merely a mildly successful new toy deployed almost exclusively by mid-level management. Part of this is also the idea that digital signage is, at its core, television, and it is hard to imagine a time in the future when people will not be drawn to the lure of quality video and audio. Acceptance by audiences is another absolutely critical element possessed more and more by modern-day digital signage deployments.

Longevity

A tenth major reason to consider involvement in digital signage would be because of its *robust future*. Digital signage will be around for a long time to come, maybe forever. The combination of the above attributes and features means that there is significant cause for optimism among industry professionals. As but one example, when people walking through a mall or on a street begin relaying their own personal radio frequency identification (RFID) information to an antenna placed on or near a digital sign display, the potential to individually link to, connect with, and relate to that individual (or group of individuals), will help take advertising to a whole new level. Further, the interactive features that become more a part of digital signage allow digital signage executives to access highly desired demographic audiences. Figure 3.2 pictures a conservative estimate of revenues the digital signage industry is expected to achieve by year-end 2010.

In short, successful growth is being propelled by—and sometimes hindered by—the quality and sophistication of these different "success" components.

What's Driving the Hardware?

Implementing a successful digital signage project depends on how well creative and technical forces come together.

On the hardware side of the question, display devices, servers, and media players on the receiver side, as well as network operations centers, ad servers, control software, and monitoring devices on the transport side (e.g., satellite, Digital Subscriber Line (DSL), wireless, wireline or combinations thereof), together

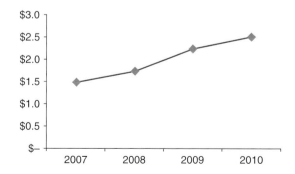

FIGURE 3.2 *U.S. Digital Signage Revenue Estimates (Copyright 2007. The Carmel Group. All rights reserved.)*

with mounting mechanisms and the other pieces of the digital signage infrastructure, are becoming easier and cheaper to build and deploy. Lifelong hardware mainte-nance is also becoming steadily more affordable. This, in turn, increases the ROI and the attractiveness of digital display for those that are deploying it.

Costs are always an important part of any digital signage experience. Yet, part of the wonder of digital signage is the variety of options, and that applies to cost recognition, as well. The following examples are the best indicators of those cur-rent fees.[2]

Outdoor Signage

Current outdoor signage costs typically depend on items such as the type of screen device and where the device is installed. They can vary greatly, dependent upon what and how many, for instance. Thus, the low-range costs for a one-color[3] out-door display device are around $10,000. Conversely, the mid-range costs for a moderately sized full-color outdoor digital display device come to around $25,000. An extra $2,000 cost for a wireless transmission device is an important option in both cases above, because wireless both (1) greatly aids the processing and deliv-ery of the data, photos, and video between the PC-based content creator and the display device and (2) reduces the cost of installing wires.[4] Otherwise, just about all other hardware costs, such as control functions and memory, are included in this total $12,000 up-front fee, because the display device itself will usually con-tain these other hardware units. Indeed, software often also is included within the price of these higher-end outdoor signage units.

Moreover, the actual outdoor installation of these types of display devices and related hardware can run as low as about $2,000, if placed on the side of an

---

2. Of course, really there is no "typical" or "standard" digital signage or digital display set-up, however, as it relates to the pricing of hardware in this instance, experts inform us that costs can, indeed, vary not only widely, but actually "wildly." One thing in particular that can vary the cost is the size and number of the monitor(s) or display device(s) deployed per site, the number of sites, and the frame refresh rates for the content. Nonetheless, the examples in this book serve as a reference to possible prices, which are expected to decline in succeeding years, and thus further drive the growth of global digital signage and display.

3. Within the digital signage industry, these types of "one-color" display devices are termed "single-" or "mono-colored" displays.

4. Note, however, that investigation of the quality of a signal sent consistently via a wireless connection is strongly recommended. Many in the telecom industry today continue to question the ability of wireless connections to deliver the same level of content quality as wired connections.

FIGURE 3.3 *A 2007 Digital Sign Installation at a Central California Coast High School in Salinas (Copyright 2008. Property of Willy Schaeffler. All rights reserved.)*

existing building. On the high-end of installation, that fee can soar to the tens of thousands of dollars, according to Salinas, CA-based Apex Sign owner, Scott Maidment.[5] Maidment cites an outdoor digital display project his company completed for Salinas High School (SHS) in 2007, which cost approximately $50,000 for two, 4-foot tall by 10-foot wide flat-screen, multicolor signs, built into a 20-foot high monument on the grass field at the front street entrance to the school (Figure 3.3). Additional installation costs for the SHS project were in the range of $5,000, Maidment notes.

Turning to a retail example, costs to deploy gas station forecourts are significantly higher than those for accompanying convenience stores. And as already noted, fees for large retailers can vary widely by the number of screens, the location of the screens, the number of channels, the refresh rates for the content, etc. Further individual hardware examples include $1,500 up front for a media player,

---

5. Installation costs also vary decidedly based upon indoor versus outdoor placement, and based upon placement on an existing wall versus a remote separate pole or monument placement on a lawn or the like. The latter involves significant engineering and construction costs. Similarly, maintenance costs can vary substantially, based upon related variables.

FIGURE 3.4 *Digital Wall Banners in New York City (Copyright 2008. Property of Jimmy Schaeffler. All rights reserved.)*

$200–$400 up front for a mounting mechanism, and $150/month for the cost of a content transport systems (e.g., satellite, DSL, or both).

Costs of digital signage in New York City are a noteworthy barometer, as well. The top of a street stairway entrance to a subway in Manhattan runs for $3,000 per month. A digital signage ad that runs for 15 minutes out of every hour on the back of the front seat in 100 New York City taxis runs for $45,000/month. A very tall digital wall banner of 30–50 feet in height (as in Figure 3.4) comes to anywhere between $20,000 and $50,000/month, dependent upon its location, size, and other elements. Plus, in central Manhattan, three large, adjacent Kodak screens in particularly high traffic and visibility corner section of the city tally $175,000/month.

In addition to those noted in this chapter's "Ten Reasons" section, other items that are typically of great concern to correctly render an outdoor digital display are the content being displayed, how far away the audience will be, what colors and quality are required, and similar display concerns.

Indoor Signage

Current *indoor* costs for hardware, on the other hand, tend to be generally lower. That is because less (or no) thought, effort, and hardware have to be put into the weather-related aspects of digital signage when the units are placed inside.

Examples of indoor digital signage vary as widely as outdoor ones. Standard classifications involve indoor digital signage that services:

- Production facilities

- Theaters

- Retail and sports facilities.

A company such as Milwaukee, WI-based Adaptive Displays suggests examples of production line digital displays that allow enhanced efficiency coming from the information they collect, display, and process. For example, a large digital display mounted between two loading docks at an express mail facility can be used not only to track the volume of packages being sorted into which trucks for delivery, but, most importantly, to direct loading personnel as to the amount of time remaining before the truck must be loaded and sent for deliveries. Depending on the size and other elements, such a single digital display device can cost anywhere from a few thousand dollars to as much as $25,000.

These "production improvement" types of digital displays are so important because of their ability to aid in the philosophy and processes that reduce factory and production operating costs, eliminate waste, and maximize ROI. Businesses ranging today from pharmaceutical to automotive are not only deploying these signs, but instituting software and information delivery systems—some of which are interactive—that make sure workers have the information flow to assure meaningful real-time data is on the board, all the time. Thus, for example, in the old days, a factory line would have to stop for resupply when a workstation ran out of a particular bolt. Using an interactive digital display device, the worker realizes the bolts are running low, touches a square on the light emitting diode (LED) screen, which then activates the request for more bolts. Without having to stop the production at any point, new bolts are delivered timely, and production is optimized. It is not atypical for a newly installed LED board to be capable of luminating for 100,000 hours, continuously, in a 24/7 production facility. In the future, these lumination times are expected to increase incrementally.

In a theater environment, digital displays are becoming more commonplace, both inside and outside. Inside displays mounted to ceilings advise cinema patrons of the movie they seek, the time, and in which theater it shows. Here, a common indoor digital display fee can range from $10,000 for a six-screen facility to more than $100,000 for a 24-plex location. Standard fees for "typical" theaters today are estimated in the $10,000–$25,000 range. Part of the value in these new theater displays is tied to the sophistication of the software deployed. Many new theaters use software that never has to be managed and which automatically ties ticket sales to other theater functions. Thus, for example, a digital display directing patrons to a particular screen will automatically display the number of tickets sold, so that patrons have an idea of how many seats are still available. The case study below featuring Logical Solutions and Carmike Cinemas highlights digital signage in this environment.

On the "typical" retail side of an indoor digital signage display, costs can run as low as a few hundred dollars for a BETAbrite screen available at any Sam's warehouse store. It exhibits limited content, typically offering only a single line of text that travels across the screen. On the other hand, these same kinds of retail signs can cost hundreds of thousands of dollars. Again, the price determinant turns on how many screens are displayed, the size of the displays, the sophistication of the back-up hardware units, what type of software is chosen, and where it is mounted

FIGURE 3.5 *An Indoor Digital Display at the San Francisco Nike Town Retail Store (Copyright 2008. Property of Jimmy Schaeffler. All rights reserved.)*

inside (as shown in Figure 3.5). On the restaurant side, a small-scale digital signage implementation will typically cost in the range of $4,000–$6,000, in 2008 currency.

Carrying the digital display concept to its biggest and most noticeable today are the large outdoor stadiums, where events are typically displayed, live, on two large screens located on opposite ends of the venue, each screen of which typically measures 30-feet by 90-feet in height and width. These screens permit those who do not have close-up views of the action on the field or stage to capture much of the events almost as effectively from afar. One of the largest of the stadium digital displays is the 50-foot by 140-foot screen at the Miami Dolphins football team's stadium. Yet another remarkable example of stadium digital display is touted by the Brookings, SD-based Daktronics Company, which has installed a 3-foot tall "ribbon" digital display at Chase Field, in Phoenix, AZ, the home of the Arizona Diamondbacks baseball team. This screen extends 1,131 feet in length (more than a quarter of a mile) around the inside edges of the stadium, between seating decks. It displays just about everything imaginable, with "fairly good" video resolution, according to Daktronics' marketing manager, Mark Steinkamp, yet it specializes in carrying advertising, photos, and lots of instant, running statistics and real-time data, including fantasy scores from other players in the leagues (Figure 3.6). Costs to purchase, install, and operate these large outdoor arena signs can run in the millions of dollars.

FIGURE 3.6 *A Ribbon Digital Signage Display at Chase Field, Phoenix, AZ (Copyright 2007. Property of Daktronics. All rights reserved. Used with permission.)*

What's Driving the Software?

On the software side of digital displays, the service is being driven by quality developments on both the on-screen content and software control systems'[6] sides of the software puzzle. Specific parts include the actual on-screen content, as well as the planning and scheduling, content security, proof of playback, dynamic screen zones, network control, and applications software. Pricing models range from fees as part of the up-front hardware payment, to those for a separate content servicing company, to other recurring or changeable cost models. Again, the fees can range from hundreds to thousands of dollars monthly, dependent upon the size and scope of the digital network.

Further, many levels of content sophistication and content delivery can cause wide swings in the prices for digital software. Thus, the combination of still photos, with live audio and video, or near-live content, plus data, delivered via wireless, wired, and/or satellite delivery systems, could cause the cost of the on-screen content to rise remarkably.

Typically, for outdoor signage, the original equipment manufacturer (OEM) of the display device will also include, without additional cost, a PC program that can be installed in just about any computer that includes adequate memory. This software becomes the internal PC operations center, where the on-screen software is created and managed and then transported either by wire, wirelessly, or by satellite to the digital display device. As an example of an additional component available for an additional $1,000, most outdoor signage suppliers offer a time and temperature software function that tracks these data points continuously and displays them on screen.

Other business models do not include software within the hardware fee, and in those instances estimates of the software prices can range from $2,000 to more than $50,000 monthly.

Usage Is Driven by Where Digital Signage Is Used

This section includes examples of the types of existing digital signage and display locales in the categories of retail, service, travel, education, and events. Specific

---

6. Although some would call this form of "software" by the term "middleware," for purposes of simplicity and clarity, the term "software control systems" will be used throughout this book.

photographic examples of digital signage and display uses in these various sectors are included.

Retail

As of year-end 2007, according to POPAI, approximately two million indoor digital signage retail displays are estimated to be in operation globally. In the United States alone, that number is estimated to approach three-quarters of a million. By another measure, the research firm iSupply estimates that by year-end 2010 the worldwide market for digital signage and professional displays will exceed $12 billion. Some prime examples are noted in this chapter, but also include others, such as the Glendale, AZ, Mall in Figure 3.7.

Besides Las Vegas, and New York City's Times Square, perhaps one of the most notable places for the deployment of digital signage has been in retail malls across the United States and, indeed, around the world. Assuming the implementation is handled in a way that is attractive to the majority of mall visitors, their retailers are finding digital signage to be a strong form of commercial communication, and its use is proliferating as consumers see more and more of it globally.

FIGURE 3.7 *The Glendale, AZ, Mall, and Its Use of Digital Signage (Copyright 2007. Property of Sean Badding, The Carmel Group. All rights reserved.)*

Service

For many who know the digital signage industry, the service industry, in the form of Las Vegas casinos, was the former's genesis. Some of the largest-sized displays in the world stand along Las Vegas' main thoroughfare, Las Vegas Boulevard (also known as "The Strip"), drawing attention to entertainment, gambling, food, beverage, and the like. Smaller-sized displays have proliferated even more of the Sin City environment, especially inside the various establishments.

Beyond the hospitality industry, convenience stores are probably one of the best examples of places where digital signage thrives within the service industry. Yet there are literally thousands of more examples. Veterinarian hospitals in southern California are implementing hundreds of digital displays aimed at calming and informing concerned pet owners in their waiting rooms. Banks, health clubs, oil-changing stations, and even government facilities (such as the Department of Motor Vehicles) are additional sites where digital signage aids in the delivery of important messages. These messages range from purely commercial ones, such as blatant advertisements for goods and services, to messages aimed at informing, setting a mood, drawing a crowd, or even dispersing one. Other existing or possible future examples of locales include gas and service stations, and even public restrooms in these and many other venues.

Restaurants are yet another locale for the burgeoning digital display phenomena. Instead of having patrons wait for seating in a vacuum of quiet and boredom, digital signage permits hospitality facility owners to positively educate, inform, and even entertain their customers. This, in turn, enhances the overall dining experience and encourages return visits (and probably better tips). Health facilities, such as sports centers, spas, and health clubs, are yet another subsector of the service industry where digital signage and displays are expected to inform, entertain, and promote.

Travel

Travel centers are key places for the deployment of digital signage displays. These include locales such as train stations, subway stations, boat launches, and airports, as well as beside freeways and other travel routes. Planes and busses themselves are yet another set of venues for the growth of travel-related digital signage.

Further, digital signage and display can be used not only in a standardized commercial sales and marketing sense (e.g., to promote the purchase of certain travel products and service opportunities), but also in the event of public safety and emergency situations. Thus, during a fire in a large building, a lobby digital display device would be ideal for communication of basic directions to first-aid locations, safe places to assemble and track loved ones, places to avoid, authorities in charge, etc.

Wayfinding, described as digital displays that guide travelers to different locales, is yet another obvious place to grow the digital signage experience. Indeed, even taxi cabs have become a home for digital signage, perhaps best indicated by the back-seat screens that have recently been installed in a large number of New York City taxi cabs (Figure 3.8). The displays face the back-seat customer and run a series of different digital content to inform, entertain, and solicit cab riders.

Educational

One of the most logical sites for the installation and usage of digital signage is in companies and institutions that wish to encourage educational growth among their members. For example, a large commercial retail operation could offer a digital display in a common meeting area, such as a cafeteria, to encourage better understanding by employees of company directives, operations products, and services. Moreover, educational institutions, such as colleges and universities, are utilizing

FIGURE 3.8 *A Digital Signage Display Monitor Mounted on the Back of the Front Seat of a New York City Taxi Cab (Copyright 2008. Property of Jimmy Schaeffler. All rights reserved.)*

digital display devices to help educators to disperse messages and improve the way the messages are delivered (Figure 3.9). It is hard to imagine a major educational institution—such as an elementary or high school, college, university, or trade school—that would not benefit from a constantly refreshed digital display device that alerts school participants to the doings and goings on associated with that institution.

Events

Almost anywhere people congregate has the potential to be a good spot for a well-implemented digital signage display. This includes smaller-sized events, such as community meetings, both in the political and religious areas.

Attend just about any major concert or sporting event globally these days and a digital display device will be there to enhance the experience. Large sums are being spent to deploy these units, in large measure because they bring the entire audience that much closer to the players, actors, and, certainly, the action. Presumably, like most other media and experiences, a favorable result ensures future participation and additional revenues and profit. A typical stadium digital signage implementation costs hundreds of thousands of dollars for the planning, hardware, software, installation, maintenance, and tracking. Moreover, it is typically just one of several such display units in a large indoor or outdoor arena.

FIGURE 3.9 *A Digital Sign at the Entrance to California Polytechnic University, Pomona, CA, Featuring the Author's Daughter, Jessica Schaeffler (Copyright 2008. Property of Diane Schaeffler. All rights reserved.)*

What is particularly impressive about these event-based digital signage and display devices is the quality of the on-screen image. Companies like Daktronics, Mitsubishi, and ANC Sports have introduced stadium screens as large as 50-feet high and 140-feet wide, which can carry live video with remarkable resolution. Trade shows are yet another event where digital displays abound, and convention centers offer similar forms of directional, commercial, and entertainment information.

Theaters might qualify best under the "Event" category, and therein lie some of the better examples of modern digital signage. In terms of variety, as a single locale, perhaps more examples of digital signage are displayed within a theater than any other. Not only are outdoor signs frequent, but also signs inside listing all the shows and show times, as well as those above the entrances to individual screens and the on-screen digital signage that so commonly precedes most movies today.

Logical Solutions, Inc., and Carmike Cinemas

Michael Barbieri, VP of Product Development, for Columbus, GA-based Logical Solutions, Inc.—calling itself a "solutions company that provides digital signage hardware and software"—has been with the company for 22 years. The company's primary digital signage involvement is in the theatrical services side; in that area, its core client is Carmike Cinemas. Logical Solutions (LSI) has more than 90 theater installations nationally in the U.S., ranging from 10 signs to 32 signs per theater. LSI also has several outdoor signs that it has deployed at retail stores.

LSI landed Carmike Cinemas' business mostly via some hard work and creative thinking. Carmike was testing out another company's LED system. When it heard of the RFP, LSI really wanted a shot at the Carmike Cinemas' business, so it approached the cinema company with some basic ideas and cost estimates. LSI was given a chance to compete against a multimillion dollar company. In turn, LSI was asked to develop a system for a single local theater, and a decision on who would get the LED signage was to be made after both rival companies completed their installations. In the end, LSI got the overall business because it "… simply developed a better animal," concludes Barbieri. "We knew our customer and the industry better than our competition, through our experience, hard work, and a great deal of research (Figure 3.10)."

LSI's actual digital signage deployment is a reaction to Carmike Cinemas' need to move customers into their auditoriums from the entrance (where tickets are purchased), then through the lobby (where concessions are purchased), and finally to the auditorium (to view the movie). Notes Barbieri, "In these larger theatres, there can be much

FIGURE 3.10 *The Exterior of a Carmike Cinemas Location and a Display of Video Content on One of Its Screens (Copyright 2007. Property of Logical Solutions. All rights reserved. Photo used with permission.)*

confusion if some sort of crowd control is not in place. It also made sense to implement that thought into our software, since it controls much of the theatres' other functions."

When attempting to assess the deployment of a potential digital signage project, LSI looks first at the size of the theater as the number one factor, which is basically done to address the issue of crowd control. The second criteria reviewed would be costs. Looking at the primary benefit to LSI and Carmike Cinemas using digital signage, Barbieri believes that the signs add professionalism to a theater. He believes that going to a movie theater should be an experience of light, sound, and visualization; something you cannot get when sitting at home. "Why do customers choose a particular store over another that sells the same products and at the same prices? I presume it is atmosphere, visual experience, and presentation! Just about anyone can make popcorn and project a movie onto a screen. It is the theater experience and presentation that make the difference," Barbieri adds.

The cost of the digital signage system was the greatest challenge in LSI's deployment of digital signage. The questions customers asked were ones like, does a sign system bring in revenue? Could LSI prove the ROI?

Fortunately, when LSI and Carmike Cinemas looked at the crowd control aspect of the digital signage system, there were real possibilities. The box office signage

FIGURE 3.11 *The Display at the Box Office Offers a List of Movies and Their Show Times, Reducing the Questions Asked by Patrons as They Make Their Ticket Purchase (Copyright 2007. Property of Logical Solutions. All rights reserved. Photo used with permission.)*

(Figure 3.11) could be used, for example, to get information to the patron about movies that were being shown, and their show times. This made the transaction of the sale move quickly. "A line of informed customers without questions will tend to move quicker than one with many questions," Barbieri observes. Next, the lobby signs inform the customers whether or not their auditorium is ready to be seated, or if they should remain in the lobby.

Barbieri notes that selling concessions is very important to a theater company. This is basically the only place where the theater will make its profit. It is important to keep the customer in the lobby as long as possible, so that the advertisements, and the smell of popcorn, can get them to purchase snacks. If the lobby becomes overcrowded, the LSI digital signage system provides a device to allow the management or cleanup crew to change the status of an auditorium, so that the customer can be seated earlier than what the system's default time states in the computer. Sometimes this kind of system override and individual choice capability is essential to a well-operating digital signage system. It also allows them to keep the customers in the lobby longer if the auditorium crew is not complete with the cleanup, and the default time has occurred.

FIGURE 3.12 *The Inside Hallway of a Carmike Cinemas Location, with Digital Signs Telling Customers in Which Theater Their Movie Is Being Shown and When It Starts (Copyright 2007. Property of Logical Solutions. All rights reserved. Photo used with permission.)*

Further, digital signs are placed over the doorways of the auditoriums (Figure 3.12), informing the customer of the movie and show time that is being shown. With a new release of a movie, there will most likely be several auditoriums showing the same movie. In the end, LSI states firmly its ability to (im)prove ROI. Adds Barbieri, "Without LED signs, a back-lit box with a sheet of Mylar displaying the movie title or other information would most likely be used in the theaters. These Mylar displays take time to order and install, and cost money to have created each week. By replacing the Mylar signs with LED signage, the ROI takes about three to five years."

LSI tells potential customers today that one of its strongest assets is the ability to offer a total package, and to offer a better solution to its customers, that is, from cost, to software, to the maintenance of the signs.

Looking at the back-end of a typical cycle of digital signage deployment, the maintenance of the system is its biggest challenge. LSI is now working with its third LED sign vendor. To get there, Barbieri explains that its first vendor had a good product, but could not do a cookie cutter (i.e., turn-key) business. "With every order, it was like getting the same product for the first time, again and again. You could imagine the lost man hours we were occurring." The second vendor lost its business after 9/11, when a recession hit. LSI is now working with its third vendor. "They are very professional and helpful. They were actually the first company I called when I was getting into the digital signage business, but the sales person would not be competitive with the pricing. Thankfully, much has changed," summarizes Barbieri.

Today, now that some of the Carmike Cinemas' LED systems are more than 10 years old, LSI is starting to see some screen failures, due to age. There are limited resources with which to purchase any more new circuit boards or components since many of them are now obsolete or no longer in production. As such, it relies on its technicians to troubleshoot the boards. LSI has spent an enormous amount of time gaining the knowledge to keep these systems running.

Additional challenges of the LSI-created and operated digital signage system in the Carmike Cinemas include getting graphic content onto the signs. Putting text onto an LED or LCD sign is easy, but putting high-quality graphics on these signs depends mainly on the talent of a theater manager or other willing individual, who must spend the time to produce an image to fit the resolution, size, and quality of the digital sign. That factor must not be overlooked when purchasing or getting into this business (especially on the theater side of the digital signage business). "Even the large sign manufacturers have called me to see if I have any new cool graphics to put on these signs when they go out to some of the theatre conventions, such as Showest in Las Vegas," offers Michael Barbieri.

The specific types of digital signage being deployed are mostly LED. LSI recently introduced a box office LCD, because the device is great for up-close, informational displays. Nonetheless, many of Carmike's lobbies are so large that an LED option is still the best choice, especially if there are multiple box offices in an open-air environment. Barbieri sums up, "We have done a few outdoor signs using Adaptive Micro Systems (AMS). They offer a great way to get information about up-and-coming events, as well as great road side signs." Organic LED signs are not yet being considered by LSI and Carmike.

The core content delivered to the cinema screens is for theater-related information, such as show times, movie titles, and the status of the auditorium. Also, LSI and Carmike do place some limited graphics on the lobby signs, because they all have a full matrix of tri-color LEDs. Barbieri believes that more can still be done to pay for these signs, if a distribution method were developed to place new content on the signs from local or national advertisers. Such a method would pay for the signage and eventually produce income. Further, since the outdoor signs are capable of 256 grayscale, the images that can be placed on these signs are, in Barbieri's words, "incredible."

LSI and Carmike have looked at scheduling mechanisms, but so far, its funding has not yet materialized. LSI investigated a project with a start-up company, called RBuzz. RBuzz tried to place high-definition screens out in public areas, such as lobbies, airports, subway terminals, and malls, where local and national advertising could be controlled in a scheduled environment. RBuzz could change the content of the advertising signs, depending on the time of day and who was the audience for the message. For example, a McDonald's breakfast biscuit was advertised at 7:00 a.m. and then the same sign changed, so that the advertisement became an Outback Steakhouse for the evening commute back home. This content not only changed due to the time of day, but also due to the location of the signage. It could all be nationally networked, back to a central location, with one marketing arm and one IT department.

The four major areas that signs are used in Carmike Cinema theaters include (1) outdoor signs, (2) the box office area, (3) the lobby, and (4) the auditoriums themselves. Additionally, all of the Carmike signs are networked locally. Because they are connected using LSI's theater solution, the two companies have the ability to see each device on the network and perform limited troubleshooting. The Carmike system is not yet being used for national, regional, or local targeting (i.e., down to a single location or single group of digital signage within a single location). Nor is LSI currently utilizing a dedicated platform solution to enable regional or national content distribution and playback. Instead, LSI uses its own dedicated platform to provide the interface that is required to manage the signs. Explains Barbieri, "We have obtained the protocols of the different manufacturers to write the drivers that are required to communicate with each system."

The LSI-developed and operated digital signage system is used primarily to influence customer behavior, such as directing customers to different areas of an establishment. Barbieri also believes that the digital signage systems' main function is to build/create brand awareness.

Barbieri would like to see more LCD units used. "We started to implement an LCD box office sign, in conjunction with LED auditorium signs. This makes so much sense. We could show video, display the current movie trailers, and advertise our latest combo snack/meal, all at the same time. What a bang for the buck!" Barbieri says. LCD technologies in the dark hallways are not as clear and cannot be seen as far away as the LED signs. The combination of the two technologies just makes sense, he reasons.

LSI invested approximately $20,000 initially. It took LSI 3–4 months to install a reliable product in the field. "For a few years running, when LSI had a large roll-out of new theater openings, its percentage of revenue for the company sales was 46% for the entire company. This is a rather large number for just one product!" summarizes Barbieri. The current ROI from the deployed digital signage project turns on collecting a small fee to support the systems in the field. Due to the slow growth of the theater industry at the time of writing, LSI is not currently installing many new systems, but when it does, the expected ROI from deployed digital signage turns mainly on the quantities of products that are being sold and/or deployed. Recently, Barbieri describes the biggest inhibitor to further digital signage deployment as that of uncertain ROI. Barbieri's explanation: "The movie industry is trying to reinvent itself after taking a beating with early release dates of DVDs and poorly made movies. New technologies like digital projectors and surround sound are being implemented. The jury is still out on whether or not these new technologies will make the difference and pump new life into the movie industry. The number of theaters that are being built are down, and there seems to be more buy-outs, trying to get markets where the companies do not yet have any presences." Initial financing of the LSI digital signage network occurred via self-financing, and, in those early days, LSI found it could get the business if it could create a better system than its competitors.

Barbieri does not necessarily feel that there is currently a need for a standards-setting body to cover all of the functions of setting technical standards, advocating and promoting, researching, educating, and networking. This is because he feels there are some established associations, such as the International Sign Association (ISA), that help companies in the truly necessary areas of promoting and advertising. Setting technical standards will only inhibit progress of new technologies. Most of these companies strive for a competitive edge. Barbieri also suggests strongly that new system operators and developers be aware of local building codes before purchasing and/or getting involved otherwise in a new sign system project. LSI has found that some local building codes play some role in the network configurations, as well as outdoor signage. For example, some jurisdictions care about what type of cable is used, that is, whether it is plenum-rated for fire codes or normal cable. And some local governments do not allow moving signs along roads or highways.

Other than these legal regulatory types of concerns up front, Barbieri, LSI, and their client, Carmike Cinemas, have observed no example of any negative reactions to their deployment of digital signage in the cinema environment. Indeed, if copying is the ultimate flattery, LSI has had lots of compliments, because many of the theater industry sign companies have copied LSI's sign configurations and the way LSI displays its information to its customers.

Miscellaneous

Some of the other "miscellaneous" versions of digital signage today include cor-porate uses, which vary all over the board. These range from corporate commu-nications aimed at large staffs, to corporate training aimed at any number of staff members. Another form that might not fit the standardized categories above is that of enhancing or influencing customer experiences, such as a post office which dis-plays information and directions on how to use the service or access the waiting lines. Many other government applications of digital signage are expected in the future, key of which will include security and safety displays. For example, used correctly, digital signage can be a great informational and crisis management tool. Numerous other sub-categories of digital signage are expected to further fill out this section in the future.

Users: Who Uses Digital Signage Is Driving Its Success

Not only is digital signage being driven by *where* it is being deployed, but impor-tantly, also by *who* is deploying it. As noted on page B-4 of *The Wall Street Journal*, October 11, 2007, in an article entitled "Password to Marketers' Meeting: Digital," the highest-level marketers at some of the world's and United States' most prominent companies—American Express, Anheuser-Busch, McDonald's, Microsoft, and Proctor & Gamble—are turning to digital signage. Their involve-ment will, undoubtedly, drive hundreds of thousands of executives from smaller marketers to venture further and more quickly into what many in marketing today believe will be a new "Holy Grail of Modern Marketing," that is, digital signage.

Business Owners

Most businesses are operated "for profit," and thus most digital displays used by business owners are used for the purpose of building that profit. These commer-cial uses are also global in scope, and constitute the strong majority of the world's digital display applications created thus far. Indeed, the commercial deployment is clearly driving the digital signage sector today and it is expected to drive this sector well into the future. Again, a key reason is the ability of digital signage to efficiently sell products and services, while also doing so in a unique and quality way that traditional advertising and media can no longer do. Of course, non-profit business owners will also drive the success of future digital display applications, as will government and other institutional players.

Brand Marketers and Ad Agencies

Beginning in the late 1990s, advertisers began losing eyeballs not only to the obvious threat (i.e., DVRs), but also to other devices that allow consumers to choose whether to view ads or not. These other devices include MP3 players, video on demand (VOD) offered by cable and telephone video service operators, and subscription VOD (SVOD) services offered by satellite video providers such as DirecTV and EchoStar. Mute buttons installed into remote control devices are yet another tool to avoid at least the audio of annoying ads. This ability to avoid ads has, in turn, created a rather chaotic and uncertain advertising environment for today's Madison Avenue community, as well as for over-the-air, cable, satellite, and telco video broadcasters and operators. The thing that is most attractive to these troubled advertisers is the prospect to regain many of those "lost" eyeballs, which is exactly the wonder of digital signage.

Digital signage is, in addition, a remarkable way to build or recapture brand awareness. The creative implementation of a digital signage display, together with live content, can uniquely attract and capture the attention and loyalty of substantial audiences. Thus, as shown in Figure 3.13, the example of the brand logos

FIGURE 3.13 *A Large Digital Sign, with Numerous Brand Logos and Messages at AT&T Park in San Francisco, CA (Copyright 2007. Property of http:// sanfrancisco.giants.mlb.com/sf/fan_forum/scoreboard.jsp. Used with permission.)*

and names that are part of the digital sign at AT&T Park in San Francisco, CA, companies such as Toyota, Safeway, Budweiser, PG&E, Sony PlayStation, Charles Schwab, and CHW Health Services and, indeed, even humble individuals such as "Nani and Nanu" on behalf of their 8-year-old grandson, Dominic, have moved to take advantage of this new form of advertising and brand awareness.

Opportunities

There are 10 key opportunities that are driving digital signage today, all of which are also detailed in this chapter at some length above. One of the best opportunities to use digital signage comes as a result of recent cost reductions on the hardware, software, installation, and maintenance sides. Thus, digital signage is no longer simply a technology application, resulting in a sales, information, or entertainment opportunity, that is available just to the "big guys," their clients, and customers.

A related opportunity is, of course, the one that turns on the opportunity to make money from those that view the content delivered to digital signs.

Challenges

Proper analysis of what is driving digital signage today involves review of not only the positives (which is a main focus of this book and this chapter), but also some intelligent analysis of the negatives. Although not complete, the list below highlights several of the key challenges faced by this new industry subsector. A proper balancing of the challenges against the opportunities recommends in many instances taking a chance on this new media called digital signage.

- *ROI skepticism*: It can often be difficult to directly connect a defined and definite ROI for digital signage. Nonetheless, one of the better views as to the real costs involved is to measure the costs of traditional advertising—especially paper signage—against the long-term costs of digital signage and display. Part of this frustration is tied to a need to obtain proper measurement data—such as audience measurement data—in a standard form followed by all research and survey entities.[7]

---

7. See article entitled "Password to Marketers' Meeting: Digital," *The Wall Street Journal*, p. B-4, October 11, 2007.

- *High installation costs*: As described earlier for both the indoor and outdoor communities, the combined hardware and software costs can be expensive, in addition to the resources required to manage the signage.

- *Content development*: One of the major concerns about the future of digital signage is that the right content must be delivered to the right people at the right time in order for the whole industry to excel. That said, the creation of the "right content" is very often a chore that is best left to, and budgeted for, those professional creators that can do it and do it well.

- *Confusion concerning system capabilities*: Users may buy a digital signage system with functions and capabilities they are unable to fully control and leverage, due to inadequate technical knowledge. The decision then becomes: should an outside vendor take over the hardware, software, installation, and/or maintenance functions, and at what cost? Also, to date, the amount of quality, reliable data about digital signage, and its capabilities is somewhat limited.

- *Scalability*: As a company's digital signage needs to grow, it faces the challenge of finding software applications that can fully integrate various types of hardware and in-house software, to communicate a company's messages onto a single network.

- *Coordinating collaboration*: Among several departments possibly affected within one organization, marketing and IT departments often have trouble working together in the implementation of digital signage, especially because their knowledge and expertise can be so different and because neither can do digital signage without the other. Thus, staff acceptance of new digital signage proposals can require significant education and patience.

- *Content management*: Buyers of digital signage are typically hesitant to develop and make their own content. This is often due to the fact that buyers lack the technological and creative expertise and talent to effectively create compelling digital content.

- *Concern about privacy*: A recent study by a respected survey organization indicated that Americans are surprisingly unconcerned about DVR operators misusing their privacy.[8] Nonetheless, all those involved in digital signage will have to be strong and disciplined when it comes to thinking through the outcomes of various campaigns that might possibly be perceived as infringing unduly on the patience or privacy rights of their constituents.

---

8. See, www.carmelgroup.com, for links to study entitled "DVRs 2007: Time in a Magic Box."

- *Concern about intrusion*: Not unlike the concerns relating to privacy and clutter, the concern for intrusion is an audience- and community-based concern. It, too, must be handled discreetly in each instance where a new digital sign is planned. For example, even one instance of the wrong sign in the wrong place and at the wrong time could send serious negatives about the industry that would require a large sum of repair to alleviate.

- *Concern about clutter*: Like privacy, people have concerns about the proper implementation of digital signage, especially in their own communities. And like privacy, the digital signage and advertising industries, especially, must be quite cautious, even sensitive, when it comes to the needs of various audiences. A proper balancing of community standards and communication with the various community groups is an ideal way to ensure the wrong examples of signage deployment do not soil the reputation of this promising industry. Legal and regulatory concerns of various communities will need to be measured carefully, especially by digital signage industry players activating systems alongside public thoroughfares.

- *Industry standards*: On its path to maturity, the digital signage industry will move toward standardization of various hardware, software, and operational elements, which it needs to do in order to begin maximizing the cost and other efficiencies that digital signage standards can offer. For example, finding common ground when it comes to fighting piracy and signal compromise would be one area where comparative telecom industries have succeeded.

- *Consumer acceptance*: Until the mass of consumers in the marketplace have overcome either a lack of understanding about or a misunderstanding about digital signage, its prospects will remain limited. In this vein, the related industries (e.g., consumer electronics, advertising, retail, travel, entertainment, service, and events) will have to be very aggressive if they wish to reap the maximum benefit in the shortest possible time frame. Also, the fact that there are few major, international digital signage providers stunts the industry's growth.

The Future Is Driving Digital Signage

When you add up the reasons for the success of digital signage, the accumulation is impressive. Indeed, there is much promise in both the present and the future of digital signage. When advertisers and their clients, especially, begin considering the prospects for digital signage, the equation is attractive: for every one reason why it may not work for them, there are easily two (or more) reasons why it will work. Thus, even without the support of the rest of the users of digital signage, the digital signage media stands a solid opportunity to succeed.

In addition, as the examples in this chapter demonstrate, visions of future examples of digital signage are incited by these examples, suggesting more and more places and applications in the future. The true challenge for every implementation of digital signage is not where to put it, but how to arrange the content so that both the digital display provider and the audience appreciate the message.

Advertising Solutions

Perhaps the primary reason digital signage is being driven into the lives of citizens globally is the erosion of traditional television habits, advertising being but one. In a most interesting article written about this topic in 2007, veteran digital signage authority David Little likens this erosion to that of New Hampshire's "Old Man of the Mountain" stone monolith, which crumbled and fell completely in May 2003.[9]

---

9. See "Digital Signage Payoff: What Is a Challenge for TV May Be a Boon for Digital Signage Networks," http://www.keywesttechnology.com/keywest-digital-signage-blog/digital- signage-payoff-what-is-a-challenge-for-tv-may-be-a-boon-for-digital-signage-networks-79.html.

4   When and Where to Use Digital Signage?

It's very clear that standard advertising today to mass millions isn't working any-more. The cost of digital signage displays is plummeting worldwide. A plasma or LCD screen is one-third the cost it was even one-and-a-half years ago. This dynamic, in conjunction with the availability of affordable broadband, has made it easier for retailers to adopt digital signage networks.

— Dick Trask, Director of Public Relations, Scala, Inc.

This chapter is intended to be used in conjunction with Chapters 6, 7, and 10. It is aimed at someone new to the digital signage industry, who is looking for the basic ideas of what makes it all tick, from a business point of view. Focus on this chapter is on keys to the (1) use, (2) display, and (3) control of a new or developing digital signage system.

The "where" of digital signage is easy: indoors and outdoors, there is a very wide range of different places where digital signage can be deployed. Indeed, as noted in Chapters 1 and 3, the better question might be to try to determine where *not* to use digital signage, because that might be a more easily accomplished task.

Put another way, as more and more marketers and entrepreneurs are discover-ing, digital signage can go just about anywhere structures exist and people con-gregate. In the future, in fact, even those limitations might not prove operable, because a digital sign, with a signal delivered to a built-in antenna and powered by a built-in solar panel, might work quite well in a remote trailhead in a busy national park. And, as noted in Lars-Ingemar Lundstrom's study of the technology behind digital signage, titled *Digital Signage Broadcasting: Broadcasting, Content Management, and Distribution Techniques*, digital signage has found its way into the home, as well. More versions are expected just about everywhere.

The tough question of digital signage is when to use it. This is because this question involves two very important, yet distinct, thoughts. First is the age-old

adage, "timing is everything." This recommends studying a given locale or scenario and acting when the elements combine to recommend digital signage. The
second part of this question involves a core message of this book, that is, do not
deploy a digital signage system of any type or size without first doing your homework. This starts, very importantly, with matching the goals of your business or
avocation with the goals you see digital signage is accomplishing.

Use

As discussed in Chapter 6, one of the four core necessities for initial implementation of a digital signage project is a commitment from one's own employees.
Typically, to be done professionally, this means a buy-in from one or several of
a business organization's internal departments. Typically, this would certainly
include the company's IT department. Yet not all that uncommonly, it would additionally include departments such as HR, corporate communications, finance,
legal, and others. Each should be brought in as a partner. Each should be queried
on the "when" and "where" to use the planned digital signage deployment. In this
measurement, considerations such as customer (or employee) traffic flow, dwell
time, and audience decision-making time would be discussed. Receiving multiple
views and contributions toward success from corporate brethren can be especially
important with a digital signage deployment that might create a challenge in terms
of proper placement of screens and the "right" content delivering the "right" message to the "right" audience.

Additionally, each department would be introduced to how it can best take
advantage of the new communications tool, and what each division needs to
give back in return. And, as pointed out in Chapter 10, it is a good idea that each
department not only knows and understands the vision statement, but also that
each department comes up with its own "mini-vision statement" as to what it, as a
department, expects the new digital signage system to do.

For those looking for a more detailed listing of the different types of uses for
digital signage, refer to Chapter 1. Nonetheless, a summary of dominant uses is
in order. These include, in no particular order: to affect the mood of an audience
and/or the ambience of the place; to build the brand of the place, a product, or service; to advertise a product or service; to deliver a message of training and/or business communications to employees; and/or to communicate important community
values, messages, or information.

Display

Any and every digital signage display needs to be well thought out ahead of time.
Ideally, each display complements the overall area, and is safe and easily seen,
but is not obstructive. In addition, part of the advanced due diligence involves
an evaluation of the new and/or existing screens vis-à-vis existing or new traditional signage, such as print or vinyl. This evaluation of the two types of signage
working together toward the same goal usually requires that location personnel
take down some of the environment's existing signage to avoid unnecessary clutter. For instance, one advantage of digital signage is that it allows—indeed, often it
demands—focus by the audience. Thus, the size of the digital signage screens and
the content that plays on them have to be appropriate for viewing, both from the
distance and the angle an audience would be observing.

Another important element of any display is to understand the importance,
and the appropriateness, of audio. A digital signage display's professional audio
needs to be loud enough, focused, and not bother either the employees or the end-
user audience. In addition, if a decision is made to avoid audio altogether, then
the video has to be easily visible, including legible and easy-to-read text, if it is to
be effective.

In the end, the ultimate key to a good digital signage display is to have good
content merge with a good display. Due diligence makes that happen, and it really
is that simple. A case study example of these criteria as practiced by a newly
planned national hair salon network follows.

The Salon Channel Network

Figure 4.1 shows the private digital signage television network, called "The Salon
Channel Network," being rolled out by Delray Beach, FL-based Airplay America. The
network focuses on 2,600 Great Clips outlets across the U.S. The Salon Channel is aimed
at consumers who dwell on an average of 20–40 minutes, and are visiting at least once
every 4–6 weeks to get their hair done. Company co-CEO Robert Cartagine touts this
particular audience as one that is "truly receptive to relevant advertising."

The service has deployed flat-screen LCD displays, together with a high-quality
audio system. The AirPlay America content is tailored to general audiences and targeted
to the salon's clientele. When fully executed, AirPlay America claims it will have the
ability to reach millions of consumers via advertising, programming, and marketing on

FIGURE 4.1 *The Salon Channel Network Is Targeted to Audiences That Are Captive for 20–40 Minutes, Every 4–6 Weeks (Copyright 2007. Property of AirPlay America. All rights reserved. Used with permission.)*

The Salon Channel. Figure 4.2 shows the basic infrastructure behind The Salon Channel Network.

Airplay manages relationships with the hair salon chains and provides programming, original content, and advertising sales. Other functions, such as installation, maintenance, and content management, are outsourced to key partners, such as X20 Media, Inc., Hughes Network Systems, LLC, Agilysys, Inc., and NEC Display Solutions. The Salon Channel Network uses Windows-based PCs and custom software furnished by X20 Media.

Installation and maintenance are provided by Agilysys and Hughes Network Systems, with Airplay supplying telephone support. Airplay maintains its works closely with its partners to strive for quality installations, ongoing reliability, and consistent performance.

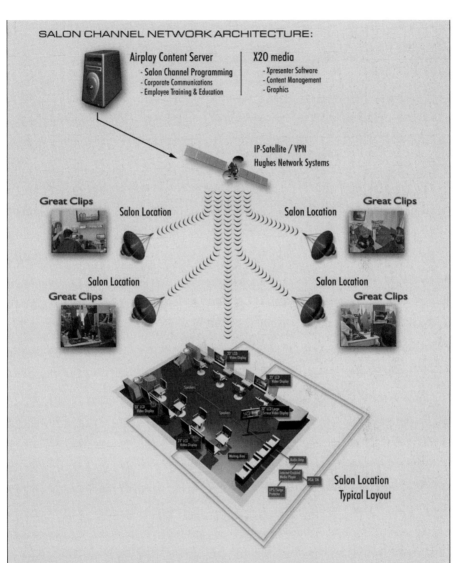

FIGURE 4.2 *The Salon Network's Infrastructure Chart Shows the Various Key Components on the Hardware Side (Copyright 2007. Property of AirPlay America. All rights reserved. Used with permission.)*

Each salon is addressable via an IP-satellite connection, which provides flexible scheduling of national, regional, or local advertising.

Content can be day-parted, week-parted, or custom-targeted to salon patrons in any or all locations. Using Multicasting over IP-Satellite, The Salon Channel provides advertisers with an attractive minimum lead time for scheduling of content (Figure 4.3).

Key to the AirPlay business model is the existence of four key stakeholders: (1) Great Clips, Inc., (2) Great Clips' franchise owners, (3) advertisers, and (4) AirPlay America. Most similar out-of-home network owners have the luxury of running a 30-minute content loop all day for as many as 30 days or more. Since The Salon Channel replaces conventional radio, the company had to place much more of an emphasis on its programming; developing short-form content, style editorials, and engaging music to entertain its viewers. AirPlay is also dealing with a much longer dwell time than most retail establishments, requiring a wider variety and quantity of content for all audiences at all times of the day. Accordingly, AirPlay America uses customer and employee satisfaction as its primary measure of success.

The Salon Channel is viewed by salon patrons, store employees, and hair stylists (who frequently work long hours). Since the program cannot be changed or turned off, it must always remain appealing and non-repetitive to everyone watching, including the salon employees, whether on a daily or a monthly basis. While advertisers want

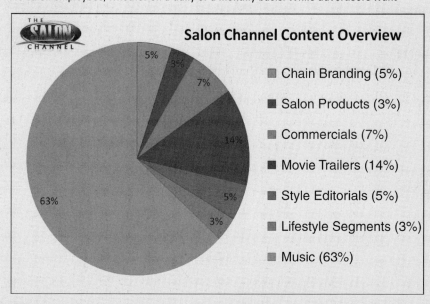

FIGURE 4.3 *The Types of Content Shown on The Salon Channel. Note the Heavier Emphasis on Movies and Music, Which the Participants Have Determined is the Right Content Vision for This Audience (Copyright 2007. Property of AirPlay America. All rights reserved. Used with permission.)*

frequency to ensure maximum recall and brand awareness, salon patrons and store employees demand programming that provides them with a positive experience during their time in the salon. AirPlay executives note that they spent numerous months designing their content formula, seeking the most engaging mix of music, entertainment, lifestyle, original programming, and advertising for viewers. When the roll-out is complete, The Salon Channel will serve millions of salon patrons and thousands of store employees nationwide. Figure 4.4 shows examples of on-screen content exhibited by The Salon Channel Network.

The Salon Channel features programming centered around four distinct themes: (1) Hair/Beauty, (2) Fashion/Style, (3) Entertainment, and (4) Music. Advertising is described as low-clutter, with only minimal avails at a quarter-hour frequency. All other content is shuffled daily, using what AirPlay claims to be a broad library of music and lifestyle

FIGURE 4.4 *A Compilation of Different Content Screens Shown Regularly to Audiences of The Salon Channel Network (Copyright 2007. Property of AirPlay America. All rights reserved. Used with permission.)*

FIGURE 4.4 (*Continued*)

programming from content providers such as CBS, Video Fashion News, and Private Label Radio.

The Salon Channel also features a variety of original "style editorials," such as Celebrity Hairstyles and Styling Secrets, Hair Tips, and Trivia. The mix of programming is intended to support AirPlay America's mission to entertain salon clients, while providing useful information that is relative to the hair salon experience.

According to Cartagine, advertisers have the unique advantage of displaying their messages to consumers, while being showcased within a genre of programming that connects them directly with the latest fashions, hair trends, and the celebrities that make those trends popular.

Control

Control of one's digital signage system is typically going to take two forms. In every instance, there will be the control exercised by the controlling company or network operator (also referred to elsewhere in this book as the "controlling stakeholder"). This is typically the "in-house control" that actually operates the system day-to-day. The other form of control—the "outside control"—is more frequent than many realize. This latter control comes from the influences of other entities, especially including governmental bodies.

In-House Control

Once the digital signage system is in place, decisions made early in the development process about control of the system can be pivotal. If control is placed in the wrong hands, then the whole system can fail, and reactions can be disastrous. Three usual control versions are typically available.

The first and the most often chosen control system for larger digital signage systems is via a single network center, which does all the work, and does not allow individual input from the separate spokes of the wheel, so to speak. Instead, everything is done from the central locale and then distributed to the tens, hundreds, or thousands of screens that make up the network. Implementation of a system like this would be a strong consideration for a convenience store system, with hundreds of stores making up the deployment.

A second version would be to have each location operate its own screen(s). Especially if the local employees are enthusiastic about the digital signage deployment and what it does for them and their customers, this do-it-in-the-store version works well. But it should be remembered that most businesses are not in the business of running the hardware, software, or operational sides of a digital signage system. That said, unless the business owner is prepared to spend additional sums on training local employees, so they can do each or all of the parts of running a digital signage deployment, it may be best to "leave it to the experts" in one main location.

A "hybrid" version of the all-at-the-headquarters and the all-at-the-single-location versions of operating the digital signage screens in a given deployment is also available. Yet, to date, there is insufficient data supporting this "hybrid" approach, and few in the industry are yet prepared to support it. In this model, most of the content is run out of one main headquarters, and individual site employees have limited input as to the software, hardware, or operational aspects of the system. Nonetheless, the one thing that does favor this approach is the idea that every once in a while, something unusual—perhaps weather or event related—comes along, and it works if the local venue personnel can adjust priorities accordingly. Thus, the local employees could step in and adjust the standard system-wide running of the day-parting (i.e., adjusting certain content for certain audiences at certain times of the day), when the need arises. The other side of this "hybrid" approach is that most systems, especially once they are up and running, are too well coordinated and too important to the overall business operation, to allow any random employee to have the chance to mess it up.

Finally, many digital signage industry experts point out repeatedly the importance of *diagnostics* and *measurements* as part of the control that is an important aspect of a good digital signage deployment. Good diagnostics built into the system, all the way down to each and every individual screen, are important to assist with maintenance. In addition, good ways to measure what actually airs on the individual screens, such as an ad playback system showing what actually played on each screen, are critical in the process of charging and collecting for advertising revenue. Professional measurement is also important when it comes to planning for the future. Without such measurement specificity, reports may come in about what was scheduled to air, but that can be wildly different than what actually aired. For example, if a screen is turned off, then what should have aired cannot match what actually aired. A valid "audited proof of actual play" should cover this concern.

Outside Control

Numbers-wise, the hundreds of thousands of screens that are the estimated universe of digital signage displays in the United States, and the millions of screens globally, will grow incrementally in the next several years. This is in no small part because digital signage works.

Nonetheless, one of the great restrictions on the growth of digital signage will come from control over its deployments that are put in place by governmental authorities. Thus, in some parts of North America today, there are blanket restrictions on the deployment of digital signage, many without any true rhyme or reason. In response, the U.S. federal government has begun undertaking to set standards and clarify the operation of digital signage along federal highways. These rules are related to restrictions on the brightness of the signs (so as to not adversely affect the safety of the driving public, based on ambient light conditions), and on their content (such that moving, flashing, intermittent, and other fast-turning distractive visuals are restricted or prohibited). It will be up to the digital signage industry—both individually, via one-by-one separate company public affairs efforts, and collectively, via trade groups' and associations' lobbying efforts—to accommodate better conditions for the development of digital signage. This will be true at the federal, state, and local levels, because all will have an impact on the growth and development of where and when to use digital signage.

5 Content

Successful—indeed just about any—content for digital signage is much more than just understanding the content, production and technical values. It is about understanding consumers—his or her needs, what he or she is doing, the environment they are in—and matching good content strategies to all of that. That's one of the biggest challenges for our industry today.

—Carre Dawson, Principal, Dawson & Company, a 12-year-digital-signage-industry veteran, and POPAI industry trade group representative

Focused and relevant content delivered to the individual by any infrastructure is called narrowcasting, because it casts a narrow message to a specific audience. This really is what quality digital signage is all about. Yet beyond the content itself is the study of the audience, the place, and the other players (or stakeholders). To do it right can take a lot of work, but doing right makes it much more likely the project succeeds, the goals are met, the audience is served, the audience reacts favorably, expected returns are achieved, and the overall digital signage industry excels.

Within the broadcasting and related realms, there's an old adage, "Content is king." Put another way, typical over-the-air broadcasting, cable, Direct Broadcast Satellite (DBS), and telco video consumers do not care about *how* they receive their content (the pictures, video, audio, animation, and data—that is actually displayed on the digital signage screen or display device), they just care about *what* content they receive. The growth of the DBS industry is a perfect example of this maxim, inasmuch as when satellite video companies such as DirecTV and EchoStar began in the 1990s delivering more channels with better digital quality for less money, consumers readily sacrificed their old cable wires and cable set-top receivers for satellite antennas and satellite set-tops.

This same adage applies to the digital signage business. Hardware, installation, distribution, maintenance, and measurement are important parts of the puzzle. Nonetheless, the true driving force behind today's digital signage is the *content* that is shown on the screens. This, then, becomes both a blessing and a bane.

The all-important content is a blessing for the digital signage industry because, literally and figuratively, the sky is the limit from a standpoint of creativity and future direction. Yet, conversely, content is a bane because if the digital signage industry slips up, and if it creates multiple disasters in the minds of its audiences, the perception (and success) of digital signage will suffer immensely. If that were to happen, not too far into the future, consumers having had or heard about bad digital signage experiences might begin driving the digital signage industry down, rather than supporting its growth.

This chapter focuses attention on an understanding of the audience, the location of the display device as it relates to the content shown, the types of content available, the applicable consumer dwell time, audio content, and future content possibilities.

Understanding the Audience

Rhetoric is the study of audiences and the impact certain messages have upon them. A basic premise of all rhetoric is that in order to speak most effectively, you speak to your audience (i.e., you address their needs). Thus, if it is late spring in the northern hemisphere and a garment retailer is trying to sell a line of clothing, if tomorrow's weather forecast is for a temperature of 100+ degrees Fahrenheit, your average audience is unlikely to be receptive to the sale of heavy wool winter coats at standard winter prices. That would be an ineffective, probably irrelevant, and maybe even offensive, message for this specific audience.

Yet, that need to "speak more effectively to your audience" is something that too few in Advertising America have dwelt upon sufficiently. Indeed, many feel that finding relevant audience messages is indeed "The Future of Advertising," around the world. The wonderful thing about digital signage is that it is developing the tools—both on the technical/hardware and on the creative/software sides— to enable this to happen, and happen quickly. Again, the important question is, can it also happen *properly* (especially as it relates to delivering an appropriate message to the audience)?

This, then, presents a clear opportunity for all future digital signers.

For example, a basic digital sign hung from a ceiling mount above the entrance to a grocery store's fruit and vegetable section would be an ideal location on which to show a special piece of content highlighting the freshness and health of bananas ... or apples ... or oranges. More aptly, this same screen would be the ideal spot to applaud the special sale of a fruit or vegetable, especially one with a short shelf life (and thus requiring a quick turnaround for the digital signage content), because to *not* do so would be to lose the product to spoilage.

Another example of digital signage that maximizes its effectiveness because of its *relevance* to the particular audience might include a tire sale advertisement on a digital sign beside a freeway, especially where traffic is frequently heavy and slowed or stopped. Conversely, an advertisement for ripe fruits and vegetables would likely be much less relevant to the freeway audience than it would be to the supermarket audience.

In this sense, the best-run and the best-implemented digital signage content will specially relate to its audience on a regular basis, probably including frequent refreshment of the content, dependent upon what is being sold, when it's being sold, and to whom and where.

As noted during an interview with the principals of the Hollywood, CA-headquartered digital signage vendor, eVision Networks, one of the better ways to ensure a proper connection with the audience is to understand and try to match and accommodate the *goals* of each of the major digital signage participants. This would include key parties such as the network owner and operator, the advertiser, the location owner, and, of course, the ultimate audience for the given content.

For example, participants would have to agree upon the purpose of the given network. Indeed, one of the best ways to address the needs of operator, advertiser, and owner is to create a strong dialog with each, both separately and collectively, and to add on a layer of adequate due diligence and data (e.g., the projected return on investment (ROI) from a given digital signage ad campaign). Chapter 8 provides more detailed information about finding these goals and building this communication among the traditional stakeholders in the digital signage industry.

Perhaps an even more important task is to gather reliable data that would offer an insight into the ultimate audience, that is, the viewer, such as any demographic details. On another level for the audience is information related to the type of audience visiting the type of locale they are frequenting at any given time.

For example, a convenience store would have a much different audience in the morning hours, as it attempts to service business people leaving early for work, than it would in the mid-afternoon, when it attempts to service mothers and their children stopping for refreshments after school or lacrosse practice. Thus, for each member of these different types of store visitors just mentioned, the proper digital signage content takes into account not only who they are and when they are there, but also things such as their budgets, what it is they are doing at the time (or have done, or will be doing next), and even what is on their minds as they patronize the business (Figure 5.1). Knowing that, the stakeholders would,

FIGURE 5.1 *Two Examples of Digital Signage Content, Targeted to Two Different Audiences. The First Is Aimed at Adults Who Might Buy Mixed Drinks (Sponsored by a Cell Phone Service). The Other Is Aimed at Women Shoppers for a Specific Line of Clothing. One Is Right for One Audience, While the Other Is Not (and Vice Versa) (First Image Is Copyright 2007. Property of Scala. All rights reserved. Used with permission. Second image is Copyright 2007. Property of Lyle Bunn. All rights reserved.)*

FIGURE 5.2 *Digital Signage Can Offer Localized Information, Such As About the Doctors and Staff at a Veterinary Office (Copyright 2007. Property of emebaVet. All rights reserved. Used with permission.)*

ideally, want to deliver different content at different times to these different audiences.

Another comment about digital signage content that appears particularly noteworthy is that it should also—wherever possible, such as local television broadcasting content—contain relevant local content. Thus, for example, a screen meeting the shoppers as they enter a target store could have a 10-second address offered by the on-duty store manager, as well as a piece of content in the meat and fish department that shows customers located in a particular region of the U.S. South that there is an exclusive, new local special on locally caught fish. Or, a screen welcoming people to a medical service clinic would have content that introduces the customer to the staff. Figure 5.2 depicts such a content display in a vet's office.

Additionally, not unlike the dilemma of the heroine as she determines just the right soup to eat in the fable of *Goldilocks and the Three Bears*, the right digital signage content mix involves just the right volume of content, not too much content and not too little. Too much content taxes the system and its employees, and wastes money on audiences that will not be appreciative. Too little content saves money and resources, yet again lapses into the ever-dangerous realm of not helping, and likely even boring or annoying, the audiences. This is something which most digital signage should never do.

Scala

Jeff Porter is the executive vice president for what is one of the more respected companies in the North American and global digital signage industries, describing itself as a "turn-key solutions provider and content management company," that goes by the name of Scala. Porter has been with Scala for more than 13 years. Porter details, "We are a software and services company. We don't have guys in trucks. We don't resell hardware. We don't sell direct. We have more than 350 partners who take our software and deliver solutions to customers around the world." Using Scala's products and services, the company has well over 50,000 systems deployed today. The size of deployments, like the one shown in Figure 5.3, ranges from one screen in the lobby of the golf manufacturing company, Taylor Made Golf, to many thousands of players operating for Shell Gas Stations. Scala's software, according to Porter, is designed to scale, both down and up.

Historically, the biggest motivator for Scala to move into the digital signage industry back in 1987 was "… the single goal of providing an easy way to manage content on a network of screens," explains Porter. "Digital Signage is not TV, nor is it the web, or print, or a billboard. It's this 'new thing,' and you need tools to manage this new media, and have it scale cost effectively."

FIGURE 5.3 *An Example of a Scala Customer, Burger King, and Its Digital Signage in a Typical Franchise (Copyright 2007. Property of Scala. All rights reserved. Used with permission.)*

When reviewing client advice on a broad scale, Porter points out that many folks new to digital signage make the mistake of focusing on the screens first (after all, that's typically the single biggest up-front cost). But he goes on to note that the piece that will "break the bank" is in "feeding the monster" and finding the right software platform to manage that task. For example, two solutions for the same deployment might involve one that is clearly right, the other that is clearly wrong. Thus, one might employ brute force, whereby one "feeds the monster" with 10,000 playlists.

And the other may involve a simple way to have the players be smart enough to play the right media at the right time with the right message. In sum, Scala has learned and practices the message of starting with the content strategy. Continues Porter, "Pick a software [management] platform that is flexible enough to deliver that content strategy, then start filling in the hardware pieces. Top down is a lot easier than bottom up. Don't make the mistake that 'someone else' will figure out where the content comes from, and 'therefore I can ignore that, and I'll instead focus on the hardware.' Bad move. You will fail. Content is King, and you need to start there, even if content is not 'your area' of responsibility" (see Figures 5.4 and 5.5).

When measuring the effectiveness of the digital signage, in retail for instance, Porter recommends simply measuring the sales lift provided to the affected products. "Put an ad up, measure the sales. Take it down, compare. You don't really need a Nielsen

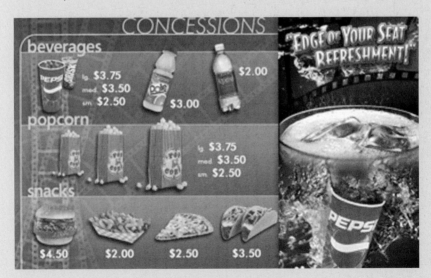

FIGURE 5.4 *An Example of the Menuboard Content Exhibited by a Typical Scala Customer, Shown in a Typical Store (Copyright 2007. Property of Scala. All rights reserved. Used with permission.)*

FIGURE 5.5 *A European Coffee House and Its Digital Signage In a Typical Store (Copyright 2007. Property of Scala. All rights reserved. Used with permission.)*

rating to tell you that you sold more. Your point of sale (POS) data will tell you that," he summarizes. Nonetheless, in a corporate environment, it's a little more difficult to measure effectiveness directly. For example, sometimes it's as simple as assessing whether the staff is better informed or educated. If yes, one's company will usually be doing better and the digital signage deployment is valuable. Scala has third-party company relationships, such as that with the company DS-IQ, so that in retail, it can provide real-time analytics to compare advertising to POS data, and thus measure the effectiveness of a campaign. But then again, this is not always necessary. As a senior executive at Lamar Digital Outdoor Advertising once told me, "If people are standing in line to buy time on my boards, we must be doing something right," Porter concludes (Figure 5.6).

Looking at the primary benefit, in Porter's eyes, of using digital signage today, he states that in today's advertising industry, traditional mass market (e.g., television) ads are costing more and more and more, while advertisers are getting less and less and less. And to make matters worse, Porter, pointing out that retail is one of the few industries where this is the case today, adds, "TiVos are a fact of life. In a recent survey

FIGURE 5.6 *Scala Customer U.K.-Based Tesco Markets, and Its Digital Signage in the Deli Section of a Typical Store (Copyright 2007. Property of Scala. All rights reserved. Used with permission.)*

published in *Business Week*, 96% of TiVo owners skipped over fast food commercials, yet, that industry still pours millions of dollars into traditional TV spots. Since 70% of all purchase decisions are actually made in the store, it seems to me that having screens in stores next to the product (that can't be TiVo-ed) make a whole lot more sense."

"We're pretty hardware agnostic at Scala. Although we test and certify a large number of hardware devices out there, we support nearly all of them. If the display has some sort of video connector, we're good to go," Porter notes. Plus, Scala is always seeking new display technologies, such as living surfaces, Organic LED screens or E-paper. Pointing, for example, to the development of new flat-screen display panels, he cheers, "It's amazing what has happened to the industry over the last five years, and I don't see any of that slowing down any time soon. We continue to keep up with the technology advances that our hardware partners are making."

Content? Which of it works for which of Scala's clients? As one would expect, this varies based on the venue. Rather, the common theme is that the content must be relevant to the venue. "Whether it's in a casino … on a gas pump, in a bank, on the factory floor, in a call center, or in the lobby. The trick is to understand that environment and come up with a content strategy that makes sense in that environment," Porter recommends.

Using Scala's software management program, InfoChannel Designer, Porter claims that clients are able to work with nearly any sort of media files presented to it, for example, MPEG, WMV, JPG, GIF, TIF, MP3, WAV, and so on, even live or streaming video. Porter goes on, "The software has to be able to integrate that with other data sources and metadata to make the playback of that media be more RELEVANT and DYNAMIC (are you catching our theme yet?)" (emphasis in original). And although some clients ask for Scala's help creating content, Porter points out that many creative people know how to use Scala's Designer tool, such as those at a graphic house but, nonetheless, Scala does have what Porter calls, "drivers on staff" to help with certain needs in the area of content creation.

Looking at content scheduling questions, Porter explains that Scala's Content Manager in Software provides an easy-to-use day-part scheduler, in an easy-to-use graphical web-based user interface. There are also sophisticated metadata filtering components for media items and players. In addition, the software responds to target triggers, such as weather/temperature, season, and so on, which can cause Scala to adapt the client's playlist. Porter's take on this topic: "You could promote umbrellas at the gas station if it's raining. You could target the right Scott's Turf Builder for your lawn, based on geography and week of the year. These are . . . very possible to easily do. . ." Moreover, the displayed content can, of course, be targeted to specific locations at specific times (Figure 5.7).

Digital signage network solutions are being used more and more for a combination of national, regional, or local targeting (i.e., down to a single location or a single group of digital signage screens within a single location). As an example, Porter lists General Motors: "General Motors has been doing this since the late 1990s. National, regional, and local content [are shown] in each factory to inform, educate and motivate their employees." And, of course, this kind of dedicated software platform can be used to enable regional or worldwide content distribution and playback.

Porter notes that Scala clients use digital signage networks in every type of venue and for every type of need, for example, use solely for in-house advertising purposes; use primarily for a targeted advertisement; use primarily to enhance customer experience; use to influence customer behavior, such as directing customers to different areas of a retail establishment; and use to build/create brand awareness.

"Assuming that [a typical client] followed at least eight out of ten of our 'Top 10 rules,' chances are ROI happens within the first 12 months (and usually by a very comfortable margin)," Porter opines. He also finds that, "Typically you'll see double

FIGURE 5.7 *A Scala Customer, a Telephone Services Provider, and Its Digital Signage in a Typical Store (Copyright 2007. Property of Scala. All rights reserved. Used with permission.)*

digit increases in sales in an advertising based network. Other networks are harder to measure, but the fact that everyone in a convention center knows where to go ... that's a good thing that might keep people coming back year after year. Without that, you're looking like yesterday's news."

Moreover, Scala recommends that clients typically have a targeted ROI plan prior to deployment. This allows them to measure their success. "Again, it gets back to having a content strategy. Without that, nothing else matters," muses Porter. ROIs are created typically based on the venue. In a bank, for instance, management may wish to have a screen to reduce perceived wait time, or to motivate customers to open a new type of account. Porter states that those sorts of performance metrics can be easily measured.

Metrics to measure the ROI depend on the venue, but many folks actually have pretty "low expectations," which are fairly easily exceeded. For instance, in QSRs, if companies can get another 2–3% growth year on year in an existing store, that's considered a significant achievement. Porter notes that Burger King Germany had increases of more than 13%, without opening any new stores. This was attributable

FIGURE 5.8 *A Scala Customer, Gas Station/Convenience Store Digital Signage Provider, FuelCast, and Its Digital Signage in a Typical Location (Copyright 2007. Property of Scala. All rights reserved. Used with permission.)*

directly to having one screen in the middle of the existing menu boards. In addition, the ROI projections are typically based on the content strategy deployed, which means each one varies—as would the content strategy—across the board (Figure 5.8).

Porter contends that the biggest inhibitor to expanding digital signage deployment for his clients is financing. To reach critical mass in many U.S. retail spaces today, a vendor needs many thousands of screens. "Compare this with the U.K., for instance. Critical mass there can be had for less than 10% of the U.S.," is Porter's generalized comparison. "The other thing that will have to change is Madison Avenue. People are very, very comfortable selling what their fathers before them have sold in advertising. It's low risk. Or so they think. We're finding that Eastern European countries are far more open to new media, since they don't have the baggage to deal with. I claim they went from 19th Century Cold War to 21st Century State of the Art (and they skipped the 20th Century all together!). There's a bit of a ball and chain in many companies in the U.S.

But, when our KIDS are calling the shots, there will be a change. 'What do you mean we're not putting screens in our stores??? Of course we are!'" (emphasis in original.)

Porter has found that many times companies seeking new digital signage deployments are finding "angel investors" to prove out their pilots, then they are using that experience to do their longer-term capital fund raising. For well-established companies, moreover, the costs are not a problem. Bloomberg, for example, has Scala in more than 100 countries around the world. "They don't think twice about it," Porter proudly exclaims.

As regards questions of digital signage regulation, an always important consideration, Porter states that Scala strongly supports POPAI. By comparison, there are some "for-profit" organizations out there, but each has some sort of position to maintain, he believes, which weakens their effectiveness. "POPAI has the infrastructure for each of its members to contribute in a non-sectarian way, for the good of the industry," suggests Porter.

Wrapping up the subject of regulatory concerns, Porter notes that people in the outdoor advertising world have to deal with regulations all the time. He quips, "It's the nature of their beast. Most other folks [in the digital signage industry] don't have a lot of regulations that they need to cope with (other than possibly the obvious safety issues)." For example, Lamar Outdoor Advertising cannot just put a digital roadside billboard anywhere. They have to get a permit for that. But they did that back in the print days too. "So it's really nothing new for them or for the industry as a whole," Porter concludes.

Content Placement

The placement of screens within a given locale is probably not as important as the actual content on the screen; however, placement can often be a key determinant in the effectiveness of the particular content. Thus, if a digital sign is located within an establishment where only half the intended audience hears and/or sees the message, then the content's impact on that audience can be no better, typically, than 50%. Money and resources would likely then be lost. As an example, if an audience of young teenage men walking through a mall is being addressed, it probably makes more sense to catch them on a screen in a Nike store, than it would on a screen in a Victoria's Secret store.

On a related note, the placement of content can be maximized if the stakeholders take into account the maximum potential of the infrastructure and content. Thus, adjusting the brightness of a particular screen, or focusing the audio into a particular section of a store, can greatly enhance the effect of the actual content on the audience.[1]

Further, because it is so dynamic and ever changing, digital signage content should be taken advantage of, although this doesn't necessarily mean spending extravagant resources on recreating content or creating new content where content already exists. Thus, tracking a theme, brand, or a certain message, companies new to digital signage can adapt shorter versions of 30- or 60-second broadcast advertisements, perhaps using 5-second clips from the former to retain that given message. Or the same company might take a video clip as the foundation for a given branding or sales message, and turn it into an animated version designed specifically for a given screen, in a given store locale, set at a given time for a specific audience. In addition to permitting lower costs, a strategy such as this permits ad agencies and their advertisers to maintain continuity in their messaging and cut the time required to go from creative idea to actual implementation.

Because so much digital signage now and in the future is and will be retail oriented, it is also important to try to achieve a handful of goals when implementing content in this environment. These include (1) stores sales, (2) product information, and (3) special events. Further, as noted throughout this book, within the study of delivering content, advertisers and their agencies should consistently strive to deliver to consumers particularly *relevant* information.

A concept known as "glance media" champions the idea that oftentimes audiences are in environments, such as grocery stores, where their time is limited and they are rushing. As such, they are unable to give any media more than a glance as they move through the environment. During this short time frame, in order to be effective, that media must deliver a quick message. In this environment, many digital signage advisers recommend giving that consumer something helpful and empowering (rather than something that either interrupts them unnecessarily or does not give them anything in return, or both). Put another way, when the consumer says, "If you are going to interrupt me, you owe me something," the digital signage providers should have content that answers, "Sure, no problem, this will satisfy your needs."

---

1. NAB/Focal Press' Publication, *Digital Signage Broadcasting: Broadcasting, Content Management, and Distribution Techniques*, contains significant additional information about the *technology* behind digital signage, should readers wish to further their understanding—and the potential of their digital signage network(s)—*vis-à-vis* the best implementation of digital signage on a technical level.

Yet another part of content placement involves combining the above-described elements to create a call to action, be it to purchase something or attend an event, or perhaps take a coupon and send in a mailer for a prize or a premium.

Interestingly, as suggested in an interview with Sam McCleery, the CEO of the virtual signage developer Princeton Video, the concept of content placement is carried one step further. McCleery's company digitally places (or replaces) advertisements on television at actual events, typically choosing locations where telecast viewing audiences would expect such an ad to appear. Thus, for the 2007 World Series telecast by Fox, Princeton Video chose a different ad for the space behind home plate for each of the separate telecasts being delivered live to Japan, Latin America, Mexico, and Canada (Figure 5.9). His company does similar digital ad placements utilizing the face-off circles in soccer matches and on the sideboards at hockey games, each adapted to the needs and goals of the many stakeholders, as well as to those of the particular telecast audiences.

Finally, placement of content means, in most cases, positioning the screen and delivering a relevant message at or near the so-called "point of purchase." Studies

FIGURE 5.9 *An Advertisement Digitally Inserted Behind Home Plate That Specifically Relates to and Is Relevant to the People Viewing That Program (Copyright 2007. Property of Princeton Video Imaging. All rights reserved. Used with permission.)*

noted in a September 25, 2005, issue of *The Wall Street Journal*, in a front-page article entitled, "In a Shift, Marketers Beef Up Spending Inside Stores," show that the "in store shelf—the point of product selection," is often the best place to attract sales and initiate a buy decision. This is where digital signage quite often best engages the audiences, especially if it involves a purchase or action decision.

Another important place of content contact is the point of purchase (POP); however, oftentimes retailers notice that unless it is for chewing gum, mints, candies, or magazines sold at the POP, it is already too late to inspire consumers to purchase an item from elsewhere in the store, if they have not already done so.

Types of Content

Six sub-topics make up the subject of content types. Five of these—stills (e.g., slides or photos), animation, video, data, and text—involve actual different versions of visual content. The sixth, audio, begs the basic question of whether and how to use it. Again, as noted in Chapter 1, it often helps to identify in the planning process the goals and purposes of the content, and then to determine if it is commercial, informational, experiential, or behavioral. Beyond that, determinations need to be made about the time of the day and the specifics of the audience to maximize the contents' effectiveness.

A mixing of these various formats adds that element of "surprise" that engages the customer; it also helps manage tight spending and time budgets. Ideally, digital signage vendors will not only pull from their traditional media assets, but also develop new content that relates specifically to the audience and environment. And as noted in the NAB/Focal Press, Sister Publication, *Digital Signage Broadcasting: Broadcasting, Content Management, and Distribution Techniques*, another layer of complexity gets added by the technologists, when items such as acceptance of standard formats, quality content standards, and maximization of bandwidth utilization are necessarily considered.

Stills

Because a single digital screen can be formatted (and usually is) so that it offers multiple zones or regions in which to place content, any one screen can be used effectively to simultaneously display many still images of anything from photos, to artwork, to PowerPoint data slides, which are also known as "stills" (Figure 5.10). Other compilations of simultaneous content might include stills, together with mixes of the other different visual content types described here.

FIGURE 5.10 *A Digital Signage Still (Copyright 2008. Property of Jimmy Schaeffler. All rights reserved.)*

Animation

Animation is an ideal place to turn creativity loose, as has been shown from the earliest days of Walt Disney and his predecessors. Within the context of digital signage, animation mixed with other media on the same screen, but using different regions (or zones), has the potential to not only engage, but also captivate, and move, various audiences to action (Figure 5.11).

Video

Probably no other type of media is more important to digital signage than video (Figure 5.12). Because the global culture is so attuned to quality (and often even lesser quality), video these days has a natural—and superior—drawing power. Yet high-quality video is also expensive and if it is too much like real, sit-at-home-and-enjoy TV, the digital signage video content will likely be boring and uninteresting, as well as irrelevant and unengaging. This, too, creates another

FIGURE 5.11 *A Digital Signage Animation on a Screen in a Hotel in Delhi, India (Copyright 2008. Property of Jimmy Schaeffler. All rights reserved.)*

FIGURE 5.12 *A Wall of Multiple Digital Signage Screens Showing Several Forms of Video Content (Copyright 2007. Property of Visual Century Research. All rights reserved. Used with permission.)*

dilemma for digital signage stakeholders, especially those responsible for creating the content.

Data

Data typically includes running tickers, at the bottoms of screens, that are used to deliver sports, or news, or stock information in a running fashion (Figure 5.13). Data works well to help maximize the effectiveness of given screens in given

FIGURE 5.13 *Data Displayed on a Large Digital Sign in New York City's Times Square (Copyright 2007. Property of Jimmy Schaeffler. All rights reserved.)*

environments, because its use permits numerous stories to be told—and rather inexpensively—on the same screen simultaneously with other content. Nonetheless, there exists the challenge of needing real-time updates with a data feed to stay relevant. Additionally, using data requires more of an infrastructure dedicated to content management than would some of the other content forms.

Miscellaneous (Text, Objects, Logos, etc.)

A fifth type of visual content combines one often-used item, that is, logos, along with other less-used items, such as full-screen written text or numbers, graphical objects, and even some not-yet-discovered-or-utilized elements. Logos and their use are obviously extremely important if the goal of the participants is to brand a place, product, service, or event (Figure 5.14).

Audio

Several important issues arise in the consideration of the ideal digital signage audio environment. First would certainly be the realization that people usually

FIGURE 5.14 *A Logo on a Digital Signage Screen beside a Freeway in California (Copyright 2008. Property of Jimmy Schaeffler. All rights reserved.)*

hear before they see, and thus audio becomes a critically important element of just about any (but not all) digital signage. Next would be the credo that the audio must match the visual message.

Yet beyond these basic concerns are others such as delivering the appropriate audio in conjunction with, or matched to, other in-house audio systems, and delivering the proper audio message to the right audience at the right time (and in the right place).

Early digital signage pioneers, such as Carre Dawson, discovered that although repetitive audio delivered in a loop was effective to address the majority of customers, that same audio later had to be removed entirely because its repetition so annoyed in-store employees, badly impacting their productivity and workplace well-being. In other instances, one or more of two or more audio systems in a given establishment was turned off, or technology was utilized allowing one audio system to be specifically delivered into a special section of the environment (while the other audio systems were delivered elsewhere).

Consumer Dwell Time

Dwell time refers to the time a viewer normally spends in an area in front of a screen. Thus, the dwell time for a patient in an emergency room waiting area might be an hour or more; whereas the dwell time for a mother with two screaming infants in a grocery store might be no more than a couple of seconds.

Dwell time is so important to content because without knowing and adapting to it, content can be served to audiences, which is completely ineffective and irrelevant, thus being a waste of stakeholder money and, perhaps more important, a waste of the consumer's time. Also related closely to dwell time would be the time of the day or week that involves a particular audience, and the realization that in many instances that audience is fluid, changing, and totally dynamic. Thus, to offer one message of a given length to one audience in the morning might be incredibly effective and relevant (and profitable), but to offer the same to an evening audience might be ridiculous. An example would be the development of a content piece for someone who visits a drug store twice a week. The second time he or she enters the store, if the same content is on the screen, the digital signage likely will be ineffective or much less effective winning the customer's attention, interest, and, ideally, action.

Taking the consumer dwell time to a whole new level, virtual advertisers and digital signage companies such as Princeton Video accept the fact that DVRs are being used by consumers to specifically avoid normal broadcast TV advertisements. They, in turn, developed digital devices, such as virtual first down lines and virtual scrimmage lines for football telecasts, and then began embedding ads into those line graphics. Thus, the dwell time of the viewer for the ad is artificially extended. Another popular use of such graphics these days—this one in the entertainment arena—is the lower screen graphical promotions for later network shows that are flashed on-screen during a separate show telecast.

Future Content

Many industry observers are of the opinion that with the inevitable advancement of technology, the scenes depicted in the movie *Minority Report* will, in fact, become reality. *Minority Report* suggested the future of advertising and product and service identity in a future America. In one instance, the computer scanned and read the proponent's eyeball and then automatically adjusted the on-screen content to his pre-supposed product and service wants and needs. Yet, despite the vision depicted in *Minority Report*, it is safe to say that it is more likely that if the digital signage industry does not properly deploy digital signage, *en masse*, that audiences will rebel in one of the most effective ways ever: they will instead turn digital signage off (and agencies and retailers will stop using it).

Thus, future content depends in large measure upon the proper implementation of the due diligence and the steps identified in this chapter, specifically, and in this book, in general.

There are many foreseeable or predictable developments that will greatly impact the creation and delivery of content to display worldwide, covered in more detail in Chapter 11. Motion detectors will work with identification devices, such as RFID, to pinpoint the individual, his or her likes, dislikes, interests, and passions. Then instantly content will be delivered and available, to turn on (or possibly even allow the consumer to turn off and/or select another message). Voice-activated devices will further allow deployment of more choices, both on the consumer and vendor sides of the digital signage relationship. Specific digital signage devices will permit consumers to transfer content to cell phones and PDAs, allowing that content to be later viewed or later used in a commercial way, for example. Touch screens and other various forms of interactivity will also proliferate and further develop, as will the quality of high-definition flat-panel screens, and the amount of content that can be transported affordably, as well as new offerings, such as 3D screens and content.

Another industry pioneer, Lyle Bunn, a strategy architect formerly with the Toronto, Canada-headquartered Alchemy organization (a digital signage content unit of the St. Joseph Content Company), offers the following advice accompanying his "White Paper," The New Madison Avenue Diet, which is applicable not only to the present—but also to the future—applications of digital signage around the world:

> Since many consumers do product research online prior to a store visit with purchase intent, it is valuable to link the Internet browsing experience with the in-store information experience to reinforce the purchase intent. From a composition standpoint, digital signage should present less information textually and more visually, while leading a consumer to a product and service selection that will fulfill their need or aspiration. The composition should also offer visual clues to nearby store sales associates, as to buyer readiness to commence the closing of the sale, up-selling and cross-selling.

Worth also noting is the idea that digital signage and the content that is so critical to its success are not the things that can achieve everything for everybody. Like any "tool," even the best digital signage content is able to achieve only certain things (and with certain people and at certain times). Thus, companies deploying digital signage should be prepared for the fact that not all departments in the company will get everything they expect or need from their digital signage department.

Perhaps further into the content crystal ball will be GPS and biometric applications, which should add even more precision to the efforts to satisfy and accommodate the individual audience member. Indeed, devices are already being developed that allow various parties to simply scan a badge or card and instantly a complete read-out of a consumer's purchasing history is available, as well as data summaries that will enable additional new advertising and other pitches. In the live video environment, those watching sports will have access to data that will permit the viewing audiences, individually, to do more and more comparisons and predictions relating to the given game, team, or player.

Yet again, in the end, only if these devices can work so that the degree of help is greater than the degree of invasion—and so that the ROI is there—will their success be longer term. Chapter 11 gives a more complete and detailed listing and description of future digital signage opportunities and applications.

6 Who's Right for Digital Signage?

Digital signage is about controlling the environment by controlling the message.
—Laura Davis-Taylor, co-author, *Lighting Up the Aisle: Principles and Practices for In-Store Media*

It's difficult to imagine a place where people congregate that could not benefit from an appropriate message delivered via a well-placed digital sign. Thus, the audience of those that can implement—and those that can receive—the digital signage experience is smaller in the beginning, but, ultimately, longer term, extremely broad based. Further, the groups of those that can benefit from digital signage deployments range from large brand marketers to advertising agencies, to retailers, to clergy, to system integrators, to investors, to travel providers, to equipment manufacturers and suppliers and, indeed, even to broadcasters and multichannel operators.

In the development, growth, and deployment of any technology, device, or even a content form, there comes a time when, to coin a phrase, the "planets begin to align." For some of these technologies or content forms, that point comes early, for others it comes much later (or never). That time of alignment in the history of digital signage happened during the period following 2005, when the elements of large and small thin digital screen displays, easy transport of instantly changeable content, higher-quality content, and a weakened ad market aligned in such a way to place digital signage on its own future fast track. As such, and as noted in Chapter 3, the better question today becomes, who can't benefit from digital signage?

The Basic Criteria

To begin with, a handful of required key ingredients is typically necessary if one is going to enter the world of a digital signage deployment.

For one, thoughts should be turned immediately to whether you have (or will have) a receptive audience. These days, this audience consideration comes down typically to two audiences: the end-user/customer and the employee base.

Next, funding is important. At minimum, quality digital signage costs are in the low thousands of dollars, and for bigger projects, millions, or tens of millions, of dollars might be required over time. Chapters 3 and 10 capture the essence of these costs and considerations.

Another set of necessities starts with a need to convey an important message to an audience. Of course, this message can range from a religious tome to a retailer's or advertiser's "purchase this now and you're brilliant" message, to a doctor's "here's how you get the most of out of this experience while you're stuck here waiting" communiqué. For everyone new to the digital signage world, each person or organization will have a different definition of just what message is important enough to reach the level of funding that is ultimately decided upon.

Probably last among the basics is an organizational buy-in. This means having the group of people around you who will create and maintain the digital signage project amply supporting what is happening. Another important gauge is whether your organization has a culture that is receptive to innovative marketing, communications, informational, and educational methods. Or, on the other side of that question, does your organization need to be? Indeed, if traditional methods of communicating with and marketing to audiences have waned or grown stale, perhaps your organization is an even better candidate for digital signage than you think.

More Ingredients

A key aid in determining if digital signage is right for your organization or locale is whether target audiences are "captive," in the sense that they are waiting in line or in a place where their movement is restricted. Some people grapple with the term "captive," noting that few real audiences these days are truly "captive," in the sense that the audience can usually leave when it wants. Put another way, this question turns on the study of why they are there and how difficult it would be to depart. If they are there to get what you are telling them (in the form of a message), and if leaving would be a hassle, then they are, in a sense, "captive," and you have something in your favor when it comes to an important audience ingredient.

Another factor to look for is whether your locale has access to large numbers of people passing by. For most messages, having larger audiences is a plus. Nonetheless, some circumstances involve specialized or limited audiences, and if the content is narrowed to address just that narrow or specialized audience, then that is what digital signers need to strive for.

A third determinant would be a place where audience measurements are easily obtained. Satisfy one or more of these "more ingredients" criteria, and you could begin to place yourself in the category of those who are right for digital signage.

Organizational Types

Presenting the picture of who's right for digital signage could merely track a listing of the stakeholders. Yet, that having already been completed in Chapter 2, the preferable form is to classify and then discuss here the types of major players, relative to the chapter heading.

The following is a listing and description of organizations and locales where digital signage applications have been commonplace, together with a briefer listing of digital signage's "miscellaneous" players and places that could come about less frequently, or are guessed about in the future.

Ad Agencies and Their Clients

No doubt the most important group of professionals to consider digital signage is the group of global ad agencies and their advertisers (closely followed by the retailers). As noted in this chapter's opening comments, advertising today is facing a watershed transition in the form of changes to the traditional print, free over-the-air broadcast TV, and even cable/satellite/telco TV advertising models.

In fact, most executives in the many industries associated with advertising would describe what has occurred during the past 10–15 years of advertising as "chaotic." For example, advertising dollars have been radically shifted from broadcast TV to cable and satellite TV, to the Internet, and many—if not most—advertisers and their clients are greatly uncertain today as to the right mix of advertising assets.

Thus, when an attractive new advertising deployment vehicle comes along, to not be at least interested is to be contemplating watching your advertising business become irrelevant (not unlike many of the irrelevant traditional advertisements and irrelevant advertising vehicles that are still dominating the telecom, commercial, and retail industries today).

Moreover, the plethora of new devices that frequently take users and viewers away from advertisements is growing substantially. Ad avoidance on U.S. broadcast and multichannel TV has become a new national pasttime, led by DVRs, MP3s, mute buttons, and other devices or technologies yet to be invented. To name but one, that is, the remarkable DVR, it is conservatively projected by media consultant and analyst The Carmel Group to have found its way into approximately 20 million U.S. TV Households (TVHHs)—or slightly less than one in five U.S. TVHHs—by year-end 2007. Yet, DVRs may end up being both the bane and the blessing of advertisers, inasmuch as studies show that most DVR users have been found to welcome personalized and on-target advertisements. Like digital signage, the real question then becomes whether the DVR industry's executive decision makers can properly introduce, acclimate, and draw DVR users to these types of data mining, personalization, customized, and pin-pointed advertising pitches. If they do, that, along with digital signage, will be another way intelligent uses of technology revive the broken advertising models.

On the digital signage side of the projections business, The Carmel Group estimates that the technology and industry subsector's overall total revenues will come in at $2.6 billion by year-end 2010. As detailed in Chapter 1, total U.S. ad market spending is estimated to have achieved $136 billion during the year 2006, according to the information service Nielsen Monitor-Plus. Of that sum, the outdoor portion came to an estimated $3.7 billion, and from that sum, the so-called "digital signage" advertising market was an estimated $1 billion, according to the data source Infotrends.

Thus, one of the first and most important questions advertisers are asking these days is, "Where can I get the most bang for the buck, when it comes to my client's ad dollars?" On that new level, digital signage advertising is being investigated for its ability to open new doors for clients. It does this by reaching new audiences, in greater numbers, and reaching audiences more effectively than before. And, it does this by offering a tremendous number of *choices* and *flexibility* in the use of the medium. That is a good part of what many believe, longer term, sets digital signage way apart from any other new advertising medium.

For example, digital signage is being looked to for its ability to meet people where they shop for a specific item, and very possibly convince them then and there to buy that item (even if it were never on the shopping list). This kind of point-of-sale sales lift can be critical to enhancing revenues, as well as numerous other objectives mentioned elsewhere throughout this book. Digital signage at the point of sales can also convince shoppers to purchase more of an item that they wanted in the first place, or better (for the advertisers and retailers), to switch to the advertiser's item or brand over the one they originally shopped for. Digital signage also has great potential to evoke other forms of a call to action, on the part of the consumer, such as when a customer is compelled—if he or she acts early—to take advantage of an advanced purchase of a not-yet-available item at a special sales price. This has the advantage of improving cash flow and heading off purchases that the same consumer might make for a competing item that later becomes available.

Other advertisers that are right for digital signage are those that are discouraged by the costs and relative ineffectiveness of traditional billboard-type signage. Poster and sign printing, distribution, installation, damage, removal, and discarding costs can be huge, especially on a regular and frequent basis. Plus, the costs of delivering signs to various locales and the long time frame required to change out an existing sign can be additional reasons to seek advertising alternatives like digital signage. Wastage of paper and related items in the "traditional" signage business is another important concern that digital signage addresses.

An advertiser's call to action in the direction of digital signage might also come from the medium's ability to help retail employees to better understand their product, services, environments, co-workers, and—most importantly—their customers.

Thus, for example, a digital signage system in a large retail outlet that is used during off hours, or used via screens placed in employee-only areas, can deliver employee training and informational content that, in turn, can make employees happier, more efficient, and generally just better at doing their jobs. Better informed and more skilled employees tend to churn (or leave the job) less often, and should make for better customer service and overall customer relations. Product knowledge, motivation, productivity, safety and compliance messages, and merchandising directives, as well as the communication of corporate values and guidelines, are some pretty compelling reasons to seek out digital signage solutions. Plus, the fact that this staff training side of the digital signage business can be accomplished using the same components and infrastructure as the consumer-focused side makes its offerings even more attractive.

JCPenney

JCPenney, headquartered in New York City, began its new generation of corporate training technology in Q1 2006. The JCPenney digital signage network services more than 150,000 of the retail giant's employees, at 1,100 locations, across the U.S. and Puerto Rico.

Because of its growth to more than a thousand locations, the company determined it needed a more cost-effective and time-efficient model to distribute critical training to its staff. JCPenney chose a software management system provided by Linden, UT-based Helius, with the ability to centrally control its training programs and distribute the same message to all locations, simultaneously, via satellite.

Going back to 1996, JCPenney has utilized interactive distance learning technology to ensure that store associates who are geographically dispersed receive necessary training in a timely manner. Using DVR-type storage on set-top boxes beside each monitor, JCPenney is able to repurpose its synchronous training and make the same class available to associates at their convenience, while maintaining the same interactive format. Store supervisors are no longer tasked with having to tape the "live" class to share it later with associates who may be working different shifts. The system is able to centrally control what gets recorded, and maintained, at the store level. This system replaces JCPenney's DVD- and CD-based "sneaker-net" delivery model, with an on-demand classroom that allows employees to receive the appropriate messages at their leisure. The software in the system also allows JCPenney to track associate training progress through an embedded learning information system that automatically captures individual trainee progress, test scores, and program completion.

Associate training is one of the most important initiatives to JCPenney leadership, and the system maximizes returns on investment (ROI), while minimizing effort and inconvenience. The software in the JCPenney system is digital IP video technology. According to Helius, that software is designed to facilitate simple integration and management, helping corporate training functions to focus more on their employees and less on logistics.

Orkin

Orkin, the 107-year-old Atlanta, GA-headquartered company that describes itself as the U.S.'s pest control leader, launched its first companywide, interactive satellite television digital signage network in mid-2006. Three digital signage industry firms provide the key ingredients for the new system. These include New York City-based GlobeCast, a subsidiary of France Telecom, which developed the platform for satellite delivery; as well as San Jose, CA-based One Touch Systems, Inc. and Linden-UT-based Helius, Inc., which collaborated to create the satellite receivers equipped with hard drives for digital video storage and software applications for the employee viewer response capabilities. Orkin has more than 400 locations serving close to 1.7 million customers annually in the U.S. and Canada.

Orkin's 8,000 employees nationwide have access to the system that is essentially a "virtual classroom," in the sense that a so-called "interactive video on demand," or IVOD, feature also allows employees to play back past programming (much like digital video recorders found in many homes), and to participate in past broadcast events. The IVOD participation is tracked and recorded in Orkin's learning management system. And although viewers of the "on-demand" video are not able to communicate live directly with the instructor, they can respond to questions in real time, and instantly view survey results. Overall, that information helps to improve employee understanding and performance of various job functions.

Because many of Orkin's employees do not have access to a personal computer at all times, the video content of the overall program is delivered to Orkin's hundreds of digital monitors that make up the national Orkin digital signage satellite TV network.

The system helps Orkin save time and monetary resources related to traditional employee training. Now new hires no longer have to travel to the company's Atlanta headquarters for initial training sessions, nor do they have to wait for an instructor to visit their region. Orkin and its partners estimate that the time needed to make a new employee productive is cut in half.

The "interactive component" of the Orkin Network involves not only the ability to respond real time to Q & A, but also to replay past sessions from the systems' set-top boxes (which also include a DVR-like hard drive for storage and playback).

Orkin leadership champions the ability of the system to address a critical need for large, nationwide companies that are growing steadily across many different regions. Further, the system is able to maintain the highest training standards, while reaching more people, more often, and at a lower cost—regardless of their location.

By adding the video on-demand component, Orkin starts training new technicians just days after they're hired. In the old system, it would take 6–8 weeks to teach employees the skills necessary to be productive and ready to work. Now, with IVOD, it takes only 3–4 weeks, a 50% savings. Because the training sessions are broadcast live to the branches and recorded digitally for on-demand playback, Orkin trainees receive consistent, uniform messaging from the company's best instructors. Finally, the system is also useful for special announcements from company executives—in the event of good news, emergencies, or other announcements.

Children's Hospital of Pittsburgh

Another large medical institution has joined the pioneering steps of the Mayo Clinic. In mid-2007, the reputable Children's Hospital of Pittsburgh of UPMC deployed a digital signage network system to more efficiently communicate with and educate hospital patients and their families, as well as employees and guests.

The initial implementation includes screens displaying content in various common areas throughout the hospital. In addition to the standard display screens, a patient TV channel was created, where patients can learn about the hospital, its facilities, and the overall patient experience. The system installed involved a custom solution that was formed to meet the unique requirements of the facility. The bottom line motivator for the hospital and its staff was the ability to speed the flow and distribution of information to all concerned parties.

Retailers

Although advertisers are identified first in this chapter, the importance of retailers is underscored. Indeed, retailers are nearly as important as a class of digital signage citizens, as are advertisers. In many instances, retailers have driven or will drive their advertising agencies to invoke digital signage. In that way, for many parts of the digital signage industry, retailers are more important to the industry and its success than their advertising agencies.

There is little question that digital signage was not only made for retailers, but that without the support of retailers, the growth of digital signage will be minimal. Most of retailing's participants have all the basic and added ingredients for successful digital signage implementation. Retailers generally have an audience that is almost always receptive to relevant and helpful messages; retailers generally have adequate funding, especially if a respectable ROI can be rationalized; retailers have an important message to convey, that is, a customer call to action aimed at purchasing something thought to be needed; and retailers—if they manage and direct their digital signage systems properly—can create a strong organizational buy-in.

Also, most retailers have their captive audiences, albeit in many instances only for a precious few seconds (so the content message has got to be quick and good). Lastly, retailers are in a position to exact quality measurements, be they through testing devices (such as eye scanners), or via tried-and-tested in-person, telephone, or Internet surveying techniques.

"Retailers" in the sense spoken of in this book, include just about every entity that has something to sell, or at least certainly organizations and individuals that have products to sell.

National Mall Owners Simon Properties, General Growth Properties, and CBL Properties

Aimed at attracting shoppers to their North American locations, regional shopping mall owners, Simon Properties, General Growth Properties, and CBL Properties, as well as other independent developers, have created extensive digital signage advertising networks across North America.

> Among the first to have the new system installed was the well-known Houston Mall in Texas. Software management was provided by Linden, UT-headquartered Helius, describing itself as "... the worldwide leader in IPTV solutions for business," in conjunction with the Jakarta, Indonesia-based advertising solutions provider, PlasMedia Productions, Inc.
>
> The goal of the digital signage deployments is to achieve the most effective way to get advertisers' messages in front of customers where they matter most (i.e., at the point of purchase (POP)), such as by informing shoppers of products and specials, and directing them to where they can purchase these items. The systems use dynamic, targeted messages displayed on strategically placed digital signage throughout stores, and communicate the malls' and stores' messages when their customers are listening—while they are actually shopping.
>
> The system involved a uniquely styled video display device, aimed specifically at appropriately attracting customers' attention. Each of the video displays is controlled by a digital signage player, and to simplify installation, regular updates are delivered to the player via a cellular IP network. Termed a "place-based media network," this set of operations offers attractive returns to these mall owners and store owners and their customers.

Inside Ads

Figure 6.1 and Table 6.1 indicate the top 10 advertisers and the overall shift in advertising that is occurring in the U.S. today. This is the graphic evidence of not only the breadth and significance of U.S. ad spending, but of the move to Internet and niche market advertising, as well.

In Figure 6.1, according to Nielsen Monitor-Plus, total ad spending in the U.S. has risen 5.1% through the third quarter of 2006, while spending on U.S. national cable TV is up 1.3%. Note that local newspapers (–3.8%) and network radio (–2.9%) lag. Regular gainers are the Internet (+40.2%) and Spanish-language TV (+16.6%).

Plus, telcos AT&T and Verizon spend their share. The two biggest U.S. telcos represent the greatest percentage gain in 2005–2006 ad spending among the top ten 2006 advertisers. AT&T (+48%) spent $1.31 billion in 2006 ad spending, equaling a third place finish; Verizon placed seventh in 2006, with ad spending of $1.03 billion (+25%).

Broadcasters and Multichannel Providers

As noted in Chapter 9, in other parts of the digital signage world, broadcasters like Mexico's Televisa are adding digital signage to their list of business and ROI

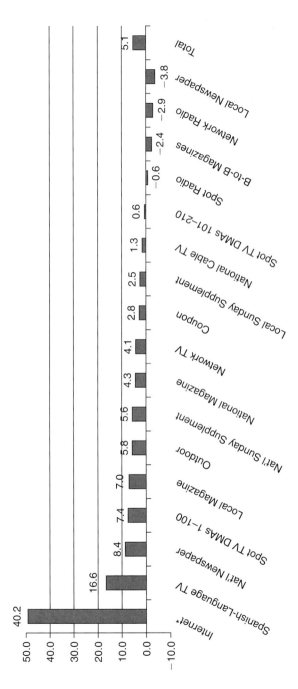

FIGURE 6.1 *Advertising Growth, January–September 2005 to January–September 2006*

	($ MIL)	2005 VERSUS 2006 CHANGE (%)
Procter & Gamble Co.	2,582	4.10
General Motors Corp.	1,774	−14.90
AT&T Inc.	1,307	47.7
Ford Inc.	1,260	12.60
Daimler Chrysler AG	1,146	−3.60
Time Warner Inc.	1,045	−10.60
Verizon Communication	1,025	24.90
Toyota Motor Corp.	975	13.90
Altria Corp.	960	0.00
Walt Disney Co.	920	2.60
Total	12,993	4.30

The top 10 U.S. Advertisers, Based on Spending Estimates in the Following Media: Network TV, Cable TV, Spot TV, Syndicated TV, Hispanic TV, National/Local Magazine, Network/Spot Radio, Outdoor, FSI (CPGs Only), National/Local Newspapers (Display Ads Only), National/ Local Sunday Supplements (Source: Nielsen Monitor-Plus)

TABLE 6.1   *Top 10 Advertisers from January to September 2006*

models. Any telecom provider with local studios is in a strong position to take those content production capabilities and fashion them toward digital signage business models. This holds particularly true for local broadcasters, wherever they are located. Actually, with today's technology, although it is very likely more of a challenge, local access and "locality" are no longer a requirement when it comes to making local content for local advertisers. The ability to send large content files via satellite and the Internet means that no longer is a face-to-face relationship necessary between a local advertiser and its content vendor. North Carolina-based Capitol Broadcasting's Microspace unit is an example of this move by a broadcaster into digital signage.

Local, regional, and national broadcasters are also in a position to become significant network operators on the digital signage terrain. Because they are already so close to the key elements that make up digital signage—the software and hardware that make up its infrastructure—broadcasters and multichannel operators already know much about the space, some even without realizing it. Broadcasters and multichannel operators can either buy or lease this equipment and the software that either helps deliver or actually is the content message. As a network operator, especially one with a large number of display sites, a broadcaster or multichannel operator has a lot to gain from an involvement in digital signage.

In short, local broadcasters and multichannel operators (such as cable and telephone video service providers) are in a unique position to easily tap into the digital signage wave. Indeed, there is a lot that local broadcasters and multichannel operators can teach the digital signage industry's forerunners, and a lot they can learn from each other.

Corporate Users

Corporate users are also in a unique position to utilize a quality digital signage system in two very effective ways. Often, as shown by this chapter's case study examples, the first intended corporate audience is the employees of the organization. The digital signage content delivered to employees takes the place of expensive and time-intensive training and other instructional material. When the travel costs for hundreds of employees can be avoided, and they can instead be trained by video distributed to scores or hundreds of locations via satellite or the Internet, the savings can be huge (see the case studies in Chapter 8 for examples). Plus, when the savings are great, corporations can justify creating content about more topics, more often.

A second use for corporate digital signage puts corporations in the same position as retailers and other users (i.e., the corporate user has something to sell). So, for example, if the corporation is a large hotel chain, a second viable use of the digital signage can be that of a sales, informational, educational, and entertainment tool linking the hotel directly to the consumer patron.

One brochure aimed at this dichotomy talks about a corporation's ability to "Inform your customers in the lobby, as well as your employees in the cafeteria."

Government Users

Not far from corporate users and their use criteria (as well as their criteria for participation in digital signage) are government users. Note that in this instance, the pool of "government" entities is intended to include schools and other educational entities, social services and related agencies, and certainly security and emergency organizations (Figure 6.2).

These organizations have audiences, occasionally large, that can be introduced and conditioned to messages that improve their lot in life, or even, in some

FIGURE 6.2 *A Digital Sign Operated by a Federal Government Agency at a Travel Facility in the Western United States (Copyright 2008. Property of Jimmy Schaeffler. All rights reserved.)*

instances, that entertain. Funding is a concern among governments on all levels, however, with a properly developed project and plan, resources are frequently available. Needless to say, governments have important messages to convey and, like corporations, governments and their employees find reasons to support digital signage systems. And governments can test their constituents' receptivity to digital signage in the same way that corporations do.

Educational Users

Certainly for those educational institutions that are not government funded and controlled, digital signage has a role to play in future development. Universities, colleges, and high schools—whether public or private—are already realizing the ability of digital signage systems to communicate important messages to interested audiences of students, parents, administrators, and the public at large. These audiences sometimes comprise thousands, and even tens of thousands, of viewers in larger metropolitan areas.

Further, almost all educational institutions are solidly funded and can argue for shifts in funding to accommodate new technology with new applications (e.g., digital signage). Educational institutions invariably have important messages to convey, and with the right content delivered at the right time to the right audiences, organizational buy-in is possible. Students in common areas, teachers in break rooms, and citizens walking or driving by on the street are the receptive—albeit not always "captive"—audiences, and the effectiveness of the message can indeed be measured in educational environments as well as any. Chapter 3 shows photos of digital signage at two west coast U.S. educational centers.

Hospitality and Entertainment

People leaving their homes and eating, traveling, and partaking of hospitality is a big part of their lives in most parts of the world. Indeed, in places like North America and Europe, as well as much of Asia and Latin America, the hospitality industry is huge. As such, it must consider the place digital signage will take in its industry.

Hospitality providers of just about every type have large, interested audiences; funding; messages to convey; employees that are eager to learn and help spread those messages; and ways to measure digital signage successes. The lineup of types of hospitality venues where digital signage (as in Figures 6.3 and 6.4) works includes restaurants, hotels, motels, coffee shops, and convenience stores (to name but the main ones). Lobbies and convention or reception centers are an attractive locale for personalized and audience-tailored messages of greeting, for example, and can be triggered to deliver customized, individualized content to those with magnetic or radio frequency identification (RFID)-activated badges. Real-time news, information, instructions, and way-finding are just a handful of the content applications that are prime for this sector and its audiences.

Transportation

Closely related to the needs of the hospitality sector are the needs of the traveling industry and its audiences. They, too, typically meet the four basic requirements for the deployment of digital signage: (1) audience receptivity, (2) funding, (3) a need to convey an important message, and (4) organizational receptivity. Additionally, audiences in the transportation sphere are frequently quite large, find themselves in confined spaces, and their responses to digital signage can be rather well managed and recorded, in most instances.

Taxis, Subways, Busses, and Trains

Tens of thousands of taxi cabs in New York City and thousands of busses in Shanghai, China, are testament to the many new and novel applications of digital signage.

FIGURE 6.3 *The Lobby of an Asian Hotel, with a Digital Sign That Is Dedicated to 24/7 Content Exhibiting Hotel-Related Events (Copyright 2008. Property of Jimmy Schaeffler. All rights reserved.)*

These, too, are obviously places where the elements of digital signage line up. Many times, the greater problems are just getting all of the involved parties on the same page, rather than determining whether digital signage is appropriate (Figure 6.5).

Airports

Airports around the world seem like the ideal places for digital signage (see Figures 6.6 and 6.7). As such, they, as an industry subsector, should take a lead toward developing the digital signage industry going forward. Again, the core message has to be, simply, to prove they are "right for digital signage, by doing it right." This means determining the needs of the hundreds of millions that make up their traveling audiences; investing proper funds into doing the digital signage well; delivering those needs in the form of quality, relevant content; and using all these measures to convince airport and related digital signage personnel of the value of the exercise.

FIGURE 6.4 *Another Example of a Hotel Lobby and Its Use of Digital Signage to Communicate with Its Guests and Employees (Copyright 2008. Property of Jimmy Schaeffler. All rights reserved.)*

FIGURE 6.5 *A Large Digital Display on an Amsterdam Train Station Platform (Copyright 2008. Property of The Carmel Group. All rights reserved.)*

ARRIVALS			10:31P - Thursday, January 25	
Arriving From	Flight	Gate	Time	Remarks
ATLANTA	1577	D4	1:44A	ON TIME
BOSTON	1732	D18	10:16P	ARRIVED
CHARLOTTE	1549	E35	10:25P	DEBRD'G
CHICAGO	5384	E1	11:28P	ON TIME
CINCINNATTI	451	E34	10:08A	ARRIVED
COLUMBUS	627	D5	10:18P	ARRIVED
DALLAS	900	E11	4:55A	ON TIME
DENVER	809	D7	12:53A	AT 1:03A
GREENSBORO	1264	D6	7:27A	ON TIME
HARTFORD	918	D17	5:45A	DELAYED
HOUSTON	234	E31	6:24A	ON TIME
INDIANAPOLIS	904	E33	5:11A	ON TIME
KANSAS CITY	1880	E1	5:40A	ON TIME
LAS VEAGAS	1273	B9	6:05A	DELAYED
LOS ANGELES	1544	C21	9:01P	CANCL'D
MEMPHIS	577	B20	7:10A	ON TIME
MIAMI	1402	C17	10:10P	AT 9:30P
NEW YORK	6699	F21	11:00A	ON TIME

FIGURE 6.6 *A Typical Flight Arrival Board at a U.S. Airport (Copyright 2008. Property of Jimmy Schaeffler. All rights reserved.)*

Health Services Providers

Taking the four main criteria above and applying them to the health services industry produces results as typically positive as for the retail industry. That is why this sector of the business world is expected to amply support digital signage implementation, as well, as shown in Figure 6.8.

Note that in this regard, the definition of health services providers is intended to throw a wide net, including (but not limited to) medical offices, hair and nail salons, veterinarians, massage therapists, spas, and retreats.

Health services providers generally have an audience that is potentially receptive to relevant and helpful messages. Be it a doctor's office, or an emergency room waiting area, these participants are generally fairly well funded and capable of continuing financial support if something like digital signage is effective.

FIGURE 6.7 *Digital Signage at Charles de Gaulle Airport in Paris, France (Copyright 2008. Property of Jimmy Schaeffler. All rights reserved.)*

FIGURE 6.8 *A Typical Doctor's Office and Its Display of Digital Signage for the Benefit of Patients and Staff (Copyright 2007. Property of emebaVet. Used with permission. All rights reserved.)*

Health care providers have an important message to convey, that is, what audiences can do to maintain or improve their health, which is probably the most important message most people ever receive. Plus, again if they manage and direct their digital signage systems properly, health services industry personnel can create a strong organizational buy-in.

Additional ingredients possessed by most health service operators include these additional items. Health care providers very often have their "captive audiences," and usually for fairly lengthy periods of time. Indeed, the U.K.-based Baby-TV service estimates that the average wait time at the doctor's office for an expectant mother is more than an hour. Plus, health services caregivers frequently have good-sized and receptive audiences. And lastly, care and health services professionals are clearly in a position to exact quality measurements, especially by way of in-person, on-premises surveys.

Houses of Worship

Not unlike the country and cultural variety suggested in Chapter 9 and what that variety will do to drive the future of digital signage globally, so, too, is there great variety among houses of worship, especially in North America, but also often around the world.

Thus, in the same way that varied forms of music make their way into various houses of worship, so, too, will various forms of technology. Technology that can fill the needs of a congregation—informational, educational, and behavioral—is being sought out by houses of worship as well, in ways never even thought of a few years ago (Figure 6.9).

Technologies for Worship magazine notes, in a 2007 interview with Alchemy's former executive, Lyle Bunn, digital signage in religious centers might include a large overhead screen showing the words to a hymn, or a live picture of the minister for the people listening to a sermon from the back of a large church:

Instead of having pamphlets sitting on a table and a sign-up sheet for a Bible study group, a church could have a flat screen display showing prospective participants what it actually looks and sounds like to be part of the group. A house of worship seeking a way to inform its congregation about the work of a missionary group could set up a system that shows some of the group's activities, on demand, with a simple press of a button instead of the cost and hassle of sending out a newsletter.... I think one of the most important aspects of the [digital signage] technology will be its ability to extend the work of the church outside of its own walls. In the same way cassette tapes allow sermons and worship services to be heard in an environment that isn't time or place dependent, digital signage can bring both sound and picture of the same things ... into places in the community the church wouldn't normally be able to reach.

FIGURE 6.9 *A Digital Sign in a Barcelona, Spain, City Cathedral Shows How Even a House of Worship Can Be a Good Spot for a Digital Sign Display. This Digital Sign Is Used Primarily to Quietly and Discreetly Convey Information to Visiting Tourists (Copyright 2008. Property of Angelina Ward. All rights reserved. Used with permission.)*

Miscellaneous

Many vendors involved in industries presently related to the digital signage industry sector are also among the list of who's right for digital signage. These include the participants listed in Chapter 2, such as mobile, interactive, touch screen, and RFID technology providers; ISPs, satellite, cable, telco, and wireless providers; traditional billboard and street furniture companies; kiosk providers; flat-panel display (and related hardware) providers; system contractors; software suppliers; store fixture providers; digital printers; audio/visual professionals; end users, buyers, and location owners; integrators; blue chip companies looking to put a network together; merchandise consultants; media directors/planners; media measurement/metrics pros; and last, but surely not least, clients looking to make investments, banks, and venture capitalists.

What will be particularly interesting to note will be the future developers of digital signage and how they adapt to become a part of the group of industries and organizations that are right for digital signage.

7 Choosing a Digital Signage Configuration

There are pros and cons to each [of the ownership] models, and we can't stress enough how critical it is for you to determine which one is right for you up front. Not only will you save yourself and your company a great deal of time, you'll also save money and hassle.

—Adrian Weidmann, co-author, *Lighting Up the Aisle Principles and Practices for In-Store Media*

Two key methods of deployment are available for those wishing to implement a digital signage system. The first involves the so-called "turn-key" plan, whereby the site owner runs the show, or one company is tasked by the site owner or controlling company to develop and implement the entire deployment of the digital signage system. A variation of this do-it-yourself model is the start-to-finish implementation that sees the site owner or controlling company usually doing no more than collecting a fee for site use. The second method of choosing your digital signage is the opposite of turn-key: typically the site owner or someone else tasked by him will pick, in "piece-meal" fashion, the individual partners that together plan, install, and operate the digital display. Nonetheless, whatever the protocol chosen, it is always important to keep the bigger planning picture in mind.

The choice of a digital signage system—more appropriately, for this chapter, the *choice of the components* that comprise that system—involves the key steps recommended throughout this book, but especially those in Chapters 4–6, 8, and 10.

Those beginning the investment in digital signage need to look within themselves and their organizations to grapple with and determine the recommended goals, and then see if doing all of the digital signage themselves, or having others do all or parts, is the best method toward achieving those goals.

This operational exercise should probably also be taken in conjunction with a financial exercise, including a look at various revenue models, suggested in Chapter 8. A planning exercise is obviously important because various digital signage components can be quite expensive.

Further, choosing a third-party turn-key operation is often a decision that determines how much control you may have over the content that reaches the audience. If control is particularly important for you, the end decision might lean well in the direction of running most if not all of the parts yourself, and probably investing in both the personnel to run the system, and a good budget to educate those new in-house digital signage personnel. It also means that you will end up paying for (or finding the investments for) the digital signage system yourself.

Implementing a Turn-Key Solution

There are advantages to carefully monitoring the selection and progress of the hardware, software, and operations parts of a digital signage deployment by yourself, in-house. Control is probably the most important advantage. If your organizational culture, or your organizational message, or your organizational structure is such that allowing others to handle parts of that or to access that, then doing it all yourself—where your organization is the turn-key provider—could be a choice. In this case, you'd better be ready for a lot of homework and learning about digital signage, in order to get the best out of the development plans and the actual implementation of your new digital signage system.

More likely, turn-key will mean that your organization has opted to have another single company do all of your digital signage deployment. Obviously, from a standpoint of smoothness of operation, having a third party run the digital system can work. This is especially the case if the third party and your organization have a good rapport and a good communication through most of the process. On a broader level, it helps if both organizations—yours and that of your turn-key vendor—have a cultural rapport, or at least if they understand one another's cultural imperatives.

Additionally, as part of the process of selecting this turn-key third party, ensure that you are working with a substantial company, one that has the resources and experience to handle it. Find this out by kicking the tires. Research references and financials, and meet with management. Give high value to experience, especially the view and opinion of objective third parties that have been part of that experience. Early in the days of the Internet explosion, this step was frequently overlooked, and that is a lesson most would not want to recall, no less repeat.

To be clear, the latter model we are talking about in this section involves pretty much stepping aside, probably collecting a revenue, and letting that third party run the show. The third party will interview and select and supervise the handful of vendors who are chosen to run the digital signage system. It typically costs more, but often the peace of mind gained from having someone run it, who knows how to do it and can do it well, is well worth the extra costs.

The case study of Gas Station TV (GSTV) provides an interesting snapshot of a company that has allied with varied vendors to implement its digital signage solution in a rather unusual locale, that is, on both sides of thousands of gas station pumps across the U.S.

Gas Station TV

GSTV is an Internet Protocol (IP)-based digital television network with screens built into gas pumps at gas stations/convenience stores, across the U.S. (Figure 7.1). "Captive" consumers (in the sense that they are tied for a short time to what they are doing, in one place) are engaged for four and a half minutes, on average, during their pump transactions. As they pump their gas, they find that with GSTV, there is only one channel. There are no remote controls, no DVRs, and there is no PC-multitasking to do. The gas service customers watch only what is on the screen.

FIGURE 7.1 *The View of GSTV From the Inside of a Customer's Car (Copyright 2007. Property of Gas Station TV. All rights reserved. Used with permission.)*

GSTV provides its programming experience by providing select news and entertainment content from well-known national networks, as well as local weather, intended to engage customers and to enable marketers to connect with these "on-the-go" consumers, probably like no other media. The content, programmed for what CEO David Leider describes as a "highly desirable and captive audience," can be specifically tailored to certain geographies and times of the day.

The specific content displayed on GSTV features sports from ESPN, news and entertainment from the ABC-TV Network, weather from AccuWeather, and local event information produced in-house. GSTV offers both geographic and day-part brand targeting, to make most relevant the content that reaches the consumer. The content is also targeted to specific locations at specific times. For example, quick service restaurants (QSRs) can use day-parting capabilities to promote breakfast, lunch, dinner, or late night messages. Plus, the weather is updated multiple times throughout the day, and targeted by location.

GSTV is currently offered on more than 5,000 screens, in 300 cities, including top media markets such as New York City, Los Angeles, Chicago, Philadelphia, San Francisco, Atlanta, Dallas, Houston, Detroit, and Tampa. It is offered at select Chevron, Conoco-Philips, Citgo, Exxon-Mobil, Murphy USA, Shell, Speedway, Valero, and Sunoco stations. At year-end 2008, Leider predicts the GSTV service will be offered on more than 12,000 screens, at leading gas retailers in the Top 15 Designated Market Areas (DMAs) (adding another five to its current list above of ten DMAs).

GSTV is a proven tool for driving business for advertisers and increasing the revenue stream for participating gas retailers, Leider claims. (More information is available at www.gstv.com.)

Interestingly, GSTV describes itself simply as a "media company," its digital signage network being its core asset. Its biggest motivator to deploy digital signage comes, in Leider's words, in the following manner: "Technology, like Digital Video Recording devices, 500 channel cable systems, and the increased use of personal computers (while watching TV), has altered the way people consume television, especially advertising on TV. Marketers can no longer expect consumers to view their messaging the same way in this new environment. This phenomenon has created an opening in the marketplace for alternative 'broadcast' venues, to help marketers reach their marketing objectives." Essentially, GSTV is delivering TV "off the couch" to consumers on the go.

Leider was drawn to digital signage because the technology enables marketers to act both globally and locally. These marketers can use an entire network to reach a large quantity of consumers, but technology enables them to "localize down to the individual location and be far more effective than traditional media," adds Leider. The decision to deploy digital signage was made by GSTV after the company conducted a five-station pilot in Dallas, TX, during late 2005, prior to the company's April 2006 launch. This pilot proved both that consumers were engaged with the experience and that gas retailers felt that GSTV enhanced their station experience and product sales. In short, two absolutely critical elements proved present.

These days, to assess the effectiveness of each digital signage deployment, GSTV works with each gas retailer, each of which has its own criteria for success. Yet, in general, these retailers view increases in convenience store product sales and customer satisfaction surveys as a solid gauge of the effectiveness of their digital signage. For its measurement of consumers, GSTV uses Nielsen Media Research to assess the GSTV network effectiveness. Figure 7.2 highlights some of Nielsen's GSTV research.

GSTV's primary benefit to its gas retailer advertising clients is that it drives convenience store product sales. For GSTV advertisers, the service drives brand awareness, product intent, and retail promotions.

The types of digital signage currently being deployed include 20-inch high LCD TVs that GSTV installs, with audio pointed in a certain direction (termed directional audio) on each pump. Each pump unit has two screens, so consumers on each side of the pump get a full experience. A typical gas station has six pumps, meaning there are 12 screens at each station.

The GSTV digital signage is remotely controlled and delivered via satellite to each gas station. HughesNet, the leading satellite distributor, figures prominently in the GSTV infrastructure scheme. The network has the capability to target content. And, of course, third parties frequently use the digital signage for advertising purposes.

Leider summarizes that the GSTV digital signage is used primarily for targeted advertisement.

David Leider's first focus is on "… creating an environment among all the digital signage companies deriving revenue from third party advertisers, that makes it easy for advertisers to buy media." If lobbying or other advocacy to affect industry regulation, or trade group participation, is what it takes to do that, then GSTV supports that. Toward that end, GSTV is currently a board member with the Out-of-Home Video Advertising Bureau (OVAB). A pleasant surprise is also the fact that Leider claims there have been no negative reactions to GSTV deployments at their thousands of pumps nationwide.

Figure 7.2 gives several indications of the success that GSTV has had with the early implementation of its digital signage venture. Respondents gave GSTV an overall favorability score of 7.6 (out of 10).

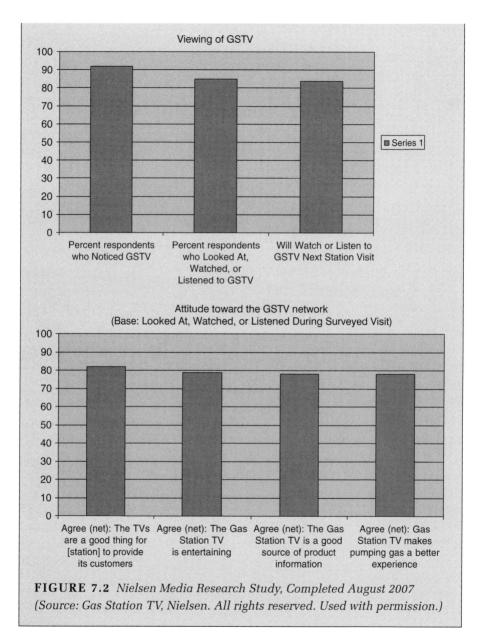

FIGURE 7.2 *Nielsen Media Research Study, Completed August 2007 (Source: Gas Station TV, Nielsen. All rights reserved. Used with permission.)*

Building a System Piecemeal

There are advantages to planning, then choosing, then implementing, and then finally operating and perhaps even expanding the digital signage system as the owner/operator. But note you are going to have a lot of researching, comparing, and interviewing to do, as well as contracts to enter into. Thus, these steps would need to be taken as part of the intense planning and development process described in Chapter 10. Moreover, these steps would need to be taken with respect to each of the component suppliers. This would include, typically, on the technical side, a review of candidates for provision of the hardware (e.g., screens, media players, servers, computers, wiring, and/or antennas); the software (e.g., the content management supplier on the one hand and the suppliers of actual on-screen content on the other); the installation; the maintenance; and the measurement.

Additionally, worth mentioning again in this context, make sure you have plenty of well-trained, well-educated, and enthused employees to help you through this maze.

Reliability

The final important part of this puzzle is *reliability*. The focus on reliability is also important because of the relative newness of the digital signage business. Many start-up companies are not yet in the position to take on serious digital signage projects. This is why pre-planning and development due diligence can make or break your future as you choose the digital signage implementation that is right for your company.

For example, bad choices of content vendors can sometimes mean that the content will either go down or it will not produce the service that was contracted for. If a screen or screens go dark, the results, in some cases, can be as damaging to a company as if the credit card system had failed.

An example on the hardware side might be a digital signage deployment for internal corporate communications, as noted by Bill Gerba, CEO of Wirespring, a software management service. In this instance, a reliable choice might be a large, eye-catching plasma display mounted in a cafeteria or break room. Depending on the size of the deployment, the owner/operator might choose for either local or remote management of the screen(s). Conversely, the owner and/or operator who is a manufacturer, might wish to improve its point-of-purchase ad exhibitions by deploying small and lightweight LCD screens, mixed together with traditional ad displays. In the latter case, it might be better and more reliable to manage the content centrally by way of a web-based interface.

A special content delivered to supermarket stores across a large area focused on the sale of fruits that quickly spoil if not quickly purchased and eaten, would, if the content is not delivered timely and properly, not only not be worth what it costs, but would also cost the loss of the fruit. Across any digital signage network, a blank screen is a worthless screen.

HughesNet's Assistant Vice President Jeff Bixler notes, "You want to work with a company that has the same attention to detail as the one managing your in-house data networks. It's that critical. If the development plan has been followed properly, video and other on-screen content often are viewed as being as important as the company's own internal data networks."

Moreover, more and more these days, newly emerging systems such as cell phones are becoming more and more important to the mass of consumers, so, too, is a well-run digital signage system becoming a part of those "must-have" systems—both for digital signers and for (some of) their audiences.

Factors for Success

Ultimately, a handful of choices and concerns arises when faced with determining how to plan and implement your digital signage system.

- Define goals for your audience and goals for your organization before choosing your turnkey vendor or separate, multiple vendors.

- Make your choices for your audience, that is, an audience that is doing what it is doing, in the specific environment, and at the specific time. Thus, do not focus on Internet-, or cell phone-, or TV-based content for in-store digital signage, when other video, data, PowerPoint, photo, or animation content files are probably the better set of choices.

- Integrate your in-store digital signage with the rest of your store and/or client's branding and product/service messages.

- Invest the time to research and find good vendor partners. This includes things like reading books and articles on the subject of digital signage and its relevant sub-parts (also financial reports, online blogs, analyst presentations, websites, and press releases, for example); checking out viable trade groups that support the digital signage industry; investigating the different vendor candidates in the different categories, as well as their experience and claims; possibly traveling to trade shows and checking out award winners and networking with speakers and other experts at these events; spending substantial time discussing the vendor's proposals with several members of the vendor team; and understanding just what it is the vendor will provide, and what the vendor will outsource or partner with third parties.

- Consider hiring consultants, especially on the technical side, who can provide instant perspective and advice, as well as recommendations of vendors and approaches, based upon your stated visions and the goals for your audience, and your own organization.

- Understand the basis for proposed vendor prices (e.g., necessary margins, industry customs or standards, competitive costs, costs of deployment, and what the market for this kind of product or service will bear).

- React to things that sound wrong. Choose to be skeptical.

- Continually maintain control over what your vendors do for you (and your audiences), especially if you are paying the freight.

- Ensure that you will receive good measurements and data supporting the success of your goals. This is part of planning for the future. All parts of your digital signage development should be built with the future in mind.

- Always keep three critical objectives in mind: your needs, the needs of the audience, and content that achieves both those needs.

8 Business Models and Benefits

When evaluating the return on investment (ROI) of a digital signage system, it is crucial to bear in mind the business model we are dealing with, which must be in line with the goals and strategy of the company. The business model will determine the speed and the magnitude of the ROI.

—Xavier Orriols, Founder, Principal, VisualCentury,
Barcelona, Spain

Once the all-important digital signage goals are set, a thorough review of the "cost versus the benefit" needs to be completed for every new digital signage deployment. On a macro scale, return on objectives (ROO)[1] is that "cost versus the benefit" digital signage measurement, and it becomes the wheel, inside of which the "spokes" represent specific goals (such as the subset called ROI). In addition, other less "money-tangible" goals (such as the other subsets of branding, merchandising, audience loyalty, employee training, ambience, audience well-being, and company image) are also used to measure the cost versus the benefit—and ultimately the success—of any digital signage operation.

Cost versus Benefit: it's the key economic equation in the determination of ROO/ROI and business models. How much must the entity making its digital signage deployment invest in the project, in order to reap a given desired goal or return? Almost every new digital signage project should be seen—very early on—through a lens that clearly distinguishes between these two critical elements (i.e., investment versus return). To not take this step is to invite early frustration, wasted energy and investment, and possibly even total failure.

---

1. The digital signage industry term, "return on objectives" (ROO), was originally made mainstream (and made commonplace within the digital signage industry) by Lyle Bunn and Lauren Moir. That use was supplemented in their "white paper" entitled, "The New Madison Avenue Diet." The author of this book toyed with the idea of instead utilizing an original, new term, such as "return on deployment," however, in the interests of clarity and simplicity, ROO was deemed the better term to describe this concept of *measuring the results*—including non-monetary ones—achieved from the goals set as part of a digital signage deployment.

The strong majority of digital signage implementations will involve "for-profit" systems, where ROI measurements come from actual commercial deployments. These are frequently the result of projects initiated and implemented by advertising agencies, retailers, and others wishing to drive the success of their businesses. They also are frequently and readily calculable, because they typically are measured in standard economic terms (e.g., dollars spent, units sold, impressions delivered, and cost per thousand viewers (CPMs)). The majority of this chapter focuses on ROI as it relates to commercial, for-profit business models.

Accountants define ROI through a rather simple, yet universally known and understood, formula, which reads:

$$\text{ROI} = \frac{(\text{GAIN FROM INVESTMENT} - \text{COST OF INVESTMENT})}{\text{COST OF INVESTMENT}}$$

Stated in words, this formula reads "ROI equals the gain from the investment minus the cost of investment divided by the cost of investment."

Yet, interestingly, the digital signage industry seems to have long ago noticed the fact that not every digital signage project involves a clear money-making or profit-oriented equation. Instead, many digital signage deployments are done for other goals and for reasons other than easily tracked and determined dollars. For example, a non-profit community hospital would utilize digital signage in part to inform and educate its patients and its employees, goals which might be quite difficult to measure in a simple dollars and cents calculation. Or a county school system would utilize digital signage in an effort to more efficiently communicate with and educate all in the community about the developments centered around the county educational system.

In these examples, measuring ROI, in a monetary sense, may not be relevant. But to seek to measure how well the digital signage met the goals of enhancing the environment around the digital sign, or, as noted above, of educating and informing customers and end-users, would be totally apropos. In this instance, the better measure is something the digital signage industry has come to know as ROO. And although it is typically more difficult to measure, there are ways to assess the impact and success on an ROO basis, and it is important to seek to regularly do so, in order not only to assess past performance, but also to calculate plans for future digital signage performance.

In addition, even in the for-profit realm, ROO is occasionally the better measure for even the most sophisticated retail manager. This is because many brand managers and visual merchandisers seem willing to treat the indirect positive effect of digital signage content on the overall store environment as a sufficient "ROI," even if there are no specific numbers to back it up.

Return on Objectives

ROO is the actual measurement of the success of the goals that were set, ideally, at the beginning of every new digital signage project. In the broadest terms, typically, these goals include one or more of the following:

- ROI

- Enhanced branding

- Sales or merchandising uplift

- Employee training

- Customer information, education, action, and satisfaction

- Ambience.

As noted above, every digital signage deployment features an ROO, although not every digital signage deployment involves a clearly measured or clearly defined ROI. That is because some digital signage systems are based upon goals other than revenue-based instant profit. When this is the case, other data, such as surveys on customer satisfaction and surveys on employee productivity, might be the better measures. Indeed, this type of ROO is an area where there are real grounds for enhanced creativity when it comes to understanding and measuring the real mid-to-long-term value of digital signage.

That said, because most of digital signage today is run by commercial entities focused on economic gain and quarterly or annual profits, the remainder of this chapter is focused on that audience, and their specific interest in measuring true ROI.

Return on Investment

"You get what you pay for" is an adage that was not made for the commercial side of the digital signage industry. That's because to properly manage digital signage, one must look for more than just a break-even, or a "get what you paid," return. Instead, the for-profit entrepreneur or corporation must look for the balance between costs and returns to tip decidedly in favor of a profit. Profits lead to enhanced support for the digital signage system, which, in turn, creates increased budgets to augment its growth, and new or additional investment by investors, both on the inside and on the outside of the company. Conversely, any solution in the commercial space should be able to pay for itself faster than it depreciates; otherwise, the system becomes less of an asset and more of a liability.

Looking at ROI, it is best to first decide which of the two business models discussed next is preferable, or if the third model—a mix of the first two—is desired. This choice determines how one best measures ROI. These calculations follow the core recommendations from the 2004 digital signage industry "white paper" authored by the Barcelona, Spain-based company, Visual Century Research, S.L., entitled "Digital Signage ROI" (www.visualcentury.com).

Business Models

What companies typically find after implementing a business model is that most of the costs of digital signage occur up-front. This involves investment in the screens, servers, and other hardware, as well as in the technical aspects of setting-up a digital signage system. It also involves investment in the software, both on the system management and on the on-screen content sides. Indeed, the total costs of creating original content can be significant, and much of this, also, is up-front.

Nonetheless, once that up-front cost has been mastered, very often digital signage owners and developers find that while the costs decline in time, the profits go in the reverse direction.

Both of the main business models (not including the "hybrid") discussed in this chapter turn on just how the digital signage content value chain shown in Figure 8.1 is managed by a company that is controlling and implementing the digital signage system. Thus, if the controlling company/network operator stakeholder wishes to manage and direct the entire content value chain itself, the costs will be different than if that controlling entity[2] chooses to outsource one, several, or all of the content value chain functions.

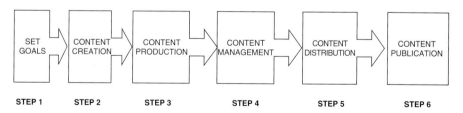

STEP 1   STEP 2   STEP 3   STEP 4   STEP 5   STEP 6

FIGURE 8.1 *The Digital Signage Content Value Chain (Copyright 2008. Property of Jimmy Schaeffler. All rights reserved.)*

---

2. Henceforth, the company that is determining whether it will develop and/or implement a digital signage system will be called the "controlling stakeholder."

It is commonly understood that the role of content management in this value chain plays a critical transition role between the "technical" or hardware side of the digital signage business, and the "creative" or software side of content development. Put another way, the content manager is the equivalent of the transmission that makes the car run, operating in between the engine that is the hardware and the wheels that represent the creative software.

ROI Business Model #1: Content Developer and Owner Model

The first business model, and the most common one in the digital signage arena, involves a controlling stakeholder wishing to use its owned content to increase sales, build a brand, or improve communications (both with employees and with consumers). The controlling stakeholder will then pay for and handle, by itself, the creation, management, and distribution of the content it owns. Typical goals of companies deploying this digital signage business model include:

- Brand enhancement

- Lower costs (as opposed to outsourcing via the second model below)

- Targeting customers at the point-of-sale

- Enhancing the customers' in-store activities.

Figure 8.2 is a graphical depiction of this first key digital signage business model. Note first that at the very top of the "chain" is the audience of consumers. They are the most important player in this system, and ultimately the one for whom everything is done. This is true because not only is that consumer's receptivity critical to the next step desired (i.e., getting them to buy the product), it is also important because by buying the product, the consumer then economically drives the business model toward success.

Looking at the middle horizontal bar stretching across Figure 8.2, the controlling stakeholder (e.g., an ad agency or retail outfit) works with the entities and/or processes indicated below that bar to create content that is then distributed to the consumers. Going from the top bar to the right and then to the bottom in the chart, the satisfied customer or end user is consequently called to action via successful content depicted properly on quality digital displays. Money is then spent on products and services, which is one form of desired customer or end-user action (or reaction). This money spent is the key measure of ROI in this model.

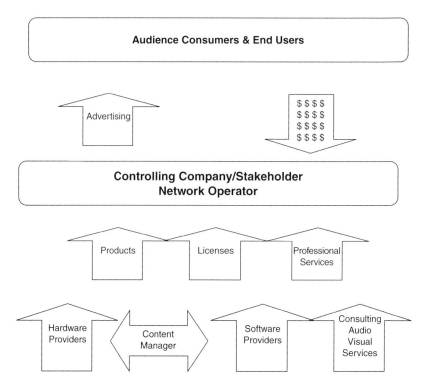

FIGURE 8.2 *Content Developer and Owner Business Model (Copyright 2008. Property of Jimmy Schaeffler. All rights reserved.)*

Figure 8.2 shows the major parts and players involved in the first of three digital signage business models, as well as the top-to-bottom time frame that this digital signage ROI Model #1 follows. The first steps to be taken following the identification of the controlling stakeholders, goals are those on the bottom of the chart; the later steps are those on the top that deliver the content to the consumer, who then is, ideally, compelled to buy the product or service. This puts the money into the pocket of the controlling stakeholder, which drives the model forward.

Yet before that top-level content can be delivered to that top-level recipient (i.e., the consumer), the controlling stakeholder must manage the development of the content in such a way as to create a strong communication between those on the technical and those on the content sides of the digital signage system. This includes finding the right hardware and software providers, the right audio/visual services provider, and making sure that the adequate products, licenses, and professional services, respectively, are timely, professionally, and cost-effectively delivered.

Note that unlike ROI Model #2, titled "Leasing Advertising Space," this first model does not anticipate income coming in from third-party sources. The controlling stakeholder company seeks to manage the content, probably looking to simplicity and greater control over the entire process, and is thus willing to sacrifice the potential economic and other uplift from an outside vendor wishing to gain advantage by using the controlling stakeholder's digital signage system.

As Figure 8.2 indicates, this first main digital signage business model shows the controlling stakeholder paying, by itself, for the system hardware, software, installation, and maintenance costs, as well as for the content development, management, and publication. In these cases, the ROI is simply a measure of all the costs involved in creating and implementing the digital signage system, subtracted from the additional revenues obtained via increased sales coming from the digital signage advertising.

European Retail Banking

This case study examines the experience of a European-based banking establishment. It is an example of ROI Model #1, titled "Content Developer and Owner" business model. The bank offers customers throughout the continent branches in which to conduct their business. It also offers branch locations in Latin American countries. Figure 8.3 shows six digital signage screens in a branch of this European bank.

By itself, the controlling stakeholder, the bank, envisions, develops, implements, and pays for its digital signage system. It is directed toward consumers of the bank's products and services, but it also offers advantages to bank employees who are trained and notified of various bank developments via the new digital signage system. High definition plasma screens are mounted in branches throughout the system, all of which are remotely managed from the controlling stakeholder's headquarters in Europe. A one gigabit/second Local Area Network (LAN) connects all the branch offices to the European country headquarters.

The bank had a handful of key goals in place when it first implemented the digital signage system. First was to entertain customers and take positive advantage of their dwell time in line. Second was to direct those customers to other services and products the bank offered. Third was to build and reinforce the bank's brand and overall positive image. Later, the bank also found that the digital signage system did a very good job of cost-effectively training and informing the bank's thousands of employees.

FIGURE 8.3 *The Digital Signage Screens at a Major European Bank Branch (Copyright 2007. Property of Visual Century Research. All rights reserved. Used with permission.)*

To be clear, the bank assumed all the up-front costs of the hardware, creation, software, installation, and maintenance. These costs were significant.

Nonetheless, the investment was recovered under this business model #1 in less than two years' time. This ROI analysis took into account the "soft" benefits of brand enhancement, customer "feel good," and employee notification. Noteworthy again in this model is that the controlling stakeholder was willing to forego potential income, say from third-party advertisers, in order to maintain control over its system.

ROI Business Model #2: Leasing Advertising Space Model

ROI Model #2 Figure 8.4, the "Leasing Advertising Space" business model, involves the controlling stakeholder looking outside, to others, to add additional content and, in turn, help pay for the posting of that content. This can be a symbiotic relationship that assists both the controlling stakeholder, as well as the advertisers and/or their clients. Advertisers looking to reach larger audiences in places like travel centers, malls, and event arenas are particularly attracted to this model.

Similarly, owners and operators of these locales are particularly keen to develop such systems and relationships. Thus, for example, a large airport might develop a digital signage system utilizing this symbiotic business model, involving informational and educational content which is "sponsored" by the advertising agency's clients. Figure 8.6 represents the players and processes supporting this digital signage business model.

In Figure 8.4, the consumer is at the top of the chain, because the consumer is still the most important party in the overall system, in that his or her response governs what the advertiser and its client are ultimately willing to do toward less or more spending using this model. Yet, the line around the consumer is a broken line, indicating a lack of relative economic importance in this model. Instead, the advertiser is truly at the "top of the food chain" in ROI Model #2, because, economically, it is the advertiser that pays for the business model.

Figure 8.4 shows the major parts and players involved in the second of three digital signage business models, as well as the top-to-bottom time frame that this digital signage ROI Model #2 follows. The first steps following the identification of goals are those on the bottom of the chart; the last steps are those on the top that deliver the content to the consumer, who then is ideally compelled to buy the product or service.

From a standpoint of the immediate economic "oil" that makes this machine operate, ROI Model #2 is clearly driven directly by advertisers and their clients' spending. Put another way, in this second business model, the revenues from advertising obtained through media buying agencies are the main business driver. Note that this model assumes that the consumer is basically receptive to and satisfied by content he or she is receiving, otherwise the model breaks down on that level, the advertiser is unhappy, and then stops paying for the advertising.

Note that in Figure 8.4, the controlling stakeholder undertakes the same basic steps as in main ROI Model #1, early on, to set up the new digital signage system. Then, in ROI Model #2, the controlling stakeholder takes an additional step: it turns to a media planning and buying agency, which then reaches out to its clients (i.e., companies that advertise). Those advertisers in turn advertise and make the payments that then flow back to the media planning and buying agency. Similarly, payments also flow to the controlling stakeholder. This is the basis for their symbiotic economic relationship.

In this digital signage ROI Model #2, the controlling stakeholder asks the third-party suppliers of advertising to pay for some or all of the system. In fact, dependent on the system and the relationship of the parties, sometimes the

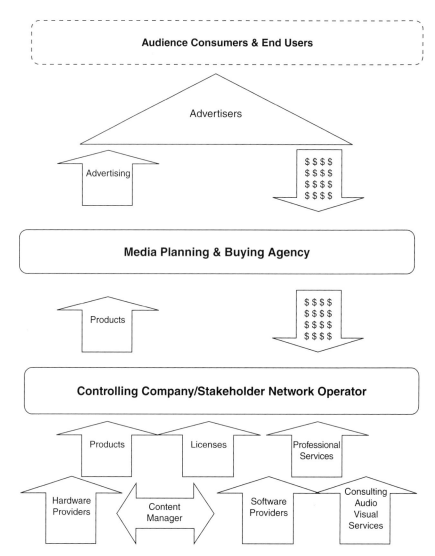

FIGURE 8.4 *Leasing Advertising Space Business Model (Copyright 2008. Property of Jimmy Schaeffler. All rights reserved.)*

third-party ad supplier will pay, up front, all or most of the initial costs of creation and implementation, including hardware, software, installation, and maintenance. The rationale behind this third-party pay-for-all system is typically that both parties will share in the benefits of the system. Again, these benefits will range from better branding, to sales uplift, to success in calling consumers to action. Plus, there is also the all-important benefit of revenues from the digital signage deployment.

Worth also recognizing as it relates to ROI Models #2 and #3 in this chapter, is the need to install high-quality measuring devices, and ideally ones which measure actual on-screen content airings. Without this data, it becomes exceedingly difficult for the parties to have reliable criteria by which to measure future opportunities and responsibilities, as well as past performance.

As is relates to content, industry experts further recommend adequate content customization to the site, as a critical means by which improved ROI can be obtained.

European Airport

This case study examines the experience of a European airport.

Because travelers typically spend hours in airports, they are considered particularly good subjects for some advertisers and retailers. Many travelers yearn to be entertained while waiting for their next flight. Many like to shop. This airport recognized a particularly favorable opportunity to take digital signage to these customers at its heavily used facility. This airport averages more than 40 million passengers annually. It also serves more than 100 airlines and offers visitors more than 10,000 square meters of retail shopping space.

Figures 8.5 and 8.6 show two different versions of digital signage in an overseas airport utilizing main business model #2.

This airport's experience is an example of a controlling stakeholder taking advantage of ROI Model #2, "Leasing Advertising Space."

After determining its goals, the airport management company went out to the industry and did deals up-front to have advertising companies and their clients invest up-front in paying for the total system costs.

One hundred plasma screens were initially purchased for installation in departure lounges, which number increased to over 1,000 in less than a year. The airport offered the advertising to 15 advertisers occupying 15 different categories, each on an exclusive category basis. Each advertiser was assured its ads would air on screen at least six times per screen per hour. A flat fee was charged by the airport managing company to every advertiser for every screen used.

FIGURE 8.5 *An Airport Digital Signage System Where the Screens Hang From the Ceiling in an Entry Area (Copyright 2007. Property of Visual Century Research. All rights reserved. Used with permission.)*

FIGURE 8.6 *An Airport Digital Signage System Where the Content Is Displayed at the Departure Gate (Copyright 2007. Property of Visual Century Research. All rights reserved. Used with permission.)*

The screens were turned on for approximately 20 hours per day, every day of the year, and are only dark from 2 a.m. to 6 a.m. The programming involved news and travel information half the time, and advertising time the other half. If that time is divided into 20 seconds per advertisement, it produces a total of 90 ad spaces per hour. It also adds up to 1,800 total ad impressions per day per screen, every day of the year.

The estimated ROI for this investment came in at eight months. As noted, some of the revenues were immediately invested into purchasing and installing an additional 900 screens over the ensuing four months. This is an example of one of the faster ROIs that come from commercial deployment of digital signage systems.

ROI Business Model #3: Hybrid Model

ROI Model #3 is the hybrid, or converged, digital signage business model. It combines parts of the "Content Developer and Owner" model with parts of the "Leasing Advertising Space" model. This is the digital signage business model that appeals to most companies deploying digital signage on a commercial level. It is attractive because it speeds up the ROI, but it also shares the risks and costs of the system, especially what can be substantial up-front costs. Nonetheless, its "sharing" aspects mean that it sometimes compromises the controlling stakeholder's control over the message and the medium.

In this model, the promotion of in-house brands and messages is frequently mixed, appropriately, with informational, behavioral, and educational content, as well as with advertisements supplied by media buying agencies. The accompanying case study of a European mall/supermarket does a good job of presenting and helping define the elements of this "hybrid" model. Indeed, the other two case studies—the bank and airport—also do a solid job of helping explain the important dynamics of ROI.

European Mall/Supermarket

This case study examines the experience of a European-based mall/supermarket. Its digital signage deployment experience involves the creation of an in-store TV network.

It shows the ROI on a business model that is a combination of the two other distinctly different ROI business models depicted in this book. For this reason, it is called a "hybrid" digital signage business model. The hybrid model involves elements of a system that is paid for, owned, and controlled by one controlling stakeholder, together with a system that is paid for primarily or entirely by advertisers.

The content in this digital signage system featured music clips, information about key brands, and special promotions. These features were aimed at differentiating the specific products in an increasingly price-competitive marketplace (Figure 8.7).

Plasma screens were eventually deployed in all of the hundreds of mall/supermarkets within the chain, though initially only a pilot program in a handful of the company's main flagship stores was implemented. In cases involving pilot programs, if the results of any pilot are measured against similar locations without pilots, the reliability of the pilot program data is markedly enhanced.

Key messages were aimed at customers while in the mall and/or store, intended to influence them at or very near the point-of-purchase. This is important because as POPAI estimates, 75% of retail purchase decisions are made in the store. Content for the

FIGURE 8.7 *The Digital Signage Screen Placed in the Mall and Super-market Area (the "Hybrid" Digital Signage Business Model) (Copyright 2007. Property of Visual Century Research. All rights reserved. Used with permission.)*

screens was updated regularly and it was possible to update it quickly, plus the content could be customized for the location. Indeed, the software and hardware backing up the system were rather complex, especially because each location had, on average, six total floors, and each floor's products had to match the content shown on the screens on that floor level. The content was chosen, organized, and distributed to all the floors in all the stores from a central location, however, occasional text could be added by individual store employees to accommodate specific store offers and information. Chain-wide, the supermarket used the digital signage system to extend the in-store radio system, informing customers of new product arrivals, special offers, and in-store events.

Advertisers worked with and supplemented the investment and efforts of the mall/supermarket company(ies). Approximately 50% of the broadcast time was sold to advertisers running promotional campaigns inside the store; this percentage rose to 85 on the supermarket's ground level, due to advertising agreements with perfume and cosmetic companies.

The ROI in this "hybrid" model came in at a bit over one year.

Also worth noting was the importance of measuring devices that actually count when an ad is telecast. Without this, advertisers are without a reliable data point with which they can verify that their ads were actually shown. In order for the digital signage industry to grow, it is essential that logging tools connected to billing systems operate in a trustworthy fashion.

Pilot Programs

Digital signage professionals with extensive experience and years in the know suggest outright that most significant expenditures of digital signage resources be initiated via a test, or pilot, program. In fact, these same pros would uniformly insist on such an initial pilot program for just about all larger-sized digital signage systems.

Not unlike one's goals and plans for the entire large-scale deployment, so, too, should realistic goals and careful plans be set for a pilot program. Then, it is important to allow the pilot program to operate, and to not be too quick to measure its success or lack thereof. Without enough reliable baseline data about the system, it becomes very difficult to use that data to later determine if a change in content or hardware placement or scheduling is necessary (or if the system in a fuller implementation stage might work at all). Once the pilot program has been in place for a given time—which will vary dependent on the model, operator, and partners chosen, as well as a dozen other criteria—then it is time to measure the effect it has had on traffic flows and store performance, as well as employee and customer well-being.

That said, pilot programs can typically be implemented in a rather short period of time, especially if those involved have done their due diligence and the system begins returning remarkable revenues or other desirable results quickly.

Importantly, digital signage pilot programs answer critical questions, such as,

(1) How many screens are enough in any given establishment or system?

(2) What content should be displayed?

(3) How should the content be displayed?

(4) Who is the real audience and are they being properly impacted?

In short, the pilot program begins to answer the all-critical question behind any digital signage deployment, that is, are the core goals of the controlling stakeholder being achieved? In the end, if the answer to this question is "maybe," perhaps it's time to either drop the system plans altogether, tweak the pilot program and try it again, or move ahead toward a larger-scale implementation.

Testing of various protocols during the pilot phase is highly recommended. Thus, based upon the audience dwell time, numerous different measurements should be made about how often the content rotates. The length of the pilot and the number of locations are up to the implementer, however, a measured industry recommendation suggests approximately a handful of sites (e.g., three to five), and a total pilot test time of approximately 1–2 months. Obviously, this is the stage at which hardware, software, and various operational aspects are honed. Further, employees and audiences are introduced to the digital signage concept, and their respective reactions and recommendations are considered. Note, too, that via cameras, survey, and/or other testing criteria, data is then also made available to help sell the digital signage implementation to advertisers and other stakeholders. Finally, the pilot stage is an ideal time to be thinking about growing the digital signage project with the information learned, ideally to several more, incremental, stages of total system growth during the ensuing years.

A particularly helpful series of articles about ROI, pilot programs, and measuring the success of various digital signage implementations are available online by visiting the writings of Bill Gerba, at www.billgerba.com, or by doing an Internet search using a search engine and typing in the words, "digital signage ROI." Additionally, the magazine, *Digital Signage Today*, offers a particularly on-point article, entitled, "Digital Signage and ROI: How to Maximize ROI on Your Digital Signage Deployments," at www.digitalsignagetoday.com.

9   International Digital Signage

Imagine the head of a mega retailer directly addressing shoppers at all of its retail outlets. The rapport between the retailer and buyer is immediate. The [same effect is achieved with] the sales force, the marketing team, and the rest of the staff, when the head of the organization shares his message directly with his employees at the same time across geographical territories. Retailers already have very advanced IT infrastructure. Building digital signage on the existing platform doesn't cost that much. Besides, look at the benefits. The reach of the retailer is phenomenal ... that's where the market will go.

—Joe Rossi, Hong Kong-based, managing director, Asia,
U.K.-based global digital media retail network enabler, Digital View

Across the globe, we are seeing the emergence of a new breed of direct broadcasting from digital signage networks that provide relevant information where and when it matters most. In retail and banking, it's advertising at the point of sale; in communities, it's a promotional city network; in corporate facilities, it's an internal information network.

—Keith Carlson, CEO, founder, The Mediatile Company

A look around the world at digital signage helps not only to put the industry into perspective, but also to see what novel implementations of digital signage are taking place globally. Additionally, those in different parts of the world get an opportunity to see what their counterparts—often their competitors—are undertaking in their own environments overseas.

In the same way that Asia has led the world in many facets of modern-day telecom development (e.g., it was the first area of the world to offer its public smaller-form cell phones and HDTV), it is not surprising that Asia is also a strong base for the development of digital signage. Further, many who have traveled and seen the deployment of digital signage in both places also rank Europe well ahead of North America, when it comes to the overall deployment of digital signage networks and infrastructure. Nonetheless, there are other parts of the world, places such as Latin America and Africa, where digital signage has new legs, too. This chapter identifies various notable applications of digital signage in countries where the cultures can help make for very different approaches to these dynamics between the digital signage presenter and its audience. Thus, Asia, Europe, and Latin America, and maybe even Africa (with their many different countries and regional cultural choices), are expected to be a front of future digital signage creativity and development (Figure 9.1).

POPAI, the global association that many credit as one of the digital signage industry's lead industry trade supporters, offers a global digital signage study, sponsored by big-time digital signage industry players, HughesNet and Publicis. The POPAI study submits a global view of the size, the players, and the issues involving the global digital signage industry. Information about this first-of-its-kind study may be accessed by visiting the POPAI website at www.popai.com.

Note, finally, and quite importantly, that for the foreign-based executive looking to move his or her company into another country, and/or looking for digital signage in that new jurisdiction to be part of the move, cultural understandings are

FIGURE 9.1 *A Freeway Roadside Commercial Digital Sign on a Main Artery Leading into Paris, France (Copyright 2008. Property of Jimmy Schaeffler. All rights reserved.)*

absolutely essential. Thus, for a U.S.-based concern, looking to establish a beach-head using digital signage in India's capital, Delhi, appreciation for the differences in language and culture, as well as for different decisions relative to all of the business basics (i.e., finance, marketing, technology, hardware, software, operations, and measurements) are imperatives. For example, a U.S.-based non-profit organization hired to fight smoking by the Indian state governments of Delhi, and its surrounding states of Haryana, Punjab, Uttar Pradesh, and Rajasthan, might rely on celebrity anti-smoking endorsements, realizing that the people of India are so strongly influenced by celebrity endorsements. Other factors that might influence the content that gets displayed on a digital screen on a Delhi street corner or a Delhi soccer stadium might include the local religions, gender perspectives, the importance of emotional values, the use of local statistics, local politics, and the importance of various foreign influences. In addition, other local matters, such as how to hire the right local contractor for installation and maintenance, are, without question, going to vary from what the U.S. non-profit organization knows and is used to. Finding an appropriate company based locally with strong ties and understandings of local matters is very likely going to mean the difference between success and failure.

Asia

Asia presents fascinating opportunities for digital signage, if for no other reason than the fact that the two countries of China and India account for more than two billion people. Indonesia has more than 200 million inhabitants, which makes it the fourth largest country in the world, population-wise. Thus, the area harbors a huge population, relatively speaking, a large percentage of which are potentially receptive to well-created digital signage content. In addition, Asia covers a large area with more than 20 countries making up the region, suggesting that there will be a lot of individual opportunities, by a lot of different companies in each country, to properly deploy what can become a successful digital signage system. Because each country can be so very different from the others—in terms of rules and regulations, as well as historical, social, and developmental mores—the chances are great that what can't be tried in one locale, may be tried in another.

India

In six metropolitan areas of greater India, the Sydney, Australia-based digital signage company, Future Media India, Inc., has deployed a 1,000-screen, 35-retail store digital signage deployment planned to meet and greet an estimated two million Indian people weekly. Possible store deployments include retail chains Pantaloons,

Big Bazaar, Food Bazaar, and Central stores. The new Indian network is described in press releases as "… the first branded out-of-home (OOH) TV network across retail outlets in India." Future Media's Chief Executive Partho Dasgupta summarizes, "When you get people to notice your brand or product in-store, the intent to buy will always be much higher."

Other Indian locales planned for digital signage include private banks, although national banks in that country are also expected to join the digital signage movement. Because digital signage costs are much less when compared to broadcast advertising costs, and because banks are typically quite solvent economically, financial institutions in India will be the early takers of digital signage.

Government entities and schools are expected to be another strong sector of growth for India's digital signage. This is, in part, due to the fact that large groups of India's people are illiterate and audio/visual ways of delivering health, emergency, or similar types of important information will be favored. Also, current trends imply that because India's business people are eager to see quick ROIs from things like digital signage, areas such as government, education, and banking—where ROOs other than ROI will justify deployments—will succeed first.

India's first deployment of on-board digital signage has recently been introduced on the Mumbai–Ahmedabad train route. India's airports, malls, highways, and theaters are expected to be additional locales for healthy digital signage growth. Further, the 2010 Commonwealth Games in Delhi, India, is the goal of a large kiosk-based digital signage project, centered on visitors to such locations as refreshment booths, waiting areas, restrooms, staircases, and near auditorium doors. The content featured will include news, information about movies, corporate sponsorship messages, and third-party advertising.

Figure 9.2 shows the author standing beneath a digital signage screen in a hallway of the Swiss-based Novotel Hotel, located in Hyderabad, India. The screen is used to display both mood-enhancing and scheduling information for guests and employees. Note that behind the author is the presence of traditional vinyl signage that the hotel has chosen to mix with the digital signage in this area.

China

Thousands of miles northwest from India, China, the larger country both population-wise and area-wise, offers a number of important digital signage projects, focused initially on major transportation firms and locations. In Macau, on the southeastern shores of China's mainland, the world's largest casino features digital signage at numerous locations inside, and at the main entrance, a giant outdoor LED display toils 24/7.

FIGURE 9.2 *This Indian Hotel Has Integrated Digital Signage into Its Public Spaces but Also Uses Traditional Printed Signs (Copyright 2007. Property of Lloyd Guiang. All rights reserved. Used with permission.)*

Shanghai's nearly one hundred subway stations, and the system's 4,000 flat-screen monitors, are the focus of a November 1, 2007 article by James Areddy in *The Wall Street Journal*. A Pepsi–Starbucks joint venture involves a soap-opera-like video story lasting 40 consecutive weekdays, about a Chinese country girl who moves to the big city to discover love, blogging, and, of course, Starbucks (Figure 9.3). The "subopera" (as it has been nicknamed) addresses an estimated 2.2 million subway users daily, who are expected to closely follow and relate to the daily segments of a few minutes each. Each time a train pulls into a station, new video updates are instantly relayed via Wi-Fi to an on-board server that broadcasts the new content to monitors in the cars. Subtitles offer dialog above the subway noise, and multiple rebroadcasts, as well as Internet tie-ins, are also offered.

The "subopera" is a unique new play on digital signage, which blends drama and advertising in a campaign that introduces bottled Frappuchino drinks into the Chinese marketplace. Jason Jiang, head of a Shanghai company that places ads in elevators, summarizes a theme of the new venture, which is that "ads beat boredom." Other in-subway content comprises emergency broadcasts, train arrival data, soccer and fashion highlights, news, and advertising. To date, the principles

FIGURE 9.3 *A Scene from the "Subopera" In Shanghai, China, Shown Daily on Hundreds of Digital Signage Displays in the Subway There (Copyright 2007. Property of Gobi Partners. All rights reserved. Used with permission.)*

behind this Chinese digital signage deployment tout over four million people who went online, using the Internet to view the episodes of this advertisement mixed cleverly with video storytelling (and vise versa).

Figure 9.4 shows a typical subway digital display in Shanghai, China, hundreds of which are witnessed daily by several million riders. The content on the screen shows an American football player, suggesting this media is being studied and used by international corporations to deliver their messages effectively to audiences in other countries.

Throughout mainland China, plans are underway for a digital signage project that runs regular TV shows and advertisements on 33,000 screens mounted inside public busses. A company called VisionChina Media, Inc. is behind the project, seeking additional funding and other digital signage areas to launch into.

Japan

In Japan, digital signage is finding its way into the "normal" application locales, such as those mentioned above in India and China. Yet, not surprisingly, technocrats in the Land of The Rising Sun are taking digital signage one step further. One of the world's largest telecom providers, NTT Communications, conducted a year-end

FIGURE 9.4 *A Subway Digital Sign in Shanghai, China (Copyright 2007. Property of Gobi Partners. All rights reserved. Used with permission.)*

2007 digital signage pilot study in front of the Kirin City Beer Hall in Tokyo's Yaesu underground shopping mall. Mood-heightening aromas apparently associated with beer—such as lemon and orange—are emitted by the actual screen device, and meant to attract audiences and enhance the impact of the messages (Figures 9.5 and 9.6).

Another example of cutting-edge Japanese developments in the area of digital signage is Mitsubishi Electric's new "completely seamless 340° immersive display project," which was built at the company's Kyoto factory on behalf of an undisclosed customer. Scheduled for a 2008 unveiling, additional details describe a "2 meter tall, 7.5 meter diameter display wall [that] creates a 340° panoramic experience that almost completely encircles the viewer with 27 million pixels of seamless display screen." Mitsubishi claims that it sees "great potential for the use of similar immersive technology in museums and in commercial applications, such as traffic simulations and data visualization."

Taiwan

Moving south along the China Sea to Taipei, Taiwan, a digital signage company there called Cayin Technology has implemented a large in-store network of 3,000 32-inch screens, installed across the country, in 1,500 branches of the retail chain

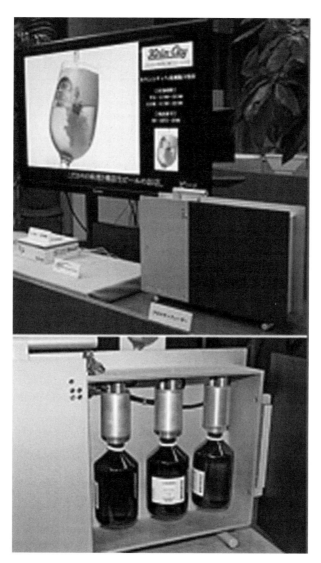

FIGURE 9.5 *The Kirin Beer Aroma-Enhanced Digital Signage Display in Tokyo, Japan (Copyright 2007. Property of NTT Communications. All rights reserved. Used with permission.)*

outlet, FamilyMart. Content includes news, commercial videos, lifestyle features, ticker tape text (e.g., RSS feeds and promotional messages), and occasional brands flashed on the screen. Each store features two screens, one in-store for shoppers, the other facing outside to draw traffic inside.

FIGURE 9.6 *The Behind-The-Scenes Workings of an Aroma-Enhanced Display (Copyright 2007. Property of NTT Communications. All rights reserved. Used with permission.)*

Philippines

In McDonald's restaurants throughout the Philippines and China, customers waiting for food in line typically have their attention fixed on plasma or LCD screens that feature video content of food items, special announcements, and marketing and product collaterals, as well as revenue-producing advertisements for other companies. In the Philippines, the Scala- and Globaltronics-installed system stretches across the island country from urban Manila and central Luzon, all the way down to the centers of Cebu and Davao City, as well as to the Visaya and Mindanao islands. The content in more than 100 McDonalds is updated an average of twice a week, according to viewer visitation patterns, or as frequently as necessary for selected outlets or occasionally even single outlets.

Singapore

In Singapore, Tel Aviv-based C-nario has helped McDonald's to deploy an SMS-controlled digital signage system in 67 of its 127 restaurants. Aimed at creating a "sense of community and enhancing patrons' dining experiences," the project allows visitors to interact by sending messages from their mobile phones to be displayed for all in the restaurant to see on an array of 42-inch flat screens in each restaurant. Guests are allowed to engage one another in chat-like conversations, respond to running content, or to a live feed, and even generate classified ads that run on a news-ticker-like service. On weekends, sports fans can watch 5-hour long streams of sports matches in better-than-broadcast quality. Ad spots are rotated at time intervals to maximize exposure, based upon the average waiting or dwell time. Touch-screen kiosks linked to point-of-sale systems issue coupons to eligible customers, who are notified via the digital signage screens. Reward points are also redeemed and gifts retrieved later at the cash register.

Singapore also offers students at its Nanyang Technological University a digital signage system to view when in high traffic areas, such as cafeterias or administrative offices. Content includes announcements of student events, as well as live webcasts showing distinguished speakers, classes, and graduations.

Malaysia

Malaysia has digital signage systems installed in its Aquaria inside the Kuala Lumpur Convention Center, as well as inside the Alamandra shopping center in Putrajaya, inside the Malaysia Tourism Center, and in restaurants comprising the Kayu Restaurant chain.

New Zealand

New Zealand reports data that shows digital signage screens and content in Auckland's International Airport are responsible for a 19% bump up in the sale of duty-free products shown. In what is a stark indication of what is to come, globally, the content on the New Zealand signage is coordinated to match the demographics of arriving and departing passengers, on each flight, to enhance the chance of a sale and overall relevance to the audience.

Europe

Bridging the landmasses (both literally and figuratively) between Asia and Europe is Turkey. As shown in Figure 9.7, a photo showing the author and his family inside a centuries-old shopping bazaar in Istanbul. The digital signage has been subtly, yet effectively, deployed in the background to the right. Overall in Europe, a wide geographical and type sampling of new digital sign projects includes

FIGURE 9.7 *The Author, Jimmy Schaeffler (on the Right), Together with His Wife, Diane, and Far Left to Right, Children Jessica, Cory, and Willy, In Front of a Discretely Displayed Digital Sign (to the Right of the Author), in an Istanbul, Turkey Shopping Bazaar (Copyright 2008. Property of Jimmy Schaeffler. All rights reserved.)*

those with Audi (the German automobile manufacturer), Aral (the German gas station operator), Dutch Railways (news and advertising on trains), Poland's The Pharmacy Advertising Channel, The Advertising Channel in Romania (retail stores and banks), Shell Retail in Norway (new displays added for carwash advertising), Hansa Banki in Lithuania, Telenor in Norway, DnB Nor Eiendom in Norway, and IKEA in the United Kingdom.

United Kingdom

Another unique example of digital signage, this time in the United Kingdom, features Baby-TV, a pre-natal content service delivered to OB–GYN offices, antenatal clinics, ultrasound departments, day assessment units, and some areas in maternity wards across the United Kingdom. From a PowerPoint presentation by Baby-TV's founder, Gavin Anderson, given at the 2007 IBC conference in Amsterdam, the following advantages of the service were highlighted: Baby-TV is (1) highly targeted, (2) with no wastage, (3) offered in a unique and exclusive antenatal hospital environment, (4) involving long-term contracts that provide the service and the partners a monopolistic advantage, and (5) offers advertisers a direct route to market. Baby-TV is offered in approximately 100 U.K. hospitals as of Q1 '08, and is negotiating with dozens more, such that it claims it will soon reach the mothers and fathers of 85% of the approximately 650,000 babies born each year in England and Wales.

The business model involves advertisements and subscriptions paid for by the owners of the Baby-TV screen and service locations. Advertisers come from local, regional, and national bases, including such well-known U.K.-located companies as Johnson's, Fisher Price, NHS, Unilever, Quinny, Maxi-Cosi, and Baby Einstein. Gavin Anderson concludes, "With this form of out-of-home digital signage—unlike broadcast TV—we get a known audience, we know when they are watching, where, who, and why, we know their mood state, and one service really fits all."

Other examples of digital signage in the United Kingdom include those deployed by Tesco, Spar, Woolworths, and The Mall. In addition, the rejuvenated U.K.-based Life Channel remains one of the largest digital signage networks in Europe.

Table 9.1 is a chart that shows three clients of U.K.-based Avanti Screenmedia, and the lessons it learned from European-based digital signage deployments it did for three key clients—Spar, Woolworths, and The Mall—during the past few years.

Further in the mode of European-based digital signage lessons, the digital signage implementation of U.K. supermarket chain Tesco is one of the better-known early models of "what not to do." Its first generation creators were too focused on the flashy new technology, and not focused enough on the true needs and interests of the shopping audience. Tesco's new agency, Dunnhumby, states that it has made some significant changes, involving software, hardware, and managements' point of view.

Germany

According to POPAI's Fabian Keller, Vice President, Digital Signage, Germany is especially poised to develop large digital signage networks in the 2008–2009 time frame. The year 2007 saw various tests of new digital signage deployments by large national chain stores (e.g., Edeka, Metro Group, Postbank). In addition, 2008 already has a couple of national roll-outs planned. These include Postbank, the largest retail bank in Germany, which is launching PostbankTV, with one million viewers projected per day in over 800 retail outlets. Postbank is expected to

	WHAT WAS DONE	WHAT AVANTI WISHED IT HAD DONE
Client #1: Mall	600 large plasma screens installed	Installed fewer big screens
	National level sales force	Local sales force, commission based
	Content updated daily	Shopping mission content
	3-year deal	5-year deal
	Lease finance agreement	Back-loaded payments to build cashflow from ad revenues
Client #2: Woolworths		
	12-store trial in 48 control stores	20-store trial in 64 control stores
	1-year test	6-month test
	6 channels	3 channels for better ROI
	15 screens	12 screens
	2.3% total stores sales uplift	Done better store selection criteria
	No ad revenue written from either third parties or suppliers	Demanded more change earlier on

(Continued)

	WHAT WAS DONE	WHAT AVANTI WISHED IT HAD DONE
Client #3: Spar		
	200 store roll-out	1,000 store roll-out
	1-year roll-out	9-month roll-out
	3 channels	2 channels—matched to the strength of the product category
	5 screens	Not installed plasma screens, because size not so critical
	No local ad sales	Should sell ad space at just one Euro per five second ad
	3.6% total store sales uplift	Enhanced even this percentage by being quicker engaging new suppliers

TABLE 9.1 *Avanti Screenmedia's Digital Signage Deployment "Wish List." Data Taken from a 2007 Presentation by Avanti Screenmedia's Stuart Chambers Before a Digital Signage Session at the 2007 IBC Conference in Amsterdam. (Copyright 2008. Avanti Screenmedia. All rights reserved. Used with permission.)*

be the first major roll-out in Germany. Meanwhile, Edeka, Germany's largest super-market, has an installation that is expected to surpass Postbank's, with its first regional roll-out in 400+ stores and about 2,500 stores targeted nationally, reaching an estimated 30 million viewers a day. Keller believes the biggest challenge for the German market will be determining the right cutting-edge concepts and content strategies.

Switzerland

Switzerland has nearly twenty digital signage networks in operation today. The third-party marketing organization Goldbach Media AG (which many describe as the leading media sales company in the country) has, according to POPAI's Keller, successfully tackled the new digital signage medium since 2003.

The Netherlands

Rabobank, the Ultrech, Netherlands-based financial institution, has a digital signage network in place that has been operational for years. Rabobank is a leading bank in the Netherlands, with more than 9 million business and private customers. The bank includes more than 1,300 independently operated local banks throughout the Netherlands. Like those in other locations around the globe, its digital signage focuses on employee training and information, and consumer advertisements and promotions. Rabobank company officials use plasma screens located within bank locations and adjacent to the bank's ATM machines. Each screen displays short, focused segments about the bank's products and services. Content is created and distributed to each locale from a central location over an ADSL telco-based infra-structure. As of late 2007, Rabobank states it has installed "hundreds and hundreds" of digital signage displays. Switzerland-based Neo Advertising recently purchased Dutch-based POSTV, the latter being the Netherlands' largest in-store digital media network, with almost 9,000 online flat screens deployed into 270 venues. (Though many of the "screens" are really walls of flat screens showing the same content in retail electronics departments, thousands of screens in almost 300 outlets is still an impressive data point.) POSTV claims that during every 4 weeks its digital signage reaches more than 6 million shoppers, which makes it the largest retail digital advertising network in the Netherlands. Network advertisers include Canon, Gillette, Heineken, Nokia, Samsung, and Unilever. Nationwide Dutch retailers using the system include Vodaphone, MediaMarkt, and Makro.

Digital signage is also making appearances in public spaces. Figure 9.8 shows a digital sign in the main city center subway in Amsterdam.

FIGURE 9.8 *As an Additional Example of How Digital Signage Is Growing in Europe and Especially in the Netherlands, the Main City Center Subway in Amsterdam Now Offers Digital Signage for Those Waiting for Transportation. Entertainment and Information, with Numerous Ads As the Key Content (Copyright 2008. Property of Jimmy Schaeffler. All rights reserved.)*

Croatia

Further east and south across Europe, Hypo Alpe-Adria Bank, in Croatia, offers a digital signage system centrally managed from Zagreb, sending bank services, new product information, and branded advertising content to the bank's 60 locations and to its sister companies. The current deployment follows a successful pilot program in Zagreb, Split, Rijeka, and Osijek, involving 42-inch Fujitsu plasma screens.

Figure 9.9 shows a hardware store in a large European city using small screen versions of digital signage at the point of purchase (POP). These types of smaller, more discrete and focused screens are expected to proliferate not only in Europe, but in most other areas of the world.

FIGURE 9.9 *A Hardware Store in Southern Europe Shows a Small, Discrete, and Focused Digital Signage Display (Copyright 2008. Property of Jimmy Schaeffler. All rights reserved.)*

Russia

Russia is a country of about 140 million inhabitants. Since the fall of communism almost 15 years ago, a freer market economy is opening unexpected possibilities for many new digital signage entrepreneurs and their applications. In digital signage terms, Russia appears to be much closer to the infancy stage than it does to the adolescent stage. Thus, the opportunities are great for digital signage applications in Russia.

A retail chain of shopping centers, supermarkets, and larger, so-called hypermarkets, titled Ramstore, runs a digital signage network centered around in-store advertising. The initial pilot project centered on high-traffic stores in cities such as Moscow, St. Petersburg, Krasnoyarsk, Kazan, Rostov, Podolsk, and Zelenograd. Content includes product information, video clips, and promotional messages, as well as significant local content, including news, sports, and weather. Content is typically changed weekly throughout the Ramstore system. Thousands of screens are planned for the multiyear roll-out of this Russian digital signage system.

Steven Keith Platt, head of the Platt Retail Institute, cites the following digital signage examples from a trip he made to Russia in October 2007, in an article titled "Russian Revolution," which was published in the *Digital Signage Weekly*. Russia's Nepkpectok supermarket chain is offering relatively simplistic digital signage deployments, showing consistent content on all screens, in the form of made-for-TV ads that have already seen their TV runs. Screens are placed in aisles and, quite cleverly, above the heads of patrons standing in check-out lines. Electronic firms such as Texhonapk have also taken to display flat-panel screens along walls and in panels in their stores. Moreover, the Russian store, Gentleman Farmer, does a good job of displaying content on a single flat panel behind the check-out counter, with 5- to 10-second spots displaying products in attractive ways.

Elsewhere

In Latin America, digital signage is now widely deployed for advertising at duty-free airport stores. Thousands of miles away, in Saudi Arabia, a new digital signage network has recently been implemented at one of the country's leading banks. The hodge-podge of examples that follows from around the globe highlights some remarkable digital signage deployments.

Mexico

Another global broadcaster, Mexico's Televisa, has joined the trend toward the business of digital signage. The system is installed in almost 300 Wal-Mart de Mexico stores, with 21–28 large-screen LCDs per store, and is made up of a total of more than 5,000 digital screen displays and touch-screen kiosks. Televisa supplies the original, retail-specific programming for the Wal-Mex Network, as it is termed, as well as the advertising spots. Florida-based Wirespring provides the software management system. The audience of shoppers enjoys a better store experience and is able to make smarter purchasing decisions, according to a September 2006 press release. Advertisers receive an additional opportunity to highlight key selling points, which also complements key traditional point-of-purchase advertising. Content is customized by store type, with multiple channels per store, including a dedicated channel for the pharmacy department in some locations. Summarizes Wal-Mex partner Wirespring's CEO, Bill Gerba, "In an industry that's often more hype than substance, [broadcaster] Televisa has taken a bold position in the world of retail media, combining digital signs and interactive kiosks to create a tightly-integrated media environment at the store level."

Another south-of-the-border example is that of Duluth, GA-based Wegener, which will deliver 1,200 digital signage deployments to the Mexican company, Satellite Store Link (SSL), for systems in Mexican banks that are focused on an audience of customers and employees. A May 2007 press release noted that employees at the Mexican display locations did not have to manage or interact with the digital signage screens or receivers in order for the devices to operate properly. Such functions and upgrades are scheduled and managed remotely from the network control center at the central operations center of the bank in Mexico.

Brazil

In Brazil, the Paris, France-headquartered digital signage company PRN has entered into a joint venture with a Brazilian company called Cereja to deploy an in-store digital signage network in more than 100 Carrefour supermarkets as of year-end 2007. According to a November 2007 press release, 42-inch plasma screens are set in special areas around each store, together with 19-inch flat-panel screens at check-out lanes, and "a video wall made up of TV monitors merchandised in the electronics section." Carrefour's so-called "hypermarkets" serve an estimated 27 million people monthly in greater Brazil.

A similar digital signage system was deployed in just over 30 locales of the retail chain Casa & Video, beginning in late 2006. Content is made up of videos produced internally as well as ad messages from suppliers.

Saudi Arabia

With the two main goals of (1) communicating more effectively with its employees and (2) improving its corporate image, The National Commercial Bank in Saudi Arabia deploys digital signage in 40 of its 300 locations in Saudi Arabia. Press releases note that employees should be able to better understand the bank's products and services, and thus the services they provide to their customers. An uplift in sales is also expected, as customers become better aware of those products and services and decide to partake. Via 42-inch flat screens, customers inside the banks are introduced to text, graphics, still images, and animation, making up the content that is delivered from the bank's corporate headquarters. That consumer content comprises information about bank services, special bank promotions, and relevant news headlines.

Africa

Focused on IP-delivered content, and simple all-in-one single box packages, the Johannesburg- and Cape Town-based Tactile Technologies has ventured with Scotts Valley, CA-based Mediatile, and Vodacom, the cell phone company, to bring a unique form of digital signage to all of greater Africa, especially its banks, retailers, financiers, pharmacies, advertisers, and members of its media and hospitality sectors. A July 2007 press release summarized that, "Mediatile's Digital-Sign-In-A-Box displays can be shipped to hundreds of locations, such as retail stores or banks, and are configured by simply plugging them into a standard power outlet. Mediatile displays instantly connect over the Internet using Vodacom mobile 3g/GPRS services, and are individually or collectively controlled through a secure web-based portal. Mediatile displays are available in 19-inch, 32-inch, 42-inch and 47-inch HD LCD sizes, including touch-screen configurations. Also available is a separate 'component player' that can be connected to almost any pre-existing display—from five-inch display panels to immense outdoor electronic billboards."

10 Where and How to Start Considering Digital Signage?

A digital signage project follows a structure similar to other application systems projects. The focus on revenue and other stakeholder benefits, however, adds additional important dimensions to a typical system development life cycle, signage project, or merchandising initiative.

—Lyle Bunn, Strategy Architect, Bunn Company

The key is to match up your customers' requirements and expectations to a solution that meets your business objectives. Once you've analyzed the business objectives, and matched them with the customer objectives, it's time to identify the unique environmental and location issues related to deploying public-space technologies.

—Brian Ardinger, Vice President, Business Development, Nanonation

Two key messages need to be remembered up front when the newcomer begins investigating digital signage: Do not be intimidated, and Do your homework.[1] From (1) initial goal and plan setting, coupled with actual growth and development of the network, then to (2) a measured test or pilot project, and finally to (3) the question of further network growth, the answers up front—or part of the answers—go a long way toward longer-term peace of mind (and profits and success). In addition, always remember: Know Thy Audience!

Like just about any new deployment or activity—especially one that involves significant expenditures of money, time, and other human resources—it's best to do your homework, prepare, and have due diligence. That makes this a particularly important chapter, and, indeed, reading this book is a good start toward all of that. The book and its chapters are written with a broad audience in mind, and focused on the core business aspects of the digital signage industry. As a neophyte, key

---

1. Note these two pieces of advise are not intended to be oxymoronic.

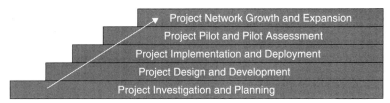

FIGURE 10.1 *On a Broad Scale, What to Consider When Evaluating a Digital Signage Endeavor (Copyright 2008. Property of Jimmy Schaeffler. All rights reserved.)*

elements to determine are (1) your goals, (2) the needs and other particulars of the specific audience, and (3) the environment in which the digital signage will be placed.

A chain of chores one would need to undertake the deployment of a digital signage solution would, of course, depend on who it was and what they wanted, as well as where they were looking to have their digital signage deployed, and who they wanted to influence. That said, there are a number of digital signage basics, highlighted in Figures 10.1 and 10.2, which should apply to just about every new digital signage participant. Note that the order of (and even inclusion of) some of these activities may also be adjusted to accommodate different entities, with different needs, for different audiences.

Key areas of investigation include content creation and delivery, hardware choices, technology, pricing and financial strategies, and measuring results, as well as, right up front, the all-important audience dynamics.

Where to Start?

Three relatively separate and important beginning stages to the digital signage process are described in this chapter. These are the processes just about every entity considering adding digital signage must take to greatly increase the probability of success. They include (1) the project beginning and development, (2) the pilot, and (3) the future growth stages. The majority of this chapter is devoted to Stage 1 activities.

Stage 1: Project Beginning and Development

Developing a digital signage project involves setting goals, developing a plan, and assessing the content, environment, and technology for the installation.

Start out by reading this book. Study these three key stages in this chapter and the other chapters covering the five or six major divisions of digital signage. These

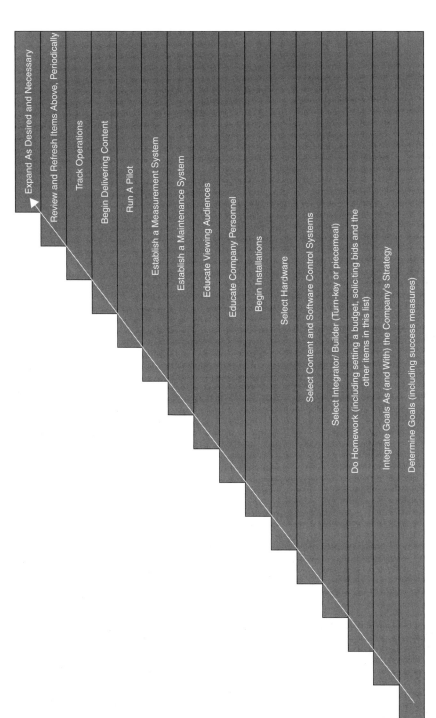

The diagram shows an ascending staircase with the following steps listed from bottom to top:

- Determine Goals (including success measures)
- Integrate Goals As (and With) the Company's Strategy
- Do Homework (including setting a budget, soliciting bids and the other items in this list)
- Select Integrator/ Builder (Turn-key or piecemeal)
- Select Content and Software Control Systems
- Select Hardware
- Begin Installations
- Educate Company Personnel
- Educate Viewing Audiences
- Establish a Maintenance System
- Establish a Measurement System
- Run A Pilot
- Begin Delivering Content
- Track Operations
- Review and Refresh Items Above, Periodically
- Expand As Desired and Necessary

FIGURE 10.2 *The More Detailed Steps in Evaluating a Digital Signage Implementation (Copyright 2008. Property of Jimmy Schaeffler. All rights reserved.)*

include things such as review of the hardware, software, installation, maintenance, measurement, and the future of digital signage. Then look to other resources, such as those referenced in the appendices of this book. Do online research, at minimum. Attend digital signage conferences, which are a great place to talk to those who understand the digital signage industry well (and where it is going). In addition, as you travel, stop to take a look at various digital signage applications, in operation. Ask those who deployed them, how does your digital signage work for you? Once the goals are set, begin the formal process of establishing a development plan.

Goal Setting, Goal Determination, and a Development Plan

The newcomer to digital signage has probably seen and/or heard a lot about the new medium before ever acting to implement it in his or her business situation. If that person or group is an advertiser, the process will involve working with the client to determine the goals and nature of the proposed experience. If that person or group of newcomers represents a retail establishment—such as a shop, a mall, or a convenience store—the process will involve lots of focus, typically, on brands, goods, products, and advertising messages. Moreover, if that neophyte is in another line of business, for example a non-commercial entity, such as a religious institution or hospital, then this chapter will guide them, as well. Yet, close on the heels of and in some cases before (or concurrently with) setting the goals, is also the critically important matter of setting and understanding the audience's goals.

Goal Setting

Business goals start with asking the big question: what is your (or your client's) vision statement? This is a key dynamic in the goal to define the scope of the entire digital signage deployment (i.e., both the pilot deployment and the later deployment of a larger digital signage model).

Typically, the vision statement can be remarkably short and sweet, perhaps even just one or two lines, for example, "to create content that informs and entertains." Various internal and external stakeholders are often invited to contribute to this stage of the preparation, to wed their views. Thus, the internal IT or HR divisions might be encouraged at this early stage to offer insights and needs (especially if either or both will be asked to contribute funds toward the budget of the digital signage system).

It is also probably not a bad idea to get that vision statement in writing. IP-based digital signage provider Helius,[2] through its CEO, Mike Tippets, further

---

2. Note that in early 2008, Helius was acquired by HughesNet.

suggests that, as common sense as it appears, do not miss this core protocol: make sure the digital signage goal is helping the business.

Another set of goals will involve the specifics of your company (or client). Beyond the vision statement, what are the specifics that bring about the success of the vision statement? Is it increased product or service sales, is it lower costs, is it less employee turnover, is it a better in-store branding experience, or is it making sure customers are knowledgeable and satisfied?

What is the real goal of the business' interest in digital signage? One great way to start is to ask, what effect do we want digital signage to have on our audience? More importantly, who do we see as the true audience, and what impact should the digital signage have on that audience? What do we believe will be the audience needs within the digital signage system?

Before positioning a new digital signage system, you must first determine the true goals of the system, very possibly in the form of short-, mid-, and long-term goals. Then, assess and decide upon the goal of the audience or end-user.

Another important item to consider in the planning process is that of success milestones, what they are, and how they will be measured, and at what points. Note that the factors identified in Chapter 8, such as new revenues, improved branding, reductions in perceived or actual waiting lines or times, greater interaction speeds, enhanced product awareness, cost reductions and, the all-important return on objective (ROO) called return on investment (ROI), can all be goals.

New ROI revenues can be sought from sales lift, sales commissions, advertisement sales, display location rentals or leases, percentages of sales from new products or services, and cross-selling. Plus, cost reductions can be sought in the areas of print and billboard costs that are no longer necessary; reduced waste of printed materials; elimination of unnecessary staff positions (such as delivery of DVDs and CDs); better assurance of actual advertisement display; maximizing earlier investments in creative development; quicker (and thus more effective) marketing of time-sensitive goods and services; and reduced staff training costs via use of the same digital signage system infrastructure for employee communications.

Note that there is evidence in spheres of real savings from digital signage, as opposed to traditional signage costs. Thus, for a "traditional" print, billboard, etc., program costing an estimated $500,000 involving a localized advertising program addressed to a mid-sized U.S. city, a replaceable digital signage cost in the same locale is estimated at 30% of the traditional signage cost, or $150,000. Put another way, the average cost savings during a 12-month period are estimated at more than 75%.

An excellent step-by-step analysis of many of these beginning development steps, titled "Planning Your Digital Signage Network," written by industry leader Lyle Bunn, is at www.signindustry.com.

Scott Stanton, from the Digital Signage Group, Inc., summarizes the goal-setting process in the Digital Signage Resource Directory: "What is needed is a balance between the initial cost of the system, the long-term operational costs, and the ability of the system to deliver the right message."

Audience Goal Determination

Presumptuous as it may sometimes seem, those wishing to step into the digital signage business must also step directly into the shoes of their customers. Often, this can be done via years of knowledge about who comes into a store or other type of venue, and what interests them. More often, these days, many believe that the only true way to measure people or groups of people is to survey them. This means asking them questions or otherwise studying them, toward the goal of truly understanding their metrics and thus what makes them tick. In this way, they tell you who they are and what they want or need.

Note, too, that the business' goals are often merged with or the same as those of the audience, and this is certainly acceptable. Thus, for a retail establishment, its goals are to sell things, which is in sync with the retail audience's goal, i.e., to buy those same things. Further, once one moves from this Stage 1 to the latter goals in this analysis, the same types of questions about the neophyte's and the audience's goals come up again and again.

Having set its goals and the goals of the target audience(s), you are in the position to look into the content and the technology that will achieve those goals. Note that here, purposefully, the first item mentioned is content. As advised by industry veteran Brian Ardinger, VP of Business Development for Nanonation, in his article of August 15, 2006, "Expert Advise: Never Start With Technology," from DigitalSignageToday.com, planners should focus first on the milestone of understanding the audience, then on the content that matches one's goals to their needs, and then on the technology to do that. Technologies such as hardware, software, networks, and systems integration come typically late in this part of the preparation process.

Development Plan

Setting the goals and thinking about and planning for the content are actually two of the first steps toward making the overall development plan for the initial digital signage deployment. Those steps are usually followed by, and eventually accompanied by, solutions to concerns such as the locating and sourcing of certain system turn-key or individual elements, operation of those elements and the overall system, and how everything will be paid for. Ideally, this developmental plan should cover the time frame from the earliest beginnings to the culmination of the pilot test project (and, ideally, the growth into a bigger and/or more sophisticated digital signage system).

Also important to the development plan will be the establishment of various milestones. Many of these will be sub-categorized as "success milestones." These step-by-step planning protocols often protect funding and spending, and make sure the project is following a professional and well-thought out pacing process. Milestones typically include items such as putting agreements into place (e.g., those with software and hardware suppliers, property and/or location owners, various system partners), acquisition of funding and other monetary resources, installation, and early testing of various technologies, to name but a few. Many experienced digital signage implementers recommend that solid business and financial plans be implemented as part of this early-stage development plan.

An important part of the business and financial plans involves creating a viable budget, which is also a good part of the dialog you must inevitably engage in with your digital signage stakeholders at this point. The completed preliminary budget then becomes part of the greater project plan. Chapter 8 provides additional practical insight into the financial parts of a digital signage project.

An early-stage budget includes things such as hardware and software costs, anticipated revenues (if any) from advertising or other sources, cash flows, and anticipated profits, if any. Various expense items are included and reviewed at this stage. These might also include labor, legal, operations, advertising (e.g., collaterals and commissions), measurement costs (e.g., viewer audits), and branding costs. Revenue sources might include advertising, sales lift bonuses, in-house content creation, production of marketing and measurement data, and commissions from coupon redemption. Although not typically "revenue," savings from costs that otherwise would have gone toward printing sales material or expensive in-person training exercises can be achieved when, for example, in systems with fifty or more locations, a satellite-delivered employee training program is also delivered (and does "double duty") as part of a digital signage system.

Similarly, typical costs must also be assessed and planned for. These would include "normal" items such as operations, administration, content acquisition, and network deployment costs.

Drilling down into the development plan, other items to consider include understanding audience demographics, the layout of the display, how often it may be changed out, an inventory list, rate cards, and advertisement sale collateral materials.

A list of 15 steps typically necessary for the proper deployment of many digital signage systems includes the following:

(1) Do a development plan.

(2) Do a financial plan.

(3) Do a business plan.

(4) Do a formal site survey.

(5) Do a budget.

(6) Put sufficient financial capital and investment in place.

(7) Identify a viable business model/ROO/ROI.

(8) Utilize consultants with experience doing the specific chores for which they are hired.

(9) Plan properly for installation, maintenance, measurement, repairs, and life expectancy.

(10) Properly match existing systems from the locale and the business with the new digital signage system.

(11) Choose quality hardware and software. Indeed, err on the side of spending a bit more to get reliable and robust hardware.

(12) Keep the first version of the implementation rather simple.

(13) Do not assume that all systems are totally reliable. Consider backups.

(14) Bring the audience toward a "call to action."

(15) Deliver active protocols for participants—including the employees and the audience of end-users—allowing them to critique (and improve) the system.[3]

---

3. The book, *Lighting Up the Aisle: Principles and Practices for In-Store Media* by Laura Davis-Taylor and Adrian Weidmann, includes 16 similar suggestions to those in this listing. In addition, the online source, "The Top 13 Deployment Mistakes … and How to Avoid Them," by Wirespring Technologies, also includes a list of "what not to do," for those seeking further guidance in this area.
See www.billgerba.com.

Assessing the Content

Chapter 5 gives a practical and concise overview of filling the rather large content vacuum, which is a typical digital signage system. Questions answered at this phase should include things like the sources of content, the types of content, who creates and finally decides upon the content, and what best fits audience needs. Concern for and attention to the cost of content—especially of licenses to acquire and use the content—are necessary, and should also be factored in sooner rather than later. Sources of content could range from in-house files to outside providers, including innumerable still and video art supply houses. Plus, if the content will be outdoors, such as along a highway or roadside, early coordination with city, state, and perhaps federal entities is advised.

Bill Gerba, CEO of Wirespring, who is a frequent blog contributor (see www.billgerba.com) and a recognized digital signage industry expert, gives a good deal of written space to the topic of content. He summarizes its importance as follows: "By custom-tailoring content to fit the ideals and preferences of the target viewer, advertisers may not only increase their chances of making a sale, but may actually strengthen their brand image and improve the overall shopping experience."

Another industry pioneer, Scala's Executive Vice President Jeff Porter, in reference to another key point about content delivery, says, "Signage must be lively, relevant, and appealing. It is not TV; it is not the Web; it is signage."

Assessing the Environment

Three core parts make up the study of the digital signage environment. These are the audience, the company and its employees, and the actual physical location of the digital signage deployment. Seen another way, it is also the physical location of the signage and those that will build, operate, and measure the screens.

The Audience

As a part of the digital signage environment, the audience must be studied once again. What is the audience in relation to the company and its employees? How often does the same audience visit? What time of day does a specific audience visit? What are they seeking when they enter? What can they expect from the store's employees? Other sections of this chapter deal more specifically with questions and concerns related to the audience (as a part of the greater digital signage environment).

The Company and Its Employees

The company behind the digital signage display may be the location owner or a network owner; it may be one company or many companies. Whatever its separate makeup, it, too, as an entity, and its specific employees, are best studied separate from, yet in relation to, the audience and physical location parts of the environment. Keeping employees happy and in sync with the needs of their customers is an important aspect of just about any digital signage location.

The Physical Location

Many kinds of physical locales make up the core of existing indoor and outdoor locations for digital signage. What an audience and a group of employees are expected to do with digital signage in a cinema locale will be entirely different from what an audience and venue employees are expected to do in a 50,000-person stadium. Coordinating the different aspects of the location, including a floor plan and retail space plan, with key aspects of the audience and the employees, creates a logical and fluid arrangement that achieves sought-after goals.

Assessing the Technology

Ideally, assessment of the technology of a developing new digital signage system will be one of the things that comes after and supports the rest of the assessments previously described. After all, technology subsumes important elements of software, hardware, the network, and systems integration.

Thus, for example, attention will be paid to the types of screens that best fit the space, those that are esthetically pleasing, those that have the proper resolution and brightness, and sometimes those that are light in weight or thin enough. Attention will be paid to whether given screens in certain locales within a digital signage facility will be the best to display a type of content that it is anticipated will be delivered to a type of audience. Attention may also be paid to specific audiences arriving at certain times of the day and to certain content day parts, or times during the day when different content needs to be delivered.

Stage 2: Pilot Program

Once the development plan is in place, it is time to move toward deployment of the development plan, which is typically best achieved via the implementation of the pilot or test program. Most digital signage experts suggest a pilot program for even the smallest of configurations, including those with just a handful of screens, or those with just one location. An ideal test protocol involves using a pilot test system in just one locale, and comparing statistics such as sales at that location to one or others without digital signage.

The deployment of the pilot program involves seeing how the installation really materialized. It also includes a view to how agreements with hardware and software suppliers, location owners, network operators, and, of course, content suppliers, have worked out.

Time-wise, for example, 1 or 2 months would be a good time frame to test a project of five stores. Assuming it will operate the same hardware and basic content (system management and on-screen content), and infrastructure as a long-term, permanent system, the pilot is a great opportunity to introduce employees and customers to the new digital signage system. Typical measurements taken during this time frame would be audience recall abilities, additional sales, improved branding experiences, and other audience impact or call-to-action criteria.

Pilots also allow the implementation team to get the bugs out, tune the system, and refine the message. A pilot is also a good way to see how a bigger system will operate.

Measurement

Measurement of viewer activity is critical at all stages of most digital signage projects, however, it is probably most important during a given time frame during the pilot phase. Testing can be done using Internet software, in-person paper surveys, or even, these days, via cameras and other on-location testing devices that measure things in the realm of audience reactions. This would include activities such as audience eye movements toward or away from a piece of digital signage content. This data is then relied upon by investors, advertisers, and location providers, to name but a few.

Stage 3: Future Growth

During the planning stage and pilot program, you will have learned how important certain parts of the puzzle really are to your individual project's success. As such, the relative functioning and importance of all the basic parts will be in greater focus. Have hardware, software, installation, maintenance, and measurement worked? Has the content motivated the audience to action? Or has it added to their well-being or to the ambience of the environment? Has the audience found it relevant? Has it achieved your goals? Indeed, thousands more questions will have been wholly or partially answered by now, and those answers will guide you to the next phase of your digital signage development.

Never underestimate the value of steady and reliable data, which measures the pilot first, and the rest of the deployment later on. In fact, as indicated in Chapter 8, even if the ROO does not include a clear ROI, it is still a good idea to try to acquire audience and content measurements, if for nothing else, to give a benchmark against which future improvements can be measured. Chapter 11 offers a more complete and detailed listing and description of future digital signage opportunities and applications.

When to Start?

The definition of a starting point for digital signage is fairly simple: he or she needs to start when the goal becomes an effort to enhance or increase the value of the messages delivered to his or her audiences. By taking steps like reading this book, capturing the other references in the appendix, talking to people who know the business, and possibly even attending some digital signage conferences, newcomers get closer to starting an actual implementation, which ties back to Stages 1 through 3, as discussed in this chapter.

Because one of the core audiences for this book is broadcasters, multichannel operators, and related others in the telecom realm, a reference is directed here toward the opportunity digital signage offers that constituency. Notes one broadcast observer, "As computers get more advanced, getting into the digital signage business is going to get easier and easier. It is a great way to diversify." Adds Capitol Broadcasting's CEO, Jim Goodmon, "We already have a lot of the content, and we are familiar with the basic equipment and the key players—advertisement agencies and advertisers—it just makes a lot of sense to work in digital signage." Goodmon's company's subsidiary, Microspace, is an early pioneer in the development of digital signage.

For advertisers (and their clients), few would doubt the importance of shifting resources to new advertising alternatives, such as Internet advertising, mobile advertising, and digital signage advertising. Most experts in and out of the ad business see digital signage as a very strong way to maintain brand presence among the general clutter of today's advertisement and TV worlds. This book is intended to clearly indicate why that is happening and how to join that process. Indeed, an old business adage recommends that, in times of stress, business people look to diversity as a hedge against the future. Beyond today's digital signage developments, actual future developments are highlighted in Chapter 11, pointing to things such as in-program placement of advertisements as a wave of the future.

Retail Banking

This case study examines the experience of a Michigan-based bank, its partnering with a Tennessee-based marketing firm, StagePost, and their alliance to develop a digital signage system they termed "Excelevision." This system was focused on delivering real-time marketing, training, and corporate communications to employees and customers at the bank's hundreds of southeastern U.S. retail banking locations. The content is delivered via an SES Americom satellite located 22,300 miles above the equator in space. The developer of new technology for the application and the provider of a content delivery solution backbone is the Raleigh, North Carolina-based Microspace.

The bank's customer strategy is to encourage customers to come personally into the retail banking locations (instead of pushing customers to use the Internet for their transactions). In fact, the bank prefers that the customer come in person to visit his/her chosen bank location at least several times in the course of a month. The bank chose digital signage content to address its customers' time waiting in line or dwell time (which tends to be a necessary part of most retail banking), rather than have that customer experience turn boring or otherwise negative.

Three components make up the "Excelevision" experience via display on large TVs or plasma screens:

- *Excelevision network*: Offers passive, one-way video-based retail advertising on the bank's products and services.

- *Customer learning terminal*: Offers an interactive two-way experience, where customers react to and request information and services.

- *Employee learning terminal*: Rather than send employees traveling long distances or trying something less effective, each location of the bank offers training content that teaches them about products and services, and allows them to interactively study and take responsive tests upon the completion of training programs. This then permits leaders at headquarters to instantly assess performance and enjoy two-way feedback.

A key challenge of the bank's digital signage project involved cost-effectively refreshing the content that is displayed for customers and avoiding the problems of old and traditional signage and communications. Those challenges included the cost of having an on-site employee to physically distribute and display content via DVDs. They also included a necessarily limited library of DVDs that could not be regularly refreshed, often leading to consumer and employee fatigue after viewing the same content repeatedly. The latter often meant an employee would simply turn the screen off altogether, which defeated the intended purpose of the system entirely.

The bank's solution was to turn to delivery of content via satellite. Satellites allow real-time delivery to any number of locations (from just one to thousands), and the price stays relatively stable as the system and the number of locales grow. Indeed, as the

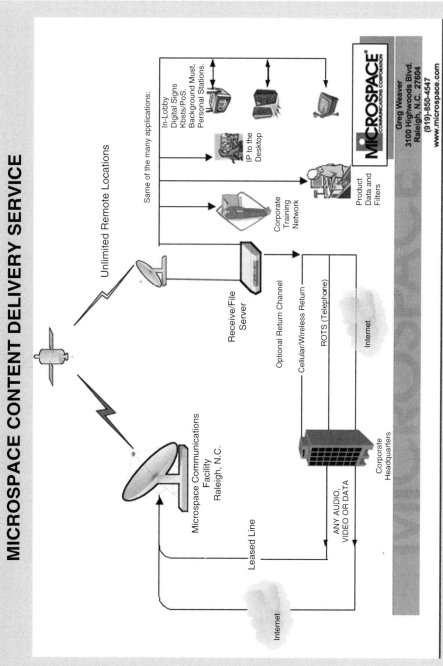

FIGURE 10.3 *Satellite Service Can Be Used to Efficiently and Securely Distribute Content for Digital Signage Networks (Copyright 2007. Property of Microspace. All rights reserved. Used with permission.)*

number of sites increases, the price per site decreases. The satellite signal distribution is also typically faster than the ground system would be, due to the complexity of the latter. Also, satellite vendors allow pricing via a traditional dedicated channel at a fixed price, or via occasional, on-demand use, paying only for what is used. The combination of pricings gives users much needed early system flexibility when assessing which is the best way to implement parts of the business model.

Further, this bank deployment affirmed the fact that a digital signage system delivered via satellite can be quite secure, and can be built to operate separately from the existing bank IT infrastructure. Most satellite vendors also offer quality-of-service insurance because they are so confident of the reliability of their systems. Germantown, MD-headquartered HughesNet is another example of a provider of digital signage whose infrastructure is based on satellite-delivered content. Figure 10.3 demonstrates how a digital signage network using satellite can be constructed. According to the bank's experience, using satellite has the added benefit of eliminating bandwidth-intensive traffic over an existing corporate network, while offering cost savings not often available using a terrestrial delivery system.

11 The Future of Digital Signage

> Some have compared the digital signage industry to the cable industry of the 1980s, and the Internet in the 1990s. Technology firms, out-of-home conglomerates, and the largest advertising agencies in the world are taking notice of digital signage as a whole new media format.
>
> —Eric Unold, co-founder, Webpavement

> Marketers used to try their hardest to reach people at home, when they were watching TV or reading newspapers or magazines. But consumers' viewing and reading habits are so scattershot now that many advertisers say the best way to reach time-pressed consumers is to try to catch their eye, at literally every turn.
>
> —Louise Story, "Anywhere the Eye Can See, It's Likely to See an Ad,"
> *The New York Times*, January 15, 2007

One can't help, after having read this far in this book, thinking of the now near-famous song lyric by the rock and roll group, Timbuk 3, which states, "The future's so bright, I gotta wear shades." Yet, in a metaphorical sense, if the digital signage industry were the singer singing that lyric, the line would, frankly, be something of an exaggeration at this point in the industry's life cycle. This would hold true both for North America and the major international markets where digital signage is burgeoning.

That is to say, the future of digital signage, both in North America and globally, is encouraging, however, that same future is fraught with concerns. These industry concerns include the top-level "paradigm matters,"[1] such as creating appropriate systems and content, and especially creating acceptable systems in public and municipal areas, where safety, clutter, and intrusion are issues. Chapters 3, 4, and 9 have thoroughly addressed many of these issues.

---

1. The term "paradigm matters" here is intended to reference the high-level importance of these concerns.

Indeed, digital signage as a medium could well end up being nothing more than an occasional niche service at best confined to but a few sectors in various commercial and non-commercial arenas. Or, rather than take over for and replace currently existing communication solutions (such as posters, point-of-purchase (POP) radio, and shelf promotions), and rather than compete with currently existing communication channels (such as TV, print, radio, and the Internet), digital signage may become much less than generally accepted (i.e., something far less than a key medium).

Yet, just looking at the current list of "future digital signage devices" does a lot to excite the imaginations of many observers. In fact, because various versions of younger people (call them Gen Y, Gen X, or Gen Whatever) are so adept at controlling the moving image, it is no wonder that digital signage is seen as a very promising medium—one that can break through the clutter that plagues just about all modern-day communicators—by most who observe and live it.

That's because things such as radio frequency identification (RFID) can be wedded to digital signage in a way that allows digital displays to instantly recognize the identity of a person approaching a digital sign. Then the sign "reacts" to the person by displaying content that is unique and relevant to that individual or the group he or she is in. Newly developed scanning devices can read a bar code or other message on a name badge or PDA and react by sending that same content to the individual's PDA for storage and later use.

Thus, for example, a digital sign might display a message in or near New York City's Times Square, advertising a product such as a premium tied to a certain brand (e.g., M & M candies). The audience member can then walk to the screen somewhere on the street, wave his/her PDA or cell phone across the message transfer point, have the information/content instantly transferred to the PDA, and later download that information on how to easily buy that premium online. This all occurs rather seamlessly, usually with a few pushes of just a few buttons or a few clicks of a mouse.

Of all the organizations interviewed and studied for this book, two of the largest, Clear Channel and the Mayo Clinic, are the more remarkable examples of an optimistic present and the enlightening future. (The Mayo Clinic case study is presented in Chapter 1; the Clear Channel case study is presented in this chapter.) These large organizations have built viable digital signage systems and built them well, albeit not without their respective share of challenges. Indeed, each has dealt with these same types of top-level "paradigm matters," that is, creating appropriate systems and content for their environments, as well as creating acceptable systems in public and/or municipal areas, where safety, clutter, and intrusion are top-level issues. In sum, it is entities such as Clear Channel and Mayo Clinic that end up truly moving the global digital signage industry into the future.

Clear Channel Outdoor

Michael Hudes is the global director of Digital Media for the large broadcasting and media conglomerate, Clear Channel Outdoor. Hudes describes his division's role within the company to be that of an "outdoor media company." Hudes estimates that by year-end 2007, his company had deployed more than 100 digital signs in North America such as the one in Figure 11.1. "We have a vast and diverse portfolio, testing digital displays in all major platforms, including airports, malls, taxis, and on street furniture."

Clear Channel has deployed the digital signage mostly in major cities; for a most recent list of those cities, go to the Clear Channel Outdoor website at www.clearchanneloutdoor.com.

What was the biggest motivator for Clear Channel Outdoor to move into the digital signage business? Hudes is rather candid, stating outright that the prime charge was to make money and to do that by generating more profits per square foot of inventory. "Our

FIGURE 11.1 *A Clear Channel Outdoor Digital Sign Located Beside a Busy Freeway (Copyright 2007. Property of Clear Channel Outdoor. All rights reserved. Used with permission.)*

goal is to create value for the real estate, for our customers, and to continue to grow out of home media, to generate more profit per square meter on a bottom line basis. We want to give customers the most flexible and targetable opportunities; we find we can make almost instantaneous copy changes, use more signage on a targeted basis, and expand the industry the way we have gone to market. We have built a network in cities that now compete more effectively for audience against TV, newspapers, magazines, and radio." Sizing up the bigger picture, Hudes and Clear Channel are so satisfied with where the digital signage business is going, the only reason they say they would exit the business is if there were some odd legal reason requiring them to do so.

The single aspect of digital signage that Clear Channel likes the most is the fact that Clear Channel can replace traditional vinyl signs with digital ones and grow its bottom line, plus expand the category for outdoor. Yet, all is not perfect. Asked what he would change in today's digital signage environment, Hudes confessed, "We'd like to be able to do our deployments more quickly, we'd love to be unfettered, and be able to judicially and intelligently deploy these signs and have fewer and less cumbersome local regulations."

Historically, Clear Channel made the move to enter the digital signage market because, as Hudes notes, the technology became more available in large measure because it became less costly. At the start-up phase, a pro forma test was conducted and, based upon its success and a conclusion that Clear Channel could thus receive the right return on investment (ROI), Hudes concludes, "We were good to go." Today, the effectiveness of the Clear Channel Outdoor signage deployments is measured in a number of ways, however, for competitive reasons, Hudes declined to detail.

Clear Channel is currently deploying predominantly LED screens outdoors, and indoors, LCD, plasma, and digital projectors. Clear Channel was one of the first to pioneer the use of digital ink in the United Kingdom, and Hudes suggested that for further notices of new technology, readers and digital signage newcomers go to the website www.magink.com. As an example of new technology being tested, Hudes cited currently deployed Bluetooth and RFID pilot programs.

Content displayed on Clear Channel's digital signage focuses mostly on the outdoors, which means mostly advertisements, but the company also does some "time- and temperature-sponsored content" (which is becoming a new "ad medium," according to Hudes); indoors, Clear Channel displays in malls, an example of which is a content sponsorship Clear Channel had until recently with Yahoo!

Clear Channel Outdoor uses advanced scheduling mechanisms for day parting, week parting, and other time-based targeting of advertising messages, and is in the process of readying its own in-house platform. It does its targeting typically based on the demands of the Clear Channel client. Hudes sees his company's role as merely providing the digital advertising screen space; the client decides much of the rest, especially in the content realm. As is true of most modern digital signage networks, control of the digital signage networks is done remotely via Internet protocol. Clear Channel also assists with the management of the content, taking the content into its servers and doing the scheduling. Further, the Clear Channel Outdoor's digital signage networks are used for worldwide, national, regional, and/or local targeting, often down to a single location or single group of digital signage within a single location.

Platform-wise, Clear Channel Outdoor is currently utilizing a proprietary, dedicated platform solution to enable regional or worldwide content distribution and playback. That system is currently based upon the use of multiple software management platforms from other vendors; however, Clear Channel has plans to consolidate all these into its own single software management platform, globally, during the next few years. The companies Clear Channel currently works with include various LED manufacturers, as well as companies such as Yesco and Daktronics in North America, and Scala in Europe.

Asked about Clear Channel Outdoor digital signage devices installed in in-store displays within a retail or service establishment (i.e., specifically related to product placement), Hudes pointed out that Clear Channel Outdoor was doing this mostly in Europe. Focus of Clear Channel Outdoor's clients' use of the digital signage product is primarily for targeted advertisements. Also the digital signage is used occasionally to build and create brand awareness. "Digital signage, because it is now so flexible and targetable, is working, and working well. So, with Macys, for example, who hasn't used outdoor because it was inflexible, they now use Clear Channel Outdoor digital signage because it is updateable, and they can buy a four-week schedule and make it work," notes Michael Hudes. He adds that also in Europe, the digital signage is used to influence customer behavior, such as by directing customers to different areas of a retail establishment, primarily located in in-store networks.

Turning to legal/regulatory matters, Hudes says Clear Channel Outdoor supports the notion of a standards-setting body to establish technical standards, advocate, promote, do research, educate, and network. He says that at this stage in the digital signage life cycle that "Standards are critical." Indeed, this is an area that Clear Channel probably has more concern over than just about any other company in today's digital signage business, because so many municipalities are in a position to control—and positively or negatively impact—what digital signage Clear Channel Outdoor is able to implement. Notes Hudes, "We are fighting every day to get the right to convert [our signs from vinyl billboards to digital signs]." The main concern for Clear Channel and its brethren is when jurisdictions make blanket prohibitions against outdoor digital signage altogether. Hudes and Clear Channel Outdoor prefer wider permissions or, at minimum, approvals based on a case-by-case review.

Advocacy-wise, to promote the use of digital signage, Hudes and his company promote in every market they enter, and the Clear Channel public affairs team zeros in on building positive relationships with every local government they are planning to be involved with. Asked about a particularly negative reaction to Clear Channel Outdoor's clients' digital signage deployment in public/outdoor locations, Hudes noted just one he can remember, that is, in Minnetonka, MN, where a refusal to allow digital signage was mandated, which has since been overturned by the ruling authorities. Hudes believes this momentum toward allowing more signage is clearly the trend for Clear Channel Outdoor and the future of digital signage (at least in North America).

The remainder of this chapter attempts to paint some of that future, and addresses that future by way of several examples of some of digital signage's most important types of constituents. Finishing up, the chapter reviews various business implications and important growth factors.

The Impact of Digital Signage

A good way to measure the future of an industry is to address its future impact relative to where it will be deployed, but, more importantly, who will deploy it.

For Advertising Agencies

As the leading stakeholders among those that are engaged in digital signage, and among those that can reasonably be expected to one day engage it, advertising agencies and their retail clients are likely the most important, at least from a standpoint of their financial deep pockets and their physical numbers. Focusing just on ad agencies, these digital signage players are certainly pleased when they look into their crystal balls and their futures inside the digital signage world.

Among all the new advertising venues—Internet and wireless cell phones included—digital signage could rival both (maybe not both together, but at least each separately). Just the fact that there is something out there such as digital signage has got to be encouraging.

History shows it's a rare time in the life cycle of the advertising industry when advertisers and their clients could look ahead and realistically say, "Digital signage...this is a great example of the medium of tomorrow." Indeed, already the industry is seeing significant shifts of advertising revenues to new alternatives, such as digital signage, IPTV, mobile, and Internet opportunities.

Future Developments

The following future digital signage developments present particular promise to advertising agencies (and by natural relationship, to their retail clients, as well):

- RFID (discussed further later in this chapter).

- Interactive (discussed further later in this chapter).

- Device-to-device downloads (discussed further later in this chapter).

- Sensory applications: as noted in Chapter 9, the Japanese beer brewer Kirin and Japanese telecom provider NTT Communications offer their recent partnership to release scents from a digital sign into a heavily trafficked area of Tokyo as an example of this new experiment in public advertising.

- The 360° "surround video" hardware, with specifically designed content: this is just one of many hardware deployments, especially on the hardware display side, that will get people on both sides of the screen more excited about what the screen can do to help send—and sell—the message.

- Seamless content in almost every instance: as exciting as the hardware potential may be, the content opportunity is even greater, again where both sides of the display unit benefit remarkably from content that engages and excites, both from the standpoint of what it says and from the standpoint of how well it was produced.

The impact of digital signage on the Madison Avenue community will eventually be huge. That is because where it is done right, it will work. As a result, billions of dollars annually will be spent by those ad agencies, on behalf of satisfied clients, getting the message out. As noted in Chapter 3, this message delivery function strikes at the core raison d'être of digital signage, which is to "...convey a message, presumably one that is important both to the displayer and to the audience."

Future Locales

Again, primarily centered around retail applications, in addition to today's primary sites indicated in Chapters 1, 3, and 6, the future of digital signage will find applications in a wide variety of locales, some suggesting remarkable growth into new deployments. The following are some noteworthy examples.

- In individual shopping carts, at every store (or at least the larger ones), instantly logging in purchases, providing data and compilations of data to assist purchases, other information, advertisements, and probably even entertainment.

- In individual vehicles, as part of their in-dash and on-screen systems.

- In (and on top of) commercial vehicles, such as on seats or on ceilings (or both) in public taxis, busses, trains, and planes.

- In lots of retail spaces, including restrooms and changing rooms, the latter being a good place to obtain additional information, both at a critical purchase time and in an important setting.

- In all travel centers, meeting the customer from when he or she arrives or at departure time.

- In all government and institutional facilities, aimed at making otherwise difficult chores that much easier.

- In houses of worship, perhaps not only via screens mounted on walls and from ceilings, but also via screens mounted on the rear of the seat in front (not unlike the more modern airplane deployments of individual passenger TV screens).

- As it relates to surfaces, digital signage will even pervade floor surfaces, whereby when one steps on a trigger, the digital signage device will, in turn, also trigger a response aimed directly at the consumer, and likely more and more in the future, at the specific consumer.

- As it relates to kiosks, they will be their own version of extreme interactivity (discussed later).

- In any place the mind can imagine (short of places where people have clearly and simply decided not to offer digital signage). Indeed, the mantra for the future deployment of digital signage globally will have to be along the lines of "Just imagine it" (but do deploy it correctly, so that the audience enjoys and appreciates the message, and you as a digital signage participant get what you need from it).

At Retail

For retailers, more and more they are individually seeking out digital signage as a new answer and alternative to traditional signage methods, such as billboards and broadcasting. In many instances, and probably as a whole, the retailers are leading their ad agencies in the move to at least investigate the new digital signage industry subsector.

The former chairman and CEO of the large and respected ad firm Digitas, David Kenny, now heads a Digitas division called "Digital Advertising Strategy." Kenny's self-stated goal is to create "a global digital ad network that uses offshore labor to create thousands of versions of ads. Then, using data about consumers and computer algorithms, the network will decide which advertising message to show at which moment to every person who turns on a computer, cell phone, or— eventually—a television."

Moreover, in the past, a major manufacturer might create a half dozen ads to target different demographics. Today, that number has moved into the thousands of ad versions. Notes digital signage guru Bill Gerba in one of his late-2007 blogs, "In the future [the number of ads for one message or product] could climb even higher, with the eventual outcome being that ads are assembled on-the-fly and customized for every viewer, based on a database of collected information that includes viewing habits, purchase histories, and the like." This viewer-by-viewer customizing and profiling is the kind that Google has been talking about for years, and more recently firms like Pick-n-Click, SpotRunner, and Visible World have investigated.

Perhaps even more tantalizing in terms of future interest and provocation is the idea of user-generated content (UGC). Rather than a professional that is paid to do so, UGC usually comes from the frequent shopper or user of a particular product or service. Recently, Apple Computer accepted an ad created by a random customer for one of its new devices and made it into a national advertising that aired thousands of times in front of tens of millions of potential purchasers. This same kind of creative development by passionate users will soon begin to populate digital signs, the result of which should be quite breathtaking (not unlike turning some digital signage systems into a commercial, corporate, and/or institutional version of YouTube).

Meanwhile, closer to what we already know today, the all-important POP within any given retail establishment (or very nearby) is where most believe the majority of purchase decisions are made (and thus where the majority of digital signage development and deployment will occur). New supermarkets, clothing stores, and malls will no longer be "retro-fitted" with digital signage in ways that appear to be after-the-fact implementations; instead, those cutting-edge shopping locales and developers will implement digital screens in many sizes, and many locales, and many form factors (e.g., flat, small, big, round, from ceilings, on floors, in walls), which are designed from the start by architects and building contractors who know the art of retail and digital signage.

In Education

Without exaggeration, the idea of the institutional use of digital signage, especially in educational centers, has got to rival even the optimism people have for digital signage in the advertising-retail space. That is because well-done digital signage does quite a good job of conveying an informational message, and that is obviously at the heart of most education.

Specifically, at colleges, for example, the entry to the campus would feature an appropriate and attractive sign, offering tasteful and extremely helpful content centered around activities, accomplishments by the community's members, directions, and the like. At parking facilities, more specific digital signage informational content would be available, as educational patrons neared their destinations.

One pundit has even suggested that in the future, campus visitors will enter a search into a browser linked to a college's website, perhaps trying to locate a particular office in a particular part of the university. Once that is done, the college then automatically populates its computer system with information about that website visitor. When the visitor arrives on campus, RFID information that was also automatically provided to the college system will trigger the front sign to read, "Welcome, Mrs. Jones. Please proceed left to Taft Hall parking lot C." Once at lot C, as Mrs. Jones walks by the digital sign there, her RFID tag in her purse would again communicate with a chip and antenna on the digital sign, which would automatically convey more information to Mrs. Jones about where she is going, what she might see there, etc.

Moreover, at every type of campus, cafeterias, waiting lounges, reception areas, gaming rooms, and many other community gathering points, digital signage will deliver institutional and individual messages (see Figure 11.2). Basic content alone will feature commercial messages (e.g., athletic event ticket sales and local community vendor sales), local city and community events, graduation and other student progress information, webcasts of speeches by famous speakers, and publicity announcements about forthcoming student, faculty, and parent events. Class rescheduling, weather delays, and event cancellations are other uses for digital signage, and digital signage networks on campus are also an ideal spot from which to communicate emergency and security messages. Moreover, although a subtle control, no less an important one is the fact that most campus digital signage screens are placed and controlled in such a way as to make turning them off or turning the audio down difficult. As in malls, campus kiosks, including interactivity, can be deployed with positive results.

In the classroom, there will be a strong digital signage presence, as well. In a NEC white paper "Benefits of Dynamic Signage in Higher Education," Russell Young

FIGURE 11.2 *A Digital Sign Display in the Reception Room of the Price Business College at the Norman Campus of the University of Oklahoma. In the Future, the University Expects to Install Digital Signs in Many More Locations, to Supplement This One and the Several That It Has Prominently Installed at the Huge 100,000+ Fan Football Stadium (Copyright 2007. Property of Jimmy Schaeffler. All rights reserved.)*

notes that large format displays will continue to take the place of standard instructional mediums, such as white boards and projectors. Young states that, "Interactive touch overlays can assist professors by providing a 'dynamic whiteboard' to allow for content and research to be saved at the touch of a button. Plus, overhead displays allow for many more uses than traditional projectors. The displays can be directly connected to the professors' laptop, campus cable network, or other multimedia input." Specifically related to enhancing the learning experience for students, those students can then use digital signage and related multimedia learning tools to directly create, collaborate, and share their work on the digital signs with others.

In Other Venues

One of the biggest developments in the outdoor or large indoor arena environment of digital signage promises to be the ability of screen makers to improve the resolution of screens, especially large ones at large venues housing or addressing hundreds of thousands or even millions over relatively short periods of time. For example, Japanese electronics maker Mitsubishi announced late in 2007 its planned deployment of a single screen digital sign with more that 27 million pixels. Yet, on the other side of this type of digital signage growth, a handful of cities such as Phoenix, AZ, have recently heard from groups of citizens concerned about "light pollution," in the form of light that negatively affects the ability of astronomers to practice their occupation or avocation. If digital signage, as an industry, is going to progress and perhaps even flourish, it will have to come to terms with people and objections such as these, probably in the form of compromises affecting how and when digital signage is utilized.

A few other types of digital signage screens are entering the market or are being talked about. For example, companies such as German-based Litefest are rolling out round screen, kiosk-like, two- or three-foot diameter, free-standing round screens, such as those shown in Figure 1.12. These are being deployed in places such as retail malls and airports, especially where high visibility is important and space is at a premium.

One particularly interesting and brilliant display of digital signage comes in the form of regular t-shirts that feature digital signage screens on either the front or the back of the t-shirt, and are operated by small batteries attached to the shirt, together with small devices that hold and convey the content to the screen. These have proved ideal for events and by specific company applications. As shown in Figures 11.3a and b, among the newest versions of digital signage implementations, these t-shirts can be a remarkable and eye-catching way of conveying important messages to important audiences.

Some today are discussing the concept of digital signage in the form of an entire side of a large, high-rise building (of tens or scores of stories), every window of which would make up a small part of the total screen. Cities such as New York, Chicago, and Tokyo are expected to be ideal candidates for major unveilings of these types of mass-image digital signage displays. In this manner, the entire skyscraper will become a new version of a digital sign.

In airports, passengers disembarking from different locations globally will have messages on lengthy walled screens, specifically aimed at them. Thus, for passengers arriving from Hong Kong on an Air China plane, some of the seamless advertising facing them as they head for customs and immigration at New York City's JFK Airport in Queens will tell them not only about the entry process, but also slip in an ad for a transportation-to-the-city service, as well as an informational piece about sightseeing in the Big Apple (such as China Town or the Feast of San Gennaro every September).

(a)

(b)

FIGURE 11.3 *Digital Signage Developed So That It Is Conveyed On The Front or Back of a T-Shirt (Copyright 2008. Property of Brand Marketers. All rights reserved. Used with permission.)*

Also, as noted in Chapter 9, travel centers, including train and subway stations, are stepping into new digital signage growth areas, such as that featured in Shanghai's subway, with its soap opera-like daily story segment about a new girl who finds a boy in the big city, and falls in love while drinking her Starbucks coffee. Note that because they often do not strictly control their environments, and because they come from different historical bases when it comes to advertising legacies and perspectives, future international digital signage country locales are expected to drive the growth of the medium, suggesting unique and extremely creative new uses that would sometimes never make the light of day in a more restrictive North America.

Most interesting is what urban planners, builders, and architects are thinking about as they get ready for much of the future. As noted in Chapter 3, the builders of the mall adjacent to the site of the 2008 National Football League's Super Bowl have done a remarkable job of interspersing digital with static (or traditional billboard) signage. So, too, will future planners for other large events—especially trade shows and sporting and other entertainment events—find an important place for digital signage among the organizational plans. A perfect example is the 2010 Commonwealth Games in Delhi, India, which, through a cinema-sponsored alliance, will offer digital signage in zones such as refreshment areas, waiting areas, washrooms, staircases, and near auditorium doors. Content will be centered around a handful of daily third-party ads, film information, and entertainment- and event-related news.

Specific Future Applications

One digital signage development that is clearly a part of the future is the overall industry effort to make each digital signage unit an all-in-one device. Thus, the operational software, the technology (possibly including a DVR-like hard drive, for example), the server, indeed, every element of a single site digital signage deployment will simply come as one unit, out of the box, and will set up on-site, almost instantly. As noted more specifically in Chapter 9, citing the "Digital-Sign-In-A-Box" product line by Mediatile in South Africa, these innovations will further ignite the future of digital signage.

Another trend that eases the stress of deployment and operation, especially as it concerns those that live with a digital signage application day to day, will be the ability to send almost every pertinent piece of content via a wireless or satellite-delivered wireless signal. Further, on the audience or end-user side, signals to and from the single unit digital signage device will be sent wirelessly to and from hand-held devices, such as PDAs and cell phones. Like the all-in-one unit innovation, this ease of access and elimination of technical barriers is a godsend to many in business, as well as their core audiences.

Kiosks promise to allow their own special version of interactivity. Combining the technology and features of digital signage, they are known in some circles as hybrid digital signs. The devices can go instantly from presentation of content to an interactive mode once someone walks nearby or touches the screen. Environmental conditions, such as a sensing of bad weather or night-versus-day, can also trigger certain reactions by the kiosk device. When shoppers navigate through the interactive branching presentation, they can get information like product recommendations, quality ratings, pricing, and availability. Some more advanced servers can not only provide information needed for the presentations, but also store information about the consumer and his or her habits, interests, likes, and dislikes. Armed with that kind of data, many servers can then be programmed to take the next logical step, that is, give the consumer recommendations for similar products and services that would fit his or her profile. Like any other digital signage device, for most users, the goal is the same: extend the scope of marketing well beyond the store, and well into the hearts, souls, and homes of shoppers who interact.

Credit cards interacting with kiosks and similar hardware such as gas station pumps are a promising future application, as well. In this model, a consumer slides a personal credit card into the pump's reader, and verifies identity via entry of a personal code, at which point the device starts delivering content that is specifically and uniquely directed to that, and only that, consumer in front of the pump. Such information might contain stock quotes, video showing specific sports of interest, news items from specific local, regional or world spots, and so on. Or better even still for the gas station pump owner, the consumer would have ads presented to him or her based upon the computer server's read of his or her interests that day, combined with an understanding of his or her prior preferences of goods, services, or even advertisements.

Predicted future applications of e-paper include e-paper books capable of storing digital versions of many books, with only one book displayed on the pages at any one time. The same will be true with e-paper magazines. Electronic posters and similar advertisements in shops and stores have already been demonstrated.

Measurement of audience interest, usage, and buying patterns, for example, is likely to also take a quantum leap when it comes to digital signage. Future forms of measurement are likely to gain significant technological sophistication, nonetheless, much will return to basic fundamental survey practices (i.e., engage the consumer and tally the answers).

RFID

When one talks RFID, typically two images come to mind. One is via the image in the movie *Minority Report*, where the potential consumer is identified and tracked, mostly for the purpose of getting that consumer to be interested in the services and products. The other image is of one being able to actually and positively react to the transfer of information that an RFID connotes. Both images can and should represent positive digital signage responses.

Concerns about privacy and piracy will both tend to continue to plague the RFID side of the digital signage industry, especially if there are negative examples of organizations or individuals taking undue advantage of consumers via the use of RFID data and resources. Technical and financial roadblocks are also anticipated (e.g., controlling the costs of the passive tags and especially the more expensive active tags, the latter of which contain their own batteries). In the end, a great deal of RFID success will turn on whether consumers are able to opt into the service voluntarily, and whether there are strict controls over the use of individualized and personal consumer data.

A good example of a RFID application that is nothing but consumer-friendly is that of a grocery store scenario, where the consumer could hold a bottle of cooking sauce in front of a kiosk. The server would then match the sauce with the ingredients needed to make a special barbeque, and direct the shopper to the specific items in the same store. Another example is an RFID tag on a product that will then read usage or pricing information to someone shopping who is blind and needs to understand data on the label by hearing instead of visually.

Interactive

For an advertiser, device-to-device interactivity could mean dozens of opportunities daily to get a particular message not only in front of a potential buyer, but also into his or her all-precious PDA and/or cellphone.

Video gaming is also thought of or described by many as a form of digital signage, and it is likely to become more so in the future, as it, too, as a medium, flexes and changes.

What should be particularly attractive to most consumers will be future interactive applications of digital signage. One of the best is the idea of "getting more." So, for example, if while quickly passing a digital sign on a street corner, the consumer wants more (but doesn't have the time just then), he or she simply activates the interactive downloading feature on his or her handheld device, and the information is sent, received, and stored for later retrieval. Mobile phones are being created to employ watermarking technology which, in turn, activates the Internet web to transfer content such as coupons or links to further offers.

Business Projections

As noted in Chapters 1 and 3, another measure of future potential for the digital signage industry and its participants is the numbers involved. Triple digit billions of dollars growth is expected sometime in the next 5–10 years. The numbers of digital signage screens will leap into the millions and tens of millions of units deployed in the same time frames, or sooner. Yet perhaps the most important measurement, which will one day be the number of people whose decisions were positively influenced by the digital signage content they viewed, will remain an elusive data point. Nonetheless, it, too, is coming closer and closer to regular measurement, and will deeply impact future business models and their subsequent business projections. This is another area where the concept of industry standards appears attractive.

Figure 11.4 shows the estimated growth of digital signage relative to traditional signage during the time period of 2007–2010. Although a conservative estimate, the 4-year growth curve rises from an estimated 4% in 2007, seven times, to 28% in 2010.

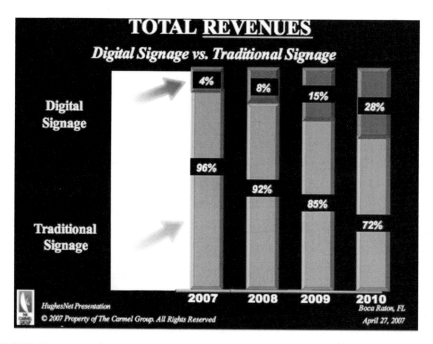

FIGURE 11.4 *Industry Experts Predict That Digital Signage Revenues Over the Next 4 Years Are Going to Significantly Erode Those of Traditional Signage (Copyright 2008. Property of The Carmel Group. All rights reserved. Used with permission.)*

Return on Investment Models/Case Studies

The tweaking of any technology tends to lower the cost of the units, as larger volumes are produced, but concurrently, it often also perfects the business models and allows for less risk and greater overall profit. Expect the same thing to occur in the realm of digital signage.

At the same time, more different and detailed business models will result from all of the new future digital signage deployments. This should put more and more business people in a position to at least consider digital signage and, if it can't work in their current business environment, for them to come back months, or years, later and try again.

As but one example, as mentioned above, especially for those subscription video operators with pre-existing local video production capacities, the transition to digital signage content production (and maybe to complete turn-key operations as discussed in Chapter 7) might be well worth investigating.

Network Integration

Once a potential patron walks into a given environment, the owner and/or controller of that space has the opportunity to influence the patron's experience, for better or worse. As more institutions, especially larger ones with deeper pockets, come to realize the potential of a digital signage network, their use will proliferate, and as a result, whatever good or even great quality content that is out there will indeed get better. And that means the pivotal consumer experience improves.

Key Growth Factors

Future key growth factors, not surprisingly, turn on both positive and negative influences. Negative influences, as noted repeatedly throughout the book, are primarily related to the changing world. Younger consumers have been given the technology to allow them to choose, and they have chosen not to have irrelevant and boring content, especially in the form of mass audience advertisements, crammed down their throats. At the same time, they have chosen, *en masse*, to have more frequent and convenient access to all types of content, which presumably includes digital signage content that is relevant and high-quality and helps the audience, wherever the audiences may be.

From a media perspective, it's important for advertisers and retailers to remember that satellite radio, digital video recorders (such as TiVo), and blockers for online advertising, for example, are increasingly eroding the value and delivery of these types of "old" advertising. This trend is likely to accelerate, as young people who are accustomed to media interactivity—and to tuning out marketing messages—enter their middle age.

Reacting to that change is the phenomena of digital signage that can be relevant and exciting to the end user. Thus, in the not-too-distant future, traditional one-way electronic media that is laced with mass audience advertising (such as multichannel and broadcast TV, as well as commercial radio) will decline in significance, leaving the retail physical location as the only place (or medium) that is likely to reach most consumers. This, in turn, suggests sink or swim opportunities for broadcasters and multichannel operators, who are now given the opportunity to find their way into these new venues. Especially for cable or telephone video providers with local production facilities, digital signage suggests a very plausible future business model. In addition, on a slightly related level, there might well be opportunities for many digital signage newcomers and existing players to move slowly into the home digital signage environment, via wireless connected devices such as digital frames, that show photos relayed to the device wirelessly from the home or another computer.

As retail stores are increasingly recognizing themselves as a medium, the value of digital signage networks and other in-store media (e.g., signage, floor decals, shelf talkers, product packaging, sampling, events, and so on) will ramp up in value within the marketing community. This will allow in-store screen networks to be regularly included in the media-planning process of both retailers and manufacturers.

Notes the U.K.'s Stuart Chambers, "People need to push back against the historical and often overly conservative inertia, and realize that digital signage is a very flexible media, companies will start making good money from it, and the technology and other costs will keep coming down. Digital signage? It's about the imaginative use of content and data."

Baby-TV's Gavin Anderson, already a wounded, yet successful, veteran of digital signage combat notes, "Digital signage is about multiples, so we publish once and use the same content many times, more interestingly, and more affordably." Anderson sees particular progress once one's content can get pushed on to people's mobile phones, especially while, as he puts it, "... they are waiting to see you. Find the space where someone is willing to engage with that video or other image, engage people in public places to be receptive to the story you tell them. People can be watching a screen everywhere they go. Find them and then package that story they want into the right format."

Summarizes Canada's Graeme Spicer, "The key is to get the right content into the right place to the right person. That is the real future of the digital signage medium."

Is it time to begin shopping for those shades?

Appendix A: Directory of North American Digital Signage

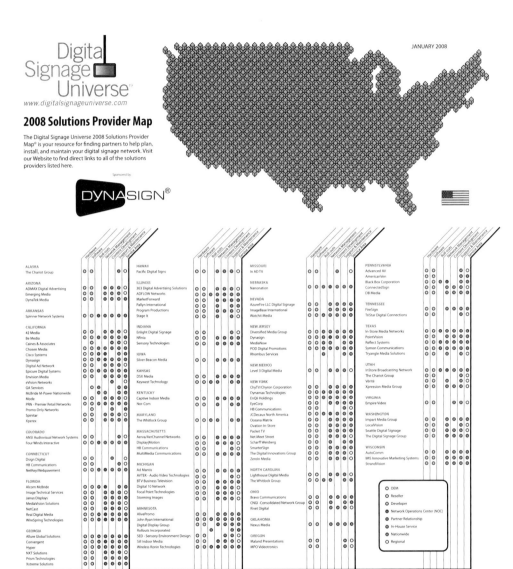

Digital Signage Universe™

www.digitalsignageuniverse.com

2008 Solutions Provider Map

The Digital Signage Universe 2008 Solutions Provider Map© is your resource for finding partners to help plan, install, and maintain your digital signage network. Visit our Website to find direct links to all of the solutions providers listed here.

Sponsored by

DYNASIGN®

JANUARY 2008

	Hardware	Software	Roll-outs	Network Management	Content Development	Support & Maintenance	Service Area
ALASKA							
The Chariot Group	◎	◎				●	○
ARIZONA							
ADMAX Digital Advertising	◎	◎		●	●	●	○
Emerging Media	◎	◎		●	●	●	○
DynaTek Media	◎	◎		●	●	●	●
ARKANSAS							
Spinner Network Systems	◎	◎	●	●	●	●	●
CALIFORNIA							
42 Media	◎	◎		●	●	●	○
Be Media	◎	◎	●	●	●	●	●
Caines & Associates		◎			●	●	○
Chosen Media	◎	◎	●	●	●	●	●
Cisco Systems	◎	◎	●	●		●	●
Dynasign	◎	◎	●	●	●	●	●
Digital Ad Network	◎	◎		●	●	●	○
Epicure Digital Systems	◎	◎	●	●	●	●	●
Envision Media	◎	◎		●	●	●	●
eVision Networks					●		○
GA Services		◎	●			●	●
McBride M-Power Nationwide			●	●		●	●
Mode	◎	◎		●	●	●	○
PRN - Premier Retail Networks	◎	◎	●	●	●	●	●
Promo Only Networks		◎			●		●
Spinitar	◎	◎		●	●	●	○
Xperex	◎	◎		●	●	●	●
COLORADO							
ANSI Audiovisual Network Systems	◎	◎				●	○
Four Winds Interactive	◎	◎	●	●	●	●	●
CONNECTICUT							
Dsign Digital	◎	◎			●		○
HB Communications	◎	◎				●	○
NetKey/Webpavement	◎	◎	●	●	●	●	●
FLORIDA							
Alcorn McBride	◎	◎	●	●		●	●
Image Technical Services	◎	◎		●	●	●	○
Janus Displays	◎	◎		●	●	●	●
MediaVision Solutions	◎	◎		●	●	●	○
NetCast	◎	◎		●	●	●	○
Real Digital Media	◎	◎	●	●	●	●	●
WireSpring Technologies	◎	◎	●	●	●	●	●
GEORGIA							
Allure Global Solutions	◎	◎	●	●	●	●	●
Convergent	◎	◎	●	●	●	●	●
Hyper	◎	◎	●	●	●	●	●
NXT Solutions	◎	◎		●	●	●	○
Prism Technologies	◎	◎		●	●	●	●
Xstreme Solutions	◎	◎		●	●	●	●
HAWAII							
Pacific Digital Signs	◎	◎		●	●	●	○
ILLINOIS							
303 Digital Advertising Solutions	◎	◎		●	●	●	○
ADFLOW Networks	◎	◎	●	●	●	●	●
MarketForward	◎	◎		●	●	●	●
Pallyn International	◎	◎		●		●	●
Program Productions	◎	◎		●	●	●	○
Stage It	◎	◎		●		●	○
INDIANA							
Enlight Digital Signage	◎	◎				●	○
Nfinia	◎	◎		●	●	●	●
Sensory Technologies	◎	◎		●	●	●	●
IOWA							
Silver Beacon Media	◎	◎		●	●	●	●
KANSAS							
DSX Media	◎	◎		●	●	●	●
Keywest Technology	◎	◎	●	●		●	●
KENTUCKY							
Captive Indoor Media	◎	◎		●	●	●	●
Nor-Com	◎	◎		●		●	●
MARYLAND							
The Whitlock Group	◎	◎	●	●		●	●
MASSACHUSETTS							
Aerva/AerChannel Networks	◎	◎		●	●	●	●
Display|Motion	◎	◎		●	●	●	○
HB Communications	◎	◎				●	○
MultiMedia Communications	◎	◎		●	●	●	●
MICHIGAN							
Ad Mantis	◎	◎		●	●	●	●
AVTEK - Audio Video Technologies	◎	◎				●	○
BTV Business Television	◎	◎		●	●	●	●
Digital 10 Network	◎	◎		●	●	●	○
Focal Point Technologies	◎	◎		●	●	●	○
Storming Images	◎	◎		●	●	●	○
MINNESOTA							
AlivePromo	◎	◎		●	●	●	●
John Ryan International	◎	◎	●	●	●	●	●
Digital Display Group	◎	◎		●	●	●	●
Rollouts Incorporated			●			●	●
SED - Sensory Environment Design	◎	◎			●	●	○
Sill Indoor Media	◎	◎		●	●	●	○
Wireless Ronin Technologies	◎	◎	●	●	●	●	●
MISSOURI							
In AD TV	◎	◎			●		○
NEBRASKA							
Nanonation	◎	◎	●	●	●	●	●
NEVADA							
AzureFire LLC Digital Signage	◎	◎		●	●	●	●
ImageBase International	◎	◎		●	●	●	●
Watchit Media	◎	◎	●	●	●	●	●
NEW JERSEY							
Diversified Media Group	◎	◎	●	●	●	●	●
Dynasign	◎	◎	●	●	●	●	●
MediaNow	◎	◎	●	●		●	●
POD Digital Promotions	◎	◎	●	●	●	●	●
Rhombus Services			●			●	●
NEW MEXICO							
Level 3 Digital Media	◎	◎		●	●	●	○
NEW YORK							
ChyTV/Chyron Corporation	◎	◎		●	●	●	●
Dynamax Technologies	◎	◎	●	●	●	●	●
EnQii Holdings	◎	◎	●	●	●	●	●
EyeCorp	◎	◎		●	●	●	●
HB Communications	◎	◎				●	○
JCDecaux North America	◎	◎	●	●	●	●	●
Oceana Matrix	◎	◎		●	●	●	●
Ovation In-Store	◎	◎		●	●	●	●
Packet TV	◎	◎		●	●	●	●
Net Meet Street	◎	◎		●	●	●	○
Scharff Weisberg	◎	◎		●		●	●
SmarterSign	◎	◎		●	●	●	●
The Digital Innovations Group	◎	◎		●	●	●	○
ZeroIn Media	◎	◎		●	●	●	○
NORTH CAROLINA							
Lighthouse Digital Media	◎	◎		●	●	●	○
The Whitlock Group	◎	◎	●	●		●	●
OHIO							
Bravo Communications	◎	◎		●	●	●	●
CNGI -Consolidated Network Group	◎	◎		●		●	●
Rivet Digital	◎	◎		●	●	●	○
OKLAHOMA							
Nexus Media	◎	◎		●	●	●	●
OREGON							
Maland Presentations	◎	◎				●	○
MPO Videotronics	◎	◎				●	○
PENNSYLVANIA							
Advanced AV	◎	◎				●	○
AmericanVen	◎	◎				●	●
Black Box Corporation	◎	◎	●	●		●	●
ConnectedSign	◎	◎		●	●	●	○
DB Media	◎	◎		●	●	●	●
TENNESSEE							
FireSign	◎	◎		●	●	●	●
TriStar Digital Connections	◎	◎				●	○
TEXAS							
In-Store Media Networks	◎	◎	●	●	●	●	●
PointVision	◎	◎		●	●	●	●
Reflect Systems	◎	◎	●	●	●	●	●
Symon Communications	◎	◎	●	●	●	●	●
Tryangle Media Solutions	◎	◎		●		●	○
UTAH							
InStore Broadcasting Network	◎	◎	●	●	●	●	●
The Chariot Group	◎	◎				●	○
Vérité	◎	◎		●		●	○
Xpression Media Group	◎	◎		●	●	●	○
VIRGINIA							
Empire Video	◎	◎			●	●	○
WASHINGTON							
Impart Media Group	◎	◎		●	●	●	●
LocalVision	◎	◎		●		●	○
Seattle Digital Signage	◎	◎		●	●	●	○
The Digital Signage Group	◎	◎		●	●	●	●
WISCONSIN							
AutoComm	◎	◎		●	●	●	●
IMS Innovative Marketing Systems	◎	◎		●	●	●	●
StrandVision	◎	◎		●	●	●	●

- ◎ OEM
- ◎ Reseller
- ◎ Developer
- ● Network Operations Center (NOC)
- ● Partner Relationship
- ● In-House Service
- ● Nationwide
- ○ Regional

Network Integration Service Providers

COMPANY NAME	HEADQUARTERED IN	WEBSITE
AMERICAVEN, LLC	Bethlehem, PA	www.americaven.com
APOLLO DISPLAY TECHNOLOGIES	Ronkonkoma, NY	www.apollodisplays.com
AUDIO VIDEO INTERACTIVE INC.	Scottsdale, AZ	www.avi-electronics.com
AVDO DISPLAYS LTD	Livonia, MI	www.avdodisplays.com
BROADSIGN INTERNATIONAL INC.	Montreal	www.broadsign.com
DG2L TECHNOLOGIES	Rocklin, CA	www.dg2l.com
DICON CO. LTD. USA	Reston, VA	www.dicon.co.kr/english
DIGITAL INNOVATIONS GROUP	Rochester, NY	www.thedigroup.com
DIGITAL VIEW MEDIA	New York, NY	www.digitalviewmedia.com
DISPLAY VISION SOLUTIONS	Piqua, OH	www.display-vision.com
HDTV SUPPLY, INC.	Thousand Oaks, CA	www.HDTVSupply.com
HUGHES NETWORK SYSTEMS	Germantown, MD	www.hughes.com
INLIGHTEN, INC.	Depew, NY	www.inlighten.net
INTERNET CONNECTIVITY GROUP	Lake Forest, CA	www.internetconnectivity group.com
MEGAGROOVES LLC	Bloomington, IN	www.megagrooves.com
NANONATION	Lincoln, NE	www.nanonation.net
NETWORK TECHNOLOGIES INC.	Aurora, OH	www.networktechinc.com
NEXCOM USA	Fremont, CA	www.nexcom.com
NEXUS DIGITAL SIGNS	Dallas, TX	www.nexusdigitalsigns.com
ONEXUM CORPORATION	Upland, CA	www.onexum.com
PREMIER STUDIOS/PREMIERI	Lenexa, KS	www.premierstudios.com
SAAZE CORPORATION	Los Altos, CA	www.saaze.com
SHERLOCK SYSTEMS	Buffalo Grove, IL	www.sherlocksystems.com
SMATTER INCORPORATED	New York, NY	www.smatter.tv

North American Network Management Service Providers

COMPANY NAME	HEADQUARTERED IN	WEBSITE
3M DIGITAL SIGNAGE	Bainbridge Island, WA	www.3MDigitalSignage.com
ABT INTERACTIVE	Chatsworth, CA	www.abtinteractive.com
AGN PROFESSIONAL	New York, NY	www.agnpro.com
ALLURE DIGITAL MEDIA, INC.	Atlanta, GA	www.alluredm.com
AUDIO VIDEO INTERACTIVE INC.	Scottsdale, AZ	www.avi-electronics.com
BROADSIGN INTERNATIONAL INC.	Montreal	www.broadsign.com
CHRISTIE	Cypress, CA	www.christiedigital.com
CHYRON CORPORATION/CHYTV	Melville, NY	www.chytv.com
CYBER OPERATIONS INC.	Pelham, AL	www.cyberoperations.com/cyberdan.html
DIGITAL VIEW MEDIA	New York, NY	www.digitalviewmedia.com
DIGITAL VIEW, INC.	Morgan Hill, CA	www.digitalview.com
DS-IQ	Bellevue, WA	www.ds-iq.com
DYNATEK MEDIA	Scottsdale, AZ	www.dynatekmedia.com
ENSEO, INC.	Richardson, TX	www.enseo.com
EYECAPTARE LLC	Milltown, NJ	www.EyeCaptare.com
FRAMERATE	Salt Lake City, UT	www.framerate.com
IMANAGEIT, INC.	Fishers, IN	www.imanageit.net
K-WILL CORPORATION	Torrance, CA	www.kwillcorporation.com
MICROSPACE COMMUNICATIONS	Raleigh, NC	www.microspace.com
MINICOM ADVANCED SYSTEMS	Linden, NJ	www.minicom.com
NAVITOUCH	Tustin, CA	www.navitouch.com
NETKEY	East Haven, CT	www.netkey.com
NEXUS DIGITAL SIGNS	Dallas, TX	www.nexusdigitalsigns.com
PLANAR SYSTEMS, INC.	Beaverton, OR	www.planar.com
SPOTMAGIC, INC.	San Francisco, CA	www.spotmagic.com/sms
THE MEDIATILE COMPANY	Scotts Valley, CA	www.mediatile.com
THE WOW FACTOR, INC	Studio City, CA	www.wowfactor.net
VIA MEDIA, INC.	Highland Village, TX	www.viamediainc.com
VISIBLEINTERACTIVE	Scranton, PA	www.visibleinteractive.com
X2O MEDIA	Montreal	www.x2omedia.com

North American Content Creation Service Providers

COMPANY NAME	HEADQUARTERED IN	WEBSITE
1STOPDIGITAL	Brentwood, TN	http://www.1stopdigital.com/
23D DIGITAL MEDIA	Atlanta, GA	http://www.23d.com/
AMX	Huntington, NY	http://www.amx.com/
BLUE PONY	Fort Wayne, IN	http://www.bluepony.com/
CHRMEDIA	Las Vegas, NV	http://www.chrmedia.com/
CUSTOMWEATHER, INC.	San Francisco, CA	www.customweather.com
DATA CALL TECHNOLOGIES	Houston, TX	www.datacalltech.com
DIGITAL VIEW MEDIA	New York, NY	www.digitalviewmedia.com
DYNATEK MEDIA	Scottsdale, AZ	www.dynatekmedia.com
EVISION NETWORKS	Los Angeles, CA	www.evisionnetworks.com
FIRESIGN INC.	Nashville, TN	www.firesign.net
FOUR WINDS INTERACTIVE	Arvada, CO	www.fourwindsinteractive.com
HUGHES NETWORK SYSTEMS, LLC	Germantown, MD	http://www.hughes.com/
LASTING IMAGE MEDIA	Baltimore, MD	www.lastingimagemedia.com
MARKETFORWARD	Chicago, IL	www.marketforward.com
MIND OVER EYE	Santa Monica, CA	www.mindovereye.com
NETKEY	East Haven, CT	www.netkey.com
NEXUS DIGITAL SIGNS	Dallas, TX	www.nexusdigitalsigns.com
PALAZZO INTERCREATIVE	Seattle, WA	http://www.palazzo.com/
POPSTAR NETWORKS, INC.	Lawrence, KS	http://www.popstarnetworks.com/
SCALA, INC.	Exton, PA	http://www.scala.com/
SPECTRUM CORPORATION	Houston, TX	http://www.specorp.com/
SPOTMAGIC, INC.	San Francisco, CA	http://www.spotmagic.com/sms
VISIX, INC.	Norcross, GA	http://www.visix.com/

North American Digital Signage Software Providers

COMPANY NAME	HEADQUARTERED IN	WEBSITE
3M DIGITAL SIGNAGE	Bainbridge Island, WA	http://www.3MDigitalSignage.com/
AGN PROFESSIONAL (AGNPRO)	New York, NY	http://www.agnpro.com/
AMX	Huntington, NY	www.amx.com
BROADSIGN INTERNATIONAL INC.	Montreal	http://www.broadsign.com/
DICON CO. LTD, USA	Reston, VA	http://www.dicon.co.kr/english
DIGITAL VIEW MEDIA	New York, NY	http://www.digitalviewmedia.com/
IDS MEDIA	New Orleans, LA	http://www.idsmedia.net/
DT RESEARCH INC.	San Jose, CA	http://www.ww.dtri.com/
DYNAMAX TECHNOLOGIES	New York, NY	http://www.dynamaxworld.com/
DYNASIGN	Fremont, CA	http://www.dynasign.net/
EASYSHADOW LLC	Bradenton, FL	http://www.easyshadow.com/
EMOTIVE RESEARCH	Burlingame, CA	http://www.emotiveresearch.com/
ET MEDIA, INC.	Newtonville, MA	http://www.etmedia.net/
FIRESIGN INC.	Nashville, TN	http://www.firesign.net/
FOUR WINDS INTERACTIVE	Arvada, CO	http://www.fourwindsinteractive.com/
DS MEDIA	New Orleans, LA	http://www.idsmedia.net/
HUGHES NETWORK SYSTEMS, LLC	Germantown, MD	http://www.hughes.com/
INMATRIX MEDIA SOLUTIONS	Haifa, IL	http://www.inmatrix.com/
KEYWEST TECHNOLOGY	Lenexa, KS	http://www.keywesttechnology.com/
MEDIATILE	Scotts Valley, CA	http://www.mediatile.com/
NETKEY	East Haven, CT	http://www.netkey.com/
NEXUS DIGITAL SIGNS	Dallas, TX	http://www.nexusdigitalsigns.com/
ONEXUM CORPORATION	Upland, CA	http://www.onexum.com/
PLANAR SYSTEMS	Beaverton, OR	http://www.PlanarDigitalSignage.com/
POPSTAR NETWORKS, INC.	Lawrence, KS	http://www.popstarnetworks.com/
REAL DIGITAL MEDIA	Sarasota, FL	http://www.realdigitalmedia.com/
REFLECT SYSTEMS INC.	Dallas, TX	http://www.reflectsystems.com/
SCALA, INC.	Exton, PA	http://www.scala.com/
SMARTERSIGN	New York, NY	http://www.smartersign.com/
SONY ELECTRONICS INC.	Park Ridge, NJ	www.sony.com/digitalsignage

SPOTMAGIC, INC.	San Francisco, CA	http://www.spotmagic.com/sms
STRATACACHE	Dayton, OH	http://www.stratacache.com/
TEQ DIGITAL	Rancho Santa Margarita, CA	http://www.teqdigital.com/
TEXAS DIGITAL	College Station, TX	http://www.txdigital.com/
THE HOWARD COMPANY	Brookfield, WI	http://www.mainstreetmenus.com/
THOMSON GRASS VALLEY	San Jose, CA	http://www.professional. grassvalley.com/
TRIVENI DIGITAL INC.	Princeton Junction, NJ	http://www.trivenidigital.com/
VBRICK SYSTEMS, INC.	Wallingford, CT	http://www.vbrick.com/
VISIX, INC.	Norcross, GA	http://www.visix.com/
WEBPAVEMENT	Alpharetta, GA	http://www.webpavement.com/
WEGENER	Duluth, GA	http://www.wegener.com/
WIRESPRING TECHNOLOGIES	Ft. Lauderdale, FL	http://www.WireSpring.com/

North American Prepackaged Software Providers

COMPANY NAME	HEADQUARTERED IN	WEBSITE
ACCUWEATHER	State College, PA	www.accuweather.com
DIGITAL VIEW MEDIA	New York, NY	www.digitalviewmedia.com
NEXUS DIGITAL SIGNS	Dallas, TX	www.nexusdigitalsigns.com
SCALA, INC.	Exton, PA	http://www.scala.com/
ASI-MODULEX	St. Louis, MO	www.asimodulex.com
AZUREFIRE LLC DIGITAL SIGNAGE	Las Vegas, NV	www.azurefire.com
DG2L TECHNOLOGIES	Rocklin, CA	www.dg2l.com
DIGITAL INNOVATIONS GROUP	Rochester, NY	www.thedigroup.com
HAWKVISION SYSTEMS	Dublin, OH	www.hawkvisionsystems.com
HDTV SUPPLY, INC.	Thousand Oaks, CA	www.HDTVSupply.com
INLIGHTEN, INC.	Depew, NY	www.inlighten.net
JANUS DIGITAL DISPLAYS	St. Petersburg, FL	www.janusdisplays.com
PREMIER STUDIOS/PREMIERIS	Lenexa, KS	www.premierstudios.com
PROUNIX S.A.	MIAMI, FL	www.prounix.com

Appendix B: Glossary

Although some of these terms are not considered specifically relevant, and some are not specifically mentioned in the book, their use will at least occasionally arise in the context of understanding digital signage. It is worth noting that many of the terms overlap the bigger TV and telecom industries, indicating how digital signage has become such a part of those industries and is expected to continue doing so.

Activation: A decision made by a consumer at the point of purchase, to purchase a product or service that has been influenced by such factors as price, promotion, convenience, or impulse.

Audience: An advertising and marketing term used to define the potential viewers of an advertisement or content displayed by a digital signage (or any other display).

Audited Proof of Display: This involves hiring an independent, objective third party to provide proof of what actually was aired on a given digital signage screen. This then serves as a means of increasing the accuracy of a play-log, showing reports that provide proof of play. This service goes beyond what content was played by the server or other playback hardware, instead focusing on what was actually paid for by the advertiser, i.e., on screen airings. Audited proof of display helps improve reporting accuracy, due to the fact that a playback device, i.e., a server, reports content delivery but individual display devices may be turned off or out of order, thus not actually displaying the all-important content.

Backhaul: A television industry term meaning to transmit coded information or data to a backbone network, which provides the means to exchange information between different Local Area Networks (LANs) or other subnetworks and central control stations. It also means to transport trafficked data between remote or distributed sites and central control sites.

Bandwidth: The measure of a communication channel's capacity to transmit data over a fixed period of time. Bandwidth is the difference between the upper and lower frequencies of a band of electromagnetic radiation over which data is transmitted. The greater the difference between the upper and lower frequencies, the higher the bandwidth's capacity to transmit data.

BETAbrite Screen: A form of digital signage that utilizes an early subset of the Alpha Sign Communication Protocol to display text on an LED screen. BETAbrite screens are also commonly referred to as scrolling message boards/screens. BETAbrite screens are relatively inexpensive compared to other more contemporary forms of digital signage, but require the manual input of code that may be quite time consuming.

Business Model: With regard to digital signage networks, the term "business model" refers to the manner in which the costs associated with the network are met, or, ideally, exceeded by the revenue for the organization deploying the network. (See Chapter 8.)

C-Band: A portion of the electromagnetic spectrum that utilizes frequencies between the 4–8 GHz range that is used in fixed satellite communications.

Clarke Ring: Also known as the Clarke Belt, The Clarke Ring is a "near-geostationary," i.e., stationary, satellite position above the earth's equator, moving at the speed of the earth's rotation. This is a desirable location for communications satellites because satellites can obtain maximum connectivity and performance when positioned in the Clarke Ring. The concept was first theorized by science fiction writer Arthur C. Clarke in the mid-1940s.

Content: The media, i.e., the video, film clips, still images, animation, audio, text, or any other form of media that is displayed on a digital signage device or network of devices.

Contrast Ratio: A means of measuring display devices by contrasting the ratio between the luminosity of the brightest and darkest colors (white and black) that a display is able to produce. A "high contrast ratio" is a desired characteristic of any display device; however, the contrast ratio reported by marketers of display devices is the ratio under ideal conditions, i.e., a controlled room in total darkness. The actual ratio when using a device outside of these ideal conditions will be significantly reduced due to reflection of ambient light.

CPM (Cost per Thousand): As M is the Roman numeral for 1,000, CPM represents the standard unit of costing used in advertising, to compare the display rates of mass media advertisement. CPM is used in the pricing of display locations for advertisement, usually increasing with the quality of the audience and scarcity of display opportunity.

Dedicated Server: Also referred to as a managed hosting service or dedicated hosting service, a dedicated server is a means of Internet hosting that provides an organization with a server (the means of providing content) that is not shared by other organizations or individuals. Dedicated servers are needed to control content distribution to large and complex digital signage networks beyond the capabilities of a personal computer.

Demand: The aggregate amount of a product or service required by a market. Demand can also be defined more specifically as the desire of consumers for a product or service.

Digital Light Processing (DLP): A technology first developed by Dr. Larry Hornbeck of Texas Instruments that is used in projectors and video projectors. DLP projectors use microscopic mirrors arranged on a semiconductor chip known as a Digital Micro-mirror Device (DMD) to create the displayed image. Each one of the microscopic mirrors represents one or more pixels in the projected image and the number of mirrors determines the resolution of the projected image. The most common projection devices using DLP technology available to the public are single DMD chip or three DMD chip projectors, which differ in the method used to produce the color, but are based on the same concept described above.

Digital Paper (Interactive Paper): Digital paper is used in conjunction with a digital pen, and is a patterned paper that can be used to create digital documents in a handwritten format. The handwriting is stored by the digital pen via the dot pattern coordinates on the paper and can then be uploaded to a computer to create a digital document. (Note this is not the same as electronic paper.)

Digital Signage: A centrally and/or remotely controlled and addressable network of typically flat-screen digital displays that deliver targeted content in the form of entertainment, information, or advertisement to a designated audience by means of a combination of software and hardware resources. Other common names for digital signage include those such as "dynamic digital signage," "digital out-of-home media network," "electronic signage," "digital media network," "digital advertising network," "narrowcasting network," and "in-store TV network." (See, Chapter 1 for a larger listing of euphemisms for the term "digital signage.")

Digital Video Compression: The compression of digital video files in order to reduce the space required to store the data on a hard drive or in the transmission of the file. Digital video compression is the process of discarding aspects of the content that are redundant and unperceivable to the human eye, such as shades of color or static content within the file, without reducing the perceived quality of the image or content. The greater the compression ratio, the greater the amount of data discarded.

DIPA (Dynamic Image Provisioning Applications): Software that is utilized in digital signage networks to control various aspects of the content distribution, including specifying which files will be played at what time in each location, partitioning electronic display screens, and controlling the characteristics of displayed content.

Display Device: The electronic device that represents the delivery component of a digital signage network, such as a flat-screen LED, LCD, plasma, or any other type of device that displays content to the audience.

Display Resolution: The number of distinct pixels in each dimension that can be displayed in a digital television or computer display system. The resolution of a digital display is an important consideration when purchasing a display and must take into account the intended use of the display device, i.e., where and how the display will be used.

Downlink: The link established by an orbiting satellite to one or more ground stations or antennas.

DSL (Digital Subscriber Line): A group of technologies that provide digital transmission of data via the infrastructure of a local telephone network. As compared to analog infrastructures, DSL substantially increases the capacity of common telephone lines to transmit data to homes and offices.

DVB-IP (Digital Video Broadcast—Internet Protocol): The internationally accepted set of standards for digital television. DVB-IP is the international equivalent of the North American digital television standard known as ATSC. DVB utilizes the 6–8-MHz channels and can be broadcast over satellite, cable, or over-the-air, using the MPEG-2 video compression format, and either Dolby or MPEG audio compression.

DVR (Digital Video Recorder): A recording device that stores data in a digital format on an internal disk drive or other storage medium. The term "DVR" may refer to a stand-alone unit with enabling software or a television that has DVR technology built into the display device. The primary advantage of DVR technology is that it allows for much longer recording times over traditional VCR or other recoding technologies, and enhanced control over the programming content by the user.

Dwell Time: The amount of time that a viewer normally spends in front of a screen. Dwell time is one measure of consideration when judging the necessary ingredients of content designed for a specific audience.

Dynamic Screen Zone: Screen zoning refers to the segmentation of screen space (on a digital signage device) into separate zones or regions, in which multiple and varied types of information can be displayed on a single screen simultaneously.

EIRP (Effective Isotropic Radiated Power): Also known as Equivalent Isotropic Radiated Power, EIRP is the amount of power an antenna must transmit to a receiver in order to produce the peak level of transmission. EIRP is typically measured in decibels over a given power level and is basically the strength of a transmission toward a receiving location. EIRP, therefore, provides a means to compare transmission strength between emitting devices, regardless of the size, form, or type of the emitters.

Electronic Paper (E-Paper): A display technology that is designed to replicate the appearance of common paper with ink writing on it. E-paper does not use backlight to illuminate its paper, unlike traditional display devices. Instead, e-paper simply reflects light just as an ordinary piece of paper would. It has the ability to display images indefinitely without a source of electricity. E-paper is flexible and can be bent, crumpled, or manipulated, much like an ordinary piece of paper. Future applications include e-books and magazines, posters, clothing, and bags. (E-paper is different from digital paper.)

Emotional Identity: The interpretation or perception of a brand by a consumer in terms of loyalty, reliability, quality, sentimentality, or other intangible terms.

Encryption: The process of transforming information or data into an unreadable form to anyone other than those possessing the key required to decrypt the information. Encryption is the most common and effective form to secure data.

Flight: The content being displayed on a digital signage device or network. Most typically, "flight" refers to an advertisement or other message content on a display device.

Footfall: A term used in retailing to refer to the amount of traffic, or number of customers patronizing a retail, or other, establishment at a given time. In reference to digital signage, footfall is typically described as the number of customers or patrons that is attracted to an establishment as a result of a digital signage display.

FTP (File Transfer Protocol): The most commonly used protocol for exchanging files over any network (e.g., Internet/intranet) between a server computer and a client computer, which allows the client to upload, download, rename, and delete files on the server.

HD (High Definition): An increase in visual or display resolution in any number of formats, including TVs, DVDs, video, and recording devices, such as cameras and camcorders.

HDTV: High Definition Television is a digital television broadcasting system offering higher resolution than traditional or standard television systems (SDTV). Introduced in the United States during the 1990s by an alliance of television manufacturers, HDTV is digitally broadcast because it requires less bandwidth when video compression is used. HDTV systems are distinguished from SDTV in the number of lines in the vertical display resolution, the scanning system, and the number of frames per second.

IDL (Interactive Distance Learning): Remote telecommunication that enables students to learn and participate from a distance via an Internet connection or satellite broadcast, combined with various forms of media, such as teleconferencing software and traditional display devices.

Interactive TV (ITV or iTV): The interaction of television viewers with television content as it is being viewed. Ranging from "low interactivity," i.e., changing volume or channels or cameras, to "moderate interactivity," i.e., video on demand (VOD), to "high interactivity," i.e., a viewer can influence the actual content as they view it. Interactive TV is generally referred to in regards to "high interactivity" television.

IP Encapsulator: As it relates to computer networking, encapsulation refers to the process of including data from an upper-layer protocol, i.e., User Datagram Protocol (UDP) or Transmission Control Protocol (TCP), into a lower-layer protocol, i.e., Internet protocol. Computer applications generally utilize the upper-layer protocols, while the Internet is based on Internet Protocol or IP. An IP encapsulator is a hardware device that carries out this process by including data from a software application to an IP format that can be delivered to a network of computers (or, in the case of digital signage, to display devices).

IPG (Interactive Program Guide): Also known as an Electronic Program Guide (EPG) or Electronic Service Guide, an IPG is an on-screen guide used to display broadcast television programming. It allows viewers to navigate content by channel, title, time, genre, or other means via a remote control, keyboard, or other device. IPGs also allow viewers to search by subject, view program reviews, and apply parental controls.

IPTV (Internet Protocol Television): Television content that is received by end users or consumers via the Internet, instead of through traditional broadcast delivery mediums such as cable and satellite. For non-commercial consumers, IPTV is generally offered in a bundled format known as "triple play," which combines IPTV, Internet access, and Voice over Internet Protocol (VoIP), which is actually Internet-based telephony.

Kbps (Kilobits per Second): Kilobits (1,000 bits) are a standard unit of information in the context of memory storage and address space size. Kilobits are used to express digital communication and transmission speeds.

Ku-Band: A portion of the electromagnetic spectrum that utilizes frequencies ranging between 10 and 17 GHz, typically used in fixed satellite communications. The symbol is a reference to "K—under," meaning the band directly under the K-Band of frequencies.

LAN/WAN (Local Area Network/Wide Area Network): Local Area Network (LAN) refers to a computer network that spans a relatively small area, such as an office, or a group of offices. LANs can be connected to one another through ordinary telephone lines or radio waves to form a Wide Area Network (WAN) over any geographic area. LANs have higher data transfer rates and are not reliant on leased communication lines to transmit data.

LCD (Liquid Crystal Display): A thin, flat display comprised of color or monochrome pixels arrayed in front of a light source or reflector that is typically utilized in battery-powered electronic devices. LCDs utilize technology that involves rod-shaped molecules (i.e., liquid crystals) that have the ability to flow as a liquid and bend light.

LED/OLED (Light Emitting Diode/Organic Light Emitting Diode): LEDs are semiconductor diodes that light up when electricity is passed through them. LEDs are typically comprised of a mix of inorganic semiconductor materials, such as aluminum, gallium, and silicone. Organic LEDs are light-emitting diodes that are made from organic compounds and have the added benefit of being flexible.

Lumination Time: The amount of time that a digital display is able to display images on its screen. This time varies greatly between and among digital signage technologies and is considered an important measure of the life of an individual digital signage screen and an overall network.

Mbps (Megabits per Second): A measure of data transfer rate that is equal to one million bits per second.

Media Player: Media players are hardware devices that are used in digital signage systems to store and then typically "push" content onto screens. They vary greatly in capacity and capability, from lower-level MPEG players to sophisticated industrial and commercial use computers that are constructed to provide reliable, secure playback concurrently sending numerous files of different forms of content.

Middleware: Software capable of connecting software components or applications via an enabling service that allows multiple processes to interact across a network. Middleware is literally in the "middle" between applications and acts as the means of connecting applications running on different operating systems, a process generally known as interoperability. The middleware classification includes content management systems, web servers, application servers, and other devices that support application development and delivery.

Mounting Mechanism: The means or method by which a display device is mounted in its environment, i.e., how the device is attached to a wall, stand, ceiling, or other physical location.

MPEG (Moving Pictures Experts Group): A joint working group of the International Standards Organization (ISO) and The International Electrotechnical Commission (IEC) that is responsible for setting international video and audio encoding standards.

MPEG-2: An encoding standard for video content and programming with broadcast TV quality, typically used for DVD, digital TV, or motion video.

MPEG-4: An expanded original MPEG standard to support 3D content, video/audio "objects," and other multimedia representation and distribution. MPEG-4 is based on Apple's QuickTime file format and offers a number of compression options.

Multicasting: In relation to digital signage specifically, multicasting is the transmission of information or data files to a network of digital signage devices, or a group of devices within a network, simultaneously, via the most efficient means of delivering the information or data file, such as satellite to many screens spread across a wide geographic area.

Multi-channel Player: A server that is capable of outputting multiple streams of unique content to multiple digital display devices, typically simultaneously. Multi-channel players may also be referred to as "site servers" or "in-store servers."

NICS (Network Interface Card): A network interface card is a hardware component that is inserted into a computer, enabling the computer to connect to and communicate over a network, typically an LAN for small groups of computers, or over protocols such as IP for larger networks.

Network Operations Center (NOC): The Network Operations Center is a central location where large and complex communications networks are controlled via highly trained staff and advanced computing systems.

PAL (Phase Altering Line): A color encoding system for broadcast television that is the European standard, and the North American equivalent to the NTSC. PAL is generally accepted as having higher-resolution quality than NTSC, and most computer screens that can also be used to view television are enabled to use PAL and NTSC formats. PAL can also be decoded into the NTSC format with the use of a PAL decoding device.

Piecemeal: A digital signage network that is developed in a piecemeal fashion, meaning that the various hardware, software, content management, or any other component of the network has been procured from separate providers. The site owner or someone else tasked by that company will pick, in a "combination" fashion, the individual partners that together install and operate the digital display network.

Plasma: A type of flat-panel display that works by sealing a mixture of cells containing a combination of neon and xenon gases between two panels of glass, with parallel electrodes deposited on their surfaces. When a voltage is passed through the cells containing the gases, ionized plasma is emitted, which creates UV radiation. The UV radiation then excites color phosphors and visible light is emitted from each cell.

Playlist: The scheduled list of content to be displayed on a digital signage network distributed by a server. Playlists define not only the order of displayed content, but also the duration of the content displayed.

Playlog: The means by which the performance of a digital signage network can be monitored and recorded. Playlogs record what content was played on which display devices for how long or how often, at what time, and on what date. Playlogs can also record other network performance information.

POP (Point of Purchase)/POS (Point of Sale): POP or POS may be defined differently by different organizations. Generally, the POP or POS is the place where a transaction occurs. It may be broadly defined, i.e., a retail store, or narrowly defined, i.e., a specific cash register within the retail store.

Proof of Play: The summary playback reports and the raw playlogs of a digital signage network. Proof of Play provides a metric for measuring the effectiveness of a digital signage network, however, it may only provide reporting on which content was played by the playback device, i.e., the server, and may not reflect which ads were actually displayed.

Protocol: The standard that allows or controls data transfers, communications, and connections between two computing devices. A protocol may be carried out via software, hardware, or a combination of hardware and software working together. Protocol is the set of rules that governs communication between computing devices. Internet protocol, or IP, enables communicable unique global addressing between and among computers.

RASables: An acronym for the key criteria used to assess the desirability of an applications system. Literally, RASables stands for Reliability, Availability, and Scalability.

Return on Investment (ROI): Return on investment is the primary monetary measurement for financial analysis of any investment. ROI, often called Rate of Return, or simply "return," is the ratio of money gained or lost on an investment in relation to the amount of money spent or invested.

Return on Objectives (ROO): Return on objectives is a term coined by digital signage industry professionals to describe the forms of return on a digital signage network other than monetary returns. Other means of return on digital signage networks are necessary because many projects are not intended or employed for monetary gain, and for those projects that are not "for-profit" networks, their returns are not easily measured in monetary terms.

RF: Radio frequency.

RFID (Radio Frequency Identification): A means of automatically identifying people, products, or animals, by storing and remotely retrieving data via a radio wave transponder known as an RFID tag. RFID can, for example, be used in digital signage applications by attaching an RFID tag to an individual, or an individual's credit card, that transmits data to digital signage devices about recent purchases or spending activity.

Sales Lift: The percentage increase in sales or revenue resulting from a specific initiative, such as the deployment of a digital signage network.

Salience: Prominent or conspicuous relevant information in content. Salience is a measure of the quality of content in terms of its ability to increase sales or brand awareness and loyalty. Horizontal salience occurs when individuals exchange information, while vertical salience refers to an individual's first-hand knowledge of a brand.

Satellite: A satellite in a telecommunications context refers to a transmission device that is stationed in space for communications purposes, and receives communications from a terrestrial "uplink" station, then sending the same communication back to the earth for receipt via an antenna. Antennas linked to a receiver that has been specified to acquire the satellite's communication are able to restructure that signal, typically for both secured and unsecured uses.

Satellite Broadband Distribution: Satellite broadband distribution refers to a means of content distribution via a high-speed satellite Internet connection that does not require a terrestrial signal (such as a mobile signal, a phone line, or a hard-wired cable connection). Satellite broadband connects a computer to a satellite via a satellite modem linked to a traditional satellite dish.

Satellite Footprint: Satellite footprint refers to an area of the earth that a satellite signal is able to access at any point in time.

SD (Standard Digital): Also known as Standard Definition TV, SD is the United States digital television standard format, created in 1998, that refers to the 525- and 625-line TV formats.

Side Server/Edge Server: Side Servers are a set of hardware components used to improve the performance of web-based systems, such as digital signage networks. In relation to digital signage networks, "side" or "edge servers" are commonly used to store and dispatch advertisement or other files to the networked devices.

Smart Card: Also known as "chip cards" or "integrated circuit cards," smart cards are any card that contains embedded integrated circuits that are able to process (receive and send out) information. Smart cards are similar in size to a typical credit card.

Streaming Video: The distribution or delivery of uninterrupted video via a telecommunications network, typically the Internet or an intranet that does not require downloading by the end user. Streaming requires an end-user medium, such as a personal computer, to buffer a few seconds of video data before being displayed on the screen, so that the medium can stay ahead of itself throughout the stream. The word "stream" refers to the delivery method and not the display or transmission devices. Streaming video will be used more and more on digital signage systems.

TCC (Technical Care Center): The TCC is a service center staffed by technical service providers that monitor network or application performance, and provide assurances of high-quality service, by responding to customer needs and questions.

TCP/IP (Transmission Control Protocol/Internet Protocol): Invented by Vinton Cerf and Bob Kahn, under contract from the U.S. Department of Defense, TCP/IP is the protocol of the Internet that has become the global standard for communications. TCP offers transport functions that ensure the total number of bytes sent by the provider is received correctly by the user.

Thin Film Transistor Liquid Crystal Display (TFT-LCD): An LCD that uses Thin Film Transistor technology to improve the quality of displayed images. TFT technology embeds transistors within the glass panel of an LCD, thus improving the stability of the image. TFT technology has been typically utilized in radiography, such as with mammograms, and is today generally utilized in all but the least expensive LCD devices. TFT-LCD devices are widely utilized in interactive touch-screen applications.

Transponder: A term that is short for "transmitter–responder," it is a device on a communications satellite that receives a signal from earth, amplifies, and then retransmits that signal on a different frequency, back to receiving antennas on the earth. Satellites typically feature several transponders.

Triggered Content: Content that can be programmed into a digital signage network, or into a single device, that overrides the scheduled content from a playlist when a predetermined condition is met. Predetermined conditions may include an emergency situation, selection of items off of a shelf, the proximity of shoppers, or the absence of attentive viewers. Content can also be triggered via an RFID transponder, a biometric identification, a barcode, or a smart card.

Turn-key: A turn-key solution is a digital signage network system in which a single company is tasked by the company triggering the digital signage system to develop and implement the entire deployment of the digital signage system. Generally, the site owner or controlling company takes over the management of the content or outsources that function to a third party. Some turn-key providers, however, also offer content management services.

Uplink: Uplink refers to a communications signal that is transmitted from the earth to a satellite. Uplink is the opposite of downlink (or the transmission of a communications signal from a satellite to the earth).

UDP/TCP (User Datagram Protocol/Transmission Control Protocol): UDP/TCP is an Internet protocol within the TCP that is used in the place of the TCP, when a reliable delivery is not required. It is typically used on networked computers to deliver short messages between them. These are referred to as datagrams.

VAR (Value-Added Reseller): A VAR is an organization that is able to increase the value of a product by either packaging separate applications together, or integrating their own applications or services into existing applications, and subsequently reselling the repackaged or integrated product to the consumer or retailer.

Virtual Private Network (VPN): VPNs are communications networks that are "tunneled" through other networks, such as the Internet, to provide enhanced security or other desired goals for communication. In digital signage networks, a VPN can be used to provide the security or connectivity reliability that a private network is capable of, but has lower associated costs than a dedicated private network. Using a VPN, a digital signage network has the ability to provide secure and reliable content delivery without delivering the content over the Internet.

VITC (Video Interval Time Code): Pronounced "vit-see," a VITC is a form of SMPTE (Society of Motion Pictures and Television Engineering) standard, which is a set of cooperating standards that allow for the labeling of individual film or video frames with a time code used in the editing process. VITC enables editors to read video or film frame by frame in the most accurate manner.

VOD (Video on Demand): VOD refers to a system that enables the user to select and watch video content, on demand, instantly, from another locale, on a television set or web browser, via a network, as a part of an interactive television system.

VoIP (Voice over Internet Protocol): VoIP refers to a category of hardware and software that routes voice conversations over the Internet or through any IP-based network, and does not require the users to incur a surcharge above the cost of the Internet service itself.

VSAT (Very Small Aperture Terminal): VSAT refers to a two-way satellite ground station, with a dish antenna (usually less than 2 meters in diameter) and a satellite receiver, both of which are used in the satellite communications of data, voice, and video signals. VSAT systems are comprised of two main parts, i.e., a transceiver that must be placed outside with direct line of site to a satellite and an indoor device that can interface the transceiver with the end user's communication device. VSAT systems are used in the distribution and delivery of digital signage content.

WDSL (Wireless Digital Subscriber Line): WDSL refers to a fixed wireless DSL technology that utilizes a stationary digital transceiver, directed at a radio transmission tower, to send and receive a signal.

Wi-Fi (Wireless Fidelity): Wi-Fi is a wireless technology brand owned by the Wi-Fi Alliance, which is used generically to refer to any type of 802.11 network or WLAN. Common Wi-Fi applications include the Internet and VoIP phone access, gaming, and network connectivity for consumer electronics, including digital cameras, DVD players, and television sets.

Index